Frank's

For The Memory

DAVE WAGSTAFFE

edited by
Steve Gordos

Thomas Publications

First published in Great Britain in August, 2014
by Thomas Publications, 26 Park End,
Newport, Shropshire, TF10 7JG

ISBN 978-0-9550585-7-8

Thomas Publications

Printed and bound by TJ International, Padstow, Cornwall

Contents

For Val

Foreword - by John Richards

Dave Wagstaffe and Frank Munro were the best of pals and had been for some years before I got to know them. They were seasoned professionals when I came to Molineux in 1969 and, to wannabes like me, they had the lot – regular first-team places, they were married with children and had nice cars and houses near to each other in the Wolves mini-enclave in Fordhouses. Frank at no 5 and Waggy at no 11 (that's their shirts, not their homes) were certainties on the team sheet that was pinned up in the home dressing room after training each Friday. They were two of the lynchpins of our early 1970s team – a side who, without argument, were second only to that of the great Stan Cullis era as being the most successful in the club's history.

Frank and Waggy were key components in that success, not least their part in helping Wolves reach their only ever European cup final by beating Juventus and Ferencvaros on the way. How fitting, also, that they should enjoy a Wembley cup final together – the one and only for both of them – with a deserved victorious outcome. At the top of their game, they were different class and, in my opinion, the two most naturally talented players in that team. To see Frank calmly guide the ball out of a frantic penalty area was a pure delight, as was watching Waggy's stuttering, stooping run followed by a drop of the shoulder and another unfortunate defender left in his wake.

Perhaps it was this affinity and recognition of each other's ability that forged their friendship at the outset as they alternated sharing lifts into work. Or, perhaps, and just as likely, it was their mutual dislike of cross country running and circuit training that brought them together. Ingenious schemers at working out short cuts to Sammy Chung's runs around Cannock Chase, they would disappear into the undergrowth and reappear, bracken-festooned, just behind the leaders! On our travels, in particular the ones on which Bill McGarry was absent for whatever reason, they were the advance party doing a recce of the area to find the places of interest, usually a bar or a pub (for soft drinks, of course) and, in the case of our occasional mid-winter trips to Southport, the opening times of the local casino.

In many ways, it was an unlikely pairing; the tough, uncompromising Scot, unafraid of giving as good as he got on the pitch and in any dressing-room disagreement with another player, or the manager for that matter; and the nervy, quiet Mancunian who was happiest sitting on the team bus doing a crossword or, later on in his life, tending his allotment or having a game of bowls. They both left Wolves in the mid-1970s and went their separate ways – Frank back to Scotland and then Australia, Waggy towards his North West roots in Blackburn and Blackpool.

For some unknown reason – some would say fate – they both decided that, after all their travelling, Wolverhampton was going to be their final home. And the friendship was renewed there as if they had never been apart. This time, however, following Frank's stroke in 1993, what was once the partners-in-crime relationship became more like the Odd Couple, with the banter just as cutting and humorous. Frank, as ever, was full of stories and regaled all who went to visit him, with Waggy as the caring support, running errands and organising outings, including regular trips to the local hostelry – Frank in a wheelchair which Waggy pushed. "I carried him on the pitch, so it's his turn to now," was Frank's usual line about the arrangement.

It is a telling mark of that relationship that Waggy wanted to write this book. After completing his own excellent Waggy's Tales, he made it a mission to chronicle Frank's life and achievements for one reason – he wanted his best friend of 40 plus years to be remembered. And what better way than this? It is said that some friendships are made in heaven. This was one of those and I have no doubt that it is continuing in its original place of manufacture.

Introduction - by Steve Gordos

This book was begun by David Wagstaffe as a tribute to his old team-mate Frank Munro. It has been published as a tribute to both players. Waggy had read through the manuscript and was satisfied he had done Frank justice. Alas, he did not live to see his work bear fruit. On August 6, 2013, he died after a short illness. Now, I hope this book will serve as a lasting memorial to both men, who were part of a superb Wolverhampton Wanderers side in the late 1960s and early 1970s, with Frank as the elegant, uncompromising central defender and Waggy the dashing left-winger. They were key members of a talent-filled team, who remain the only one in the club's history to reach a European final.

Frank's For The Memory has taken some time. It was kicked off by Waggy with a series of long chats to Frank and continued after the subject's death in 2011. As he had done with his highly entertaining autobiography, Waggy chose to do his writing-up in long hand, then I took over in an editing and research role and, in the second half of Wolves' Championship season of 2012-13, we arranged to meet Thomas Publications' David Instone in the lovely Gluttons For Nourishment coffee shop in Tettenhall. The three of us quickly agreed a way forward with the project and there was a reminder of the author's huge popularity when a lady diner recognised him from a nearby table and suggested, even a few weeks short of his 70th birthday, that she thought he would still be well up to the task of keeping the club away from the clutches of relegation – and should immediately look out his boots for that night's game at Barnsley.

By then, though, Waggy was thinking only of harking back to the past and telling the story of the lad from Dundee, who burst on to the football scene as a 16-year-old. He and I have tried to tell how Frank reached the top of the tree, first as a midfield dynamo with Dundee United and Aberdeen and finally as calm Beckenbauer-like centre-half with Wolves and Scotland. This book was a labour of love for us both. We decided from the start that all proceeds due to us would go to charity and that remains the case.

Exactly two years after his death, Frank came home to Molineux. A rare concession by Wolves allowed his sons Grant and Stuart to place his ashes below the turf behind the goal in front of the Stan Cullis Stand. Club chaplain David Wright led the memorial service, which was attended by Frank's wife Margaret

Munro and his partner in later life, Naomi Hackner. Many other relatives, former team-mates and friends were there, too, among them Val Williams, Waggy's partner of 20 years. It is appropriate that Frank's ashes are located in the shadow of the stand bearing Cullis's name. The two men shared the same birthday, October 25.

Ten days before the ceremony, Waggy had died peacefully in the arms of his beloved Val. His illness, although blessedly short, had come out of the blue. At the beginning of the year, we had a wonderful night out at Molineux, celebrating his magnificent career with Wolves when he was inducted into the club's Hall of Fame. In the second half of summer, we were mourning him.

After Frank's memorial service, relatives, old players and friends gathered in Sir Jack's Restaurant in the Billy Wright Stand. The formalities inside included a tribute to Frank that was hosted by that bundle of humorous energy, Steve Kindon, and hit just the right note. Former team-mates Mel Eves, Phil Parkes, Barry Powell, John Richards and Steve Daley each told a brief anecdote about the great man. Where there had been tears earlier, suddenly there was laughter and I guess that's how Frank would have liked it.

I just wished Waggy had been there, too.

Chapter One

From Dundee To Doc

"Born to be" is an often used phrase but, in the case of Francis Michael Munro, it really was true. He was born to be a footballer. At the age of 11, at school in Broughty Ferry, he was head and shoulders above his team-mates, in more ways than one. He told me he was not academic in any way and had no interest in school work. So it was a natural progression for him to use the sporting attributes with which he was blessed. By the time he was 14, he was a strapping lad with a physique that could quite easily cope with the rigours of the professional game. Football was his game and football was definitely his aim.

At the time, he was captain of the local Catholic school team, centre-forward and goalscorer. His side had reached the final of the Dundee Schoolboys' Trophy and, being the biggest game around in school football, it was to be played at Tannadice, the home of Dundee United. Playing for the opposition was one Peter Lorimer, another future Scottish international. Lorimer was ten months older than Frank and even then had a reputation not only for being highly promising but also for having a really powerful shot. After winning Scottish schoolboy caps, Lorimer joined Leeds and made his League debut when he was only 15.

It was decided that Frank was to be the one to try to contain Lorimer, who was undoubtedly the opposition's best player. Not only did Frank manage to do that – even though Lorimer did score with a 30-yard thunderbolt free-kick – he also helped himself to the goals which gave his team a 2-1 victory. With 22 promising players on show, the game inevitably attracted quite a few scouts, one of whom tracked down Frank to his home address. He was from Chelsea and was to launch the beginning of Francis Munro's career; a life which did not have the easiest of starts was about to change.

Frank was born on October 25, 1947, in Broughty Ferry on the outskirts of Dundee. Tragically, both his parents died early. His father passed away when Frank was six weeks old and his mother when he was two. He was brought up by his maternal grandmother, Mina Conway, whom he adored, until her death when he was only nine. Consequently, he went to live with his aunt and uncle, Mary and

Francie Conway, in Mid Craigie, another Dundee suburb. He was the youngest of four brothers after Alec, Allan and James.

The scout who knocked on the door reported, eventually, to Tommy Docherty, who had won 25 Scotland caps as a Preston and Arsenal wing-half. Arrangements were made for Frank to go for trials with Chelsea, who emerged around that time as one of the country's leading sides. Travelling to the big city was a big thing for a young boy, so it was agreed brother James would accompany him. The trials were to be held in three half-hour sessions so players could be tried in different positions and in situations in which they could be assessed to see how they coped. Frank was devastated to be withdrawn after the first session as he was convinced he had performed reasonably well. However, his disappointment did not last long because he was taken aside by Tommy Doc and told he had greatly impressed. He invited Frank, with James, into his office to discuss the possibility of him becoming an apprentice professional. The brothers then returned to Dundee while Tommy had Frank's contract drawn up and accommodation was found.

"I'll just sort out your expenses before you go," said Docherty. "Here's two weeks' wages for you." James interrupted by saying: "No, it's just two days." "It's two weeks," said Docherty with a wink. The penny suddenly dropped and the payment for taking Frank south was accepted as a much-appreciated gesture. By the time the relevant arrangements had been made, Frank had just turned 15 and was so excited at the prospect of eventually becoming a pro footballer that he did something he always regretted. Had he waited two weeks longer before leaving school and dashing off to Chelsea to chase his ambition, he would have been eligible to play in the England v Scotland schools international. He later acknowledged that it did not appear such a significant game, compared with others he did play in, but it was something he really wished he had done.

He was pleasantly surprised to discover that Chelsea had found him digs in Thornton Heath with the bonus that his landlady was Scottish. It would have been reasonable to assume that a 15-year-old moving hundreds of miles south from a small suburb to the bright lights of London would have felt lost and overawed – but it was just the opposite. He loved it. After training all day with the other youths, he used to pass away the evenings at Balham ice rink, where he was able to stand and watch a vast array of the opposite sex skate by. It was the same on the tube on his way to training. He was amazed – he had not realised there were this many women in the world! And he never saw the same ones two days running!

It was all new and exciting but, despite enjoying his football, he felt the gloss eventually wear off and he admitted to becoming lonely and depressed, especially after hearing from his brothers. They seemed so far away in Scotland and they were! Eventually, Frank had a chat with Tommy Doc to seek his advice on the situation. The Doc was sympathetic and could understand the way Frank felt, suggesting that he return home to have a break for a couple of weeks. Chelsea generously paid for his train ticket and, as a bonus, Docherty gave him £60 to spend while in Dundee – a lot of money for one so young. Arriving early at the station, Frank had time to browse around the newsagent's on the platform and, rather naughtily, bought a copy of Playboy magazine to 'read' on his long journey back to Dundee – a trip that was to turn out to be a minor disaster. As the train sped over the border, he decided it was time to dispose of the magazine so his brothers didn't find out he had bought it. He opened the window and launched it into the countryside, immediately remembering that the £60 Tommy had given him had been neatly tucked among the pages for safekeeping. It was the costliest magazine Frank ever purchased and he imagined some Scottish farmer finding something he had never seen before – and £60 into the bargain; a gift from heaven, indeed!

Refreshed after two weeks at home, Frank went back to London in pursuit of a career with Chelsea but, as time went by and not helped by many calls from back home, he decided to go and see Tommy Doc to say he was returning to Scotland permanently. Again, Docherty was very sympathetic and wished him all the best, adding the parting shot: "I hope that, in years to come, I won't have to pay a lot of money to buy you." Frank was not the only Scot to become homesick at Stamford Bridge. Tommy Doc was attracting youngsters from far and wide but it seemed Scotland was just too far away for some. John Scott and Davie Robb were another two who could not settle in the big city. Scott joined Dundee and Robb went to Aberdeen. Both had successful careers and won international caps. Two fellow Scots delighted they did stick it out were Eddie McCreadie and John Boyle.

Many years later, Frank said in an interview with David Instone in the Wolves official magazine: "I was too young for the step and became terribly homesick. I watched Arsenal and Everton at Highbury one night in probably the best match I ever saw and, a few years later, would have loved what London had to offer. But I couldn't settle at that age. My brother used to ring me from Scotland every night and that just made me worse." Frank also told David that, before he returned home for good, he went to Leeds and had a trial game, playing alongside Peter Lorimer and Jim McCalliog. But he decided that, whether or not they wanted him, the call of home was too strong.

His family were pleased to have him back but he still had a burning desire to be a pro footballer. The solution was right there on his doorstep – he was surrounded by Dundee supporters and even Frank's own favourite, centre-half Ian Ure, played for them. So where better to begin? Bob Shankly, the brother of legendary Liverpool boss Bill Shankly, was manager of Dundee, so an interview was arranged. He offered Frank £10 a week as an apprentice but there was a snag. Because Frank was still approaching his 16th birthday, the plan was to farm him out to junior club Lochee. Frank saw this as a backward step and believed the only way he could gain experience was to play with older players, so he said 'no'.

The 39 Steps is the name of a famous John Buchan novel, which later was made into a film and is set mostly in Scotland. However, to Frank and other Dundonians, 'the 39 steps' was the distance between the front door of Dens Park, the home of Dundee, and the main entrance of Tannadice, hq of Dundee United. It may have been a very short walk but it made a massive difference to Frank's career. Jerry Kerr had been manager of Dundee United since 1959 and would remain so for 12 years. He, too, offered Frank £10 a week but promised to put him straight into the reserves. Needless to say, the offer was accepted but his brothers were furious because they were staunch Dundee supporters and hated United, who Frank joined in July, 1963. As promised, he went into the reserves and held down a regular place until the end of the season. The side won the reserves cup and had a very successful campaign, which made Frank feel he was knocking on the first-team door. At a couple of months short of 17, he knew in his mind he was ready for that and his chance would come at the start of 1964-65 in the Scottish League Cup.

The tournament was played on a league basis in the early stages and began before the League season proper. United were drawn in a group with Dundee, Falkirk and Motherwell and the opening game for United was against the team from down the road. To his great delight, Frank was given the no 8 shirt and grabbed the opportunity by hitting the winning goal in a promising debut before a Dens Park crowd of nearly 17,000. At 16 years, nine months and 14 days, he remains the youngest Dundee United player to appear in a League Cup game. It looked like being a stroll when Dennis Gillespie and Lewis Thom scored with just over half an hour gone. However, Dundee reduced the deficit with an Andy Penman penalty before the break and Bobby Waddell equalised 20 minutes from time. Then came Frank's big moment six minutes from time when he met perfectly with his head a hanging cross from Johnny Graham. What a way to crown your debut! The teams on Saturday, August 8, 1964, were: Dundee: Slater, Hamilton,

Cox, Seith, Roydon, Stuart, Penman, Murray, Waddell, Cousins, Cameron. Dundee United: Davie, Millar, Dicks, Neilson, Smith, Briggs, Graham, Munro, Moran, Gillespie, Thom.

Although Frank was walking on air after his dramatic start, there were no congratulations from his family. All he received was a clip round the ear from one of his brothers for beating their favourite team. Despite this luke-warm reception from his nearest and dearest, that day was the beginning of a career which was to span many years and end on the other side of the world. He kept his place and, four days later, scored again as Falkirk were beaten 3-0 at Tannadice. He was delighted with his goal, a 25-yarder. This was followed by a 1-0 victory at Motherwell. In between those two League Cup games, Frank made his League debut in a 1-0 home defeat by Partick Thistle.

Manager Kerr may have been tempted to give the youngster a rest but a bizarre incident in training ensured he stayed in the team. The squad were doing some long distance running during which they had to pass a large country residence with several Alsatian dogs chained up outside, barking away as the players jogged past. Frank playfully grabbed the calf of Tommy Neilson in front of him and barked like a dog. Tommy reacted by jumping in the air, presuming he was being attacked by one of the Alsatians. Unfortunately, the incident backfired because Tommy pulled his hamstring and finished up on the treatment table. So he missed the return League Cup game with Dundee, which United won 2-1 with Frank again scoring the winner.

Four League Cup games had yielded four wins but the return with Falkirk brought a 5-2 defeat. A win over Motherwell at Tannadice ensured qualification for the quarter-finals, however, and United were far too strong there for Hamilton Academical. The first leg of the quarter-final, at Tannadice, saw United post what remains their biggest League Cup victory as they hit eight without reply, seven coming in the first half and two from Frank. He could be excused for feeling smug but was soon brought down to earth in a third meeting with Dundee. The arch rivals avenged their two cup defeats by winning a Scottish League Division One clash 4-1 at Tannadice. Another novice, 16-year-old Jocky Scott, hit the headlines by scoring twice in the last six minutes. Frank played in the return with Hamilton but took a knock, so Kerr left him out for the League trip to Celtic, picking a defensive line-up who earned a draw. In midweek, Frank had a game with the reserves and promptly scored a hat-trick in a 6-1 win over Hearts. That saw him restored to the first team in a 1-1 home draw with Hibernian but he would not be given the chance to display his talents on Scotland's most famous football stage.

For the League Cup semi-final against Rangers at Hampden Park, Frank was in the squad but Kerr may well have felt his inexperience weighed against him for such a big game. I am certain Frank would not have shared that view. I am sure he would have taken a semi-final in his stride because he was not the sort ever to have pre-match nerves. He gave way to Benny Rooney, son of Celtic trainer Bob Rooney, and could only look on as United took the lead through Doug Moran on 21 minutes but were finally beaten 2–1 in extra-time. Rangers, without star winger Willie Henderson, who was down with flu, were way below their best but equalised through Jim Forrest with only four minutes to go. Forrest also hit the winning goal, in the opening minute of the second half of extra-time. Had he played, Frank would have been marking the genius that was Jim Baxter, a player of immense ability and one who would go down in the folklore of Scottish football. The Kerr strategy was to have Rooney man-mark Baxter and he did succeed in curbing his menace to some extent. However, Baxter did enough in the match to impress the watching Frank. He reckoned he learned far more from watching Baxter than from all the others put together. How he would have loved to play against him. Rangers beat Celtic 2-1 in the final to retain the trophy.

When Dundee United skipper Tommy Neilson had recovered from his injury, he returned to his regular position in the no 4 shirt and Dennis Gillespie was restored to his normal position at no 10. Jerry Kerr had not written off Frank, however, and played him at no 8, so he must have done well in the manager's eyes after his introduction to the side. Following a poor start to the season, United were revived by the arrival of Swedish winger Orjan Persson and Danish striker Finn Dossing. The latter hit 21 goals in just 19 games as they finished a respectable ninth in the 18-team division, which saw Kilmarnock champions on goal average from Hearts. On a dramatic final day, Killie went to Hearts standing two points adrift of their hosts but won 2-0 to snatch the title by 0.042 of a goal. There was no such drama for Frank to savour but he had played in 20 of the 34 League games and could look back on a highly satisfactory first season as a first-teamer.

His first League goal for the club had come in a 3-2 home win over Morton towards the end of the season. It was a dramatic one as well, a header from an Orjan Persson cross three minutes from time to secure victory. He was not involved in the two League games with Rangers but at last got the chance to face the mighty Gers when he was in the side who lost 2-0 to them as 23,000 packed into Tannadice for a second-round clash in the Scottish Cup. He did not have the chance to pit his wits against Jim Baxter, however, as the great man was still recovering from a broken leg.

FROM DUNDEE TO DOC

As 1964-65 progressed, things were going well on the field for Frank but not so well off it. There were always people ready to shoot him down and hand him advice only in a back-handed sort of way. One reporter wrote: "Francis has everything that it takes to make him a great player. The brains, the physique and the ability are all there but this likeable young player is inclined to put on the beef and there are times when it affects his playing ability and makes him look ponderous." Another typical quotation came from redoubtable Dundee United full-back Jimmy Briggs when the team were travelling on a train back from a game: "Francis came into the compartment. It was like an eclipse of the sun as the 14st broth of a boy seemed to get in the way of most of the lights."

Such comments were probably made with the best of intentions but sometimes Frank did let them affect him. He had plenty of encouragement from the likes of Jimmy Briggs and Tommy Neilson about the football side of life but, as with most young men in the limelight, he had to learn by experience as to his life away from the game. Being a local lad, knowing and being known by lots of people, his audience widened the more he made the headlines. Obviously, many were a wee bit jealous when a local boy made good. So it was not long before rumours began being bandied about . . . if he laughed out loud in a pub, he was drunk. It did not help matters when he was seen to be enjoying himself as young men do. It became like living in a goldfish bowl because the more Frank played, the more people knew him.

New Year's Day in Scotland is a big deal, with a full League programme but, with the uncertainty of the weather, there were times when it was impossible for all matches to be played. It was on one of these occasions in 1966 that Frank was to find himself in hot water with the Dundee United board of directors. The team had been taken away the day before – a normal occurrence – but they found out on New Year's Eve that their match had been snowed off. Jerry Kerr, in his wisdom, allowed the married players to go home and spend New Year's Eve with their families. The single lads were confined to barracks, as it were, in the hotel. However, one of the bachelors, Ian Mitchell, was given permission to return to the house where he lodged in Dundee. That left just Frank and the Norwegian winger Finn Seeman. Obviously, they felt unfairly treated and could not see why they should not be able to join in the New Year celebrations, so off they went, not thinking there was any way they could be found out. However, found out they eventually were and they were ordered to appear before the United board, who fined them £25 each – almost a week's wages. Frank could never understand why the vast majority of the squad were allowed home and two others kept back. Kerr told the press: "We had no alternative but to discipline the players. We just cannot stand for club instructions being disregarded."

Inevitably, the incident was mulled over and one reporter remarked that part of the problem was that young footballers were being paid too much. There was too much gallivanting about in cars and that sort of thing. It is laughable now but the board of directors were so furious about the piece that they issued a statement saying that, of the £27 paid to the players, £7 was put in their wage packets and £20 paid into their bank accounts. The story about the fines broke two weeks into the new year, just before United entertained St Mirren. By coincidence, all three bachelors played a prominent part in a 3-0 win, with Frank heading two goals, one from a Seeman corner, and Mitchell scoring the third.

Although Frank was playing well and was one of the favourites of the Tannadice crowd, he did not get on well with Jerry Kerr. To be honest, he did not rate him very highly as a manager. He was constantly switched from attacking inside-forward to defensive midfield and back again. If centre-half Doug Smith had not been such a stalwart in his position, Frank was sure Kerr would have tried him at no 5 because he had captained the Scotland youth team when playing centre-half. Smith, however, was a United legend, eventually totalling over 600 competitive games for the club. Frank was forever being reminded by Kerr to keep his weight down and to watch his drinking. He had moved out of his aunt and uncle's home into the club hostel with some of the younger members of the squad, so, consequently, Kerr was able to check on his comings and goings.

A way out of this situation would soon emerge as he met Margaret Nicoll, a local girl, whom he eventually married. Her grandmother, also Margaret Nicoll, who lived around the corner, had a spare room and was looking for a lodger – and Frank fitted the bill. This gave him the independence he sought and the bonus was that new girlfriend Margaret lived within 100 yards. Margaret's grandmother turned out to be a wonderful lady whom Frank admired immensely – just like his own grandmother, who had looked after him until she died. They were two people he held in great esteem. The new arrangement had its down side, though. Manager Kerr once again called Frank into his office to express his concerns about rumours of late nights and drinking sprees. Frank tried to explain that people had become jealous of his success and could not wait to knock him down. He admitted that he did go out for a drink but did not go overboard. In Frank's opinion, it was particularly difficult for a local lad to make good, especially in football.

Even though he could not drink legally, he bought a car so he could go further afield and stem the flow of rumours. Rather naughtily, he taught himself and began driving without a licence. Some months – and a few minor bumps – later, he was given a 'producer' after being stopped by the police. He had to turn up at the nearest station with his documents and knew from that moment he was in trouble because he did not have any to produce, least of all a driving licence! It just happened that when he did call at the station, the officer at the desk was an old friend of his – one frequently on duty at Tannadice. When he found out Frank had not even got a licence, he went absolutely ballistic. "Frank," he bawled, "you could have got me the sack. I've had a lift off you many times after the match and all the time you haven't had a licence. I could have been done for aiding and abetting."

Of course, Jerry Kerr got wind of the matter and immediately impounded the car and parked it underneath the stands where, much to his amusement, Frank could catch sight of it during a game. This made Frank even more determined to take a test and be able to drive legally but that process turned into a complete shambles. Having missed his first test because he overslept, he had an early night before his second so he was refreshed and raring to go. After checking in with the examiner, they both walked outside to proceed and Frank was asked: "Where's the car?" "What car?" came the reply. He was so naïve. He thought tests were taken in the examiner's car. With a face like thunder, the examiner stormed off but I bet that didn't prevent roars of laughter when he recounted the story to his colleagues. That was it as far as Frank was concerned. He was not going to bother with tests any more. In his own mind, he could drive and it was to be another ten years before he took a test again – in Wolverhampton.

With the rest of his relatives liking a drink, the Munro name was always to the fore even if he was not drinking with them. It is difficult to stop the rumours when they start – you can hardly hand out leaflets denying every little story. Frank still did not rate Jerry Kerr but then again he really had not had anybody to measure him against, apart from that brief spell at Chelsea. Frank was only 18 and, apart from international managers at youth team and other levels, Kerr was the first boss he had. He felt Kerr was always on his back and the fact that he played him in several different positions made him think he was not rated. Frank realised many years later that the fact that Kerr trusted him in several positions and was always trying to keep him on the right road meant that the manager really did rate him. What do we footballers of 18 years of age know? All we want to do is play without anybody getting on to us about our weight or our drinking habits.

What cannot be denied is that Dundee United certainly did rate Kerr. He had taken them into the top flight and kept them there. He is credited as being the man who transformed them from an ordinary side into one who could rub shoulders with Rangers, Celtic and Aberdeen. Confirmation of his standing in their history came in 2003, when the main stand at Tannadice was renamed after him a year on from his death. Frank was among the many old United players invited back to the ground for the unveiling ceremony.

League football was put on hold for Frank for the last three games of 1964-65 – his country needed him. His progress had not gone unnoticed by the Scotland youth team selectors and he was named in the squad for the European tournament in Germany. Scotland opened with a 1-1 draw against Italy in Stuttgart after Hibernian's Jimmy O'Rourke had given them a 14th-minute lead. Petrenic levelled 20 minutes into the second half. The Scotland team in that game on April 15, 1965 was: McCloy (Motherwell), Dickson (Kilmarnock), Gartshore (Hibernian), Munro (Dundee United), Whiteford (Hibernian), Murray (Morton), Lister (Aberdeen), Jardine (Dunipace Thistle), O'Rourke (Hibernian), Law (Queen of South), Johnston (Rangers). O'Rourke was on target again in the next match thanks to Frank's precision pass as Yugoslavia were beaten 1-0 in Freiberg. However, the groups consisted of only three teams so, when the Italians then beat the Yugoslavs 2-0, goal difference saw the Scottish lads eliminated. Favourites England were beaten 3-2 by East Germany in the final. So Frank returned home with a couple of international caps to his name and he still had some action awaiting him before he could take a break.

Having played 20 League games, eight League Cup ties and two Scottish Cup ties in his debut season, he might, as a 17-year-old budding star, have been ready for a rest but Frank would have played all year if he had the chance. That is why he welcomed a further ten games in the Scottish Summer Cup. This competition, first played during the war, had been revived the previous season with the aim of raising much-needed extra revenue, although the big two, Rangers and Celtic, shunned it. Not so Dundee United and that meant matches throughout May. United were in a qualifying group of four with Aberdeen, Dundee and St Johnstone. They won all six games, hitting 21 goals and conceding only six. Those wins included a double over neighbours Dundee, 4-1 away and 3-2 at home. Frank's only goal was in the 4-1 home win over St Johnstone when he scored from the penalty spot. In the semi-final, Partick Thistle were beaten 3-0 at Tannadice after a goalless draw in the first leg. The final was also over two legs and United were on the back foot after losing the first one 3-1 at Motherwell. Finn Dossing had given them an early lead, only for Pat Delaney to cancel it out. In the second half, Motherwell went ahead through Joe McBride, a player who had been signed by Wolves several years earlier and then transferred to Luton without making a first-team appearance while at Molineux. Delaney stretched the lead 13 minutes from time but United must have fancied their chances of overturning the deficit in the second leg when their Danish winger Mogens Berg saw his 12th-minute free-kick deflected past 18-year-old goalkeeper Peter McCloy, Frank's Scotland youth team colleague. However, the youngster was not beaten again as he defied a string of efforts. The game, played on June 2, attracted a gate of over 18,000. That was a decent attendance but the Summer Cup was not played again, with Frank probably one of the few who regretted its passing.

Frank cemented his place in the team during 1965-66 by playing 28 League games and scoring 13 goals. If he scored in a match, he usually scored twice. Six times he hit a brace in League games and also netted two when Motherwell were beaten 4-1 in the League Cup. His first double came in a 5-1 Tannadice win over St Johnstone early in the season after United had lost their opening League game 4-0 at home to Celtic. The St Johnstone game was the second in a run of six successive League wins. During that run, United also beat Falkirk in a Dewar Shield match, with Frank again twice on the mark. In a seven-game sequence, United had therefore scored 34 goals.

Another two-goal contribution by Frank came in a 4-2 home win over Morton early in the season and was an example of his reluctance to miss a game unless it was absolutely essential. He had a cold but did not tell the manager and his state of health might have been why he had a poor game – apart from his goals. Unkindly, some of the home fans gave him some 'stick' yet at the end he was in a distressed state and was packed straight off home to bed. Hopefully, when the background to his display was made known, those jeering fans were ashamed of themselves. It was typical Frank, though. No way would he willingly miss playing. As a midfielder, his main role was to make goals but he soon showed he could score them as well, with both feet and his head. Frank wore the no 8 shirt for most of the season until the signing of Billy Hainey from Partick Thistle. Then, Frank was switched to no 7 and both men shone in a 1-0 win over Rangers in March, 1966. Hainey scored his first goal for the club but the Glasgow Herald reporter noted: "Munro, as linkman, distributed long accurate passes." That was a vital defeat for Rangers. They won their remaining seven games but finished two points behind champions Celtic. Dundee United were a creditable fifth. That was good enough to earn them a place in the Fairs Cup the following season, when they gained memorable home and away wins over mighty Barcelona – but Frank would have no part in games which went down in United history.

Before the sudden developments which would take his career in a new direction, though, he had a busy summer with the Scotland youth team. They were off to the UEFA under-19 championship in Yugoslavia and warmed up with a friendly against England, who had beaten them 5-3 at Hereford earlier in the season. It was a different story this time at Ibrox as the Scottish lads impressed in a 4-1 win despite playing against a side who included several players who would later establish themselves in the English game, notably Phil Summerill (Birmingham), Alec Lindsay (Liverpool), Frank Lampard Senior (West Ham), David Craggs (Newcastle), Mike Bernard (Stoke) and Jimmy Husband (Everton). The scorers for the Scots were Gordon Cumming (Arsenal, 2), Alan Campbell (Charlton) and Joe Harper (Morton). Lindsay, who was then on Bury's books, replied for England. Frank played at centre-half and was immaculate. The wonder is that no-one twigged that this was the position that was meant for him. One man who certainly did see the light was youth team boss Roy Small, who spotted Frank's potential as a pivot. Before the game against England, he said: "Frank Munro is a natural at centre-half. Though he has been played by Dundee United at inside-forward and wing-half, I reckon his build and style make him just the lad for the no 5 jersey – and the youth selectors agree with me."

So, in late May, 1966, he set off for the UEFA Under-19 Championship and was not only named as centre-half but also given the captaincy. That says much for his status in the eyes of the selectors. Small had said beforehand: "When you get a set of players together on an occasion like this, the natural captain tends to emerge." Led by Frank, Scotland went through their group stage unbeaten but drew all three games and so failed to qualify for the knockout stages. The opening match was a 1-1 draw with Spain in Pristina and it proved a tough experience for Frank and his pals, as one report confirmed. Their opponents were described in the Glasgow Herald as "far from scrupulous . . . they specialised in body checking and the tackle fractionally late. As a result, most of the Scots had bruises after the game and Leven was limping for the last 50 minutes." Arthur Duncan of Partick Thistle gave Scotland the lead on 27 minutes but Balzien levelled midway through the second half. The Scotland line-up was: Devlin (Morton), Murray (Morton), Halpin (Hamilton Academical), Purcell (Chelsea), Munro (Dundee United), Borthwick (Morton), Leven (Arsenal), Cumming (Arsenal), Harper (Morton), Campbell (Charlton), Duncan (Partick Thistle).

It was no surprise that Arsenal's battered Neill Leven missed the next game, which saw the team held 1-1 by West Germany. Duncan, on 50 minutes, again gave Scotland the lead but Schollbech equalised 14 minutes later. Only a couple of fine saves late in the game by keeper Dennis Devlin preserved a point. The Glasgow Herald report reckoned the Scottish lads were superior individually but failed because of the wrong tactics, persisting in crossing high balls into the middle, where the diminutive Joe Harper had little chance against a tall goalkeeper and bulky centre-half. Reflecting on the first two games, a so-called special correspondent in the Glasgow Evening Times wrote: "Munro, a dominating player, has proved an ideal skipper."

To have any chance of qualifying, the Scots had to beat a Dutch side who had lost their previous two games. For some reason, the selectors moved Frank to inside-right and it looked like paying off when they led 2-1 at the break through goals from Hugh McLeish and Arthur Duncan. However, the Dutch came back to draw 2-2 and the rearranged Scottish line-up lost their way. The verdict in the Glasgow Herald was: "Scotland's tactics did not seem right for this vital match. Their inside-forwards played too deep and the gamble of having Munro, the centre-half, at inside-right did not come off." Even harsher was the Evening Times correspondent, who wrote: "Rarely has a Scottish side failed so miserably as this young team in their final qualifying match in Mirovica last night. They seemed tired almost from the early minutes of the game and could do no more than draw. They could not have qualified anyway, as Spain won the section convincingly by beating West Germany 3-1. It would have at least been some consolation to say the Scots went down fighting but they simply faded away, apparently too tired and too slow to get on top of a side which had little more than enthusiasm and a brilliant right-half in Schneider. This fellow scored two goals and looked capable of running through the Scottish defence every time he got the ball. The Scots have stayed in the same hotel as the other three teams in the section, they have eaten the same food and had basically the same preparation. Yet, for some reason, they had much less stamina. The Scottish tactics were also quite baffling as, in a game where they had to win by two goals, they actually spent most of the time defending, with only Hugh McLeish up front."

They were tough words for the young Scots but the report did note that Frank's effectiveness had been curtailed by an ankle injury sustained in the first half. There was another blast at the beaten team in the final paragraph: "If the Scots were tired last night, they will be feeling a lot worse by the early hours of tomorrow morning when they expect to complete the 20-hour return trip, which will probably include six take-offs and four different planes." Not much sympathy there for a bunch of young lads who had done their best. McLeish, then on East Fife's books, had a promising career cut short through injury and later went into politics. He became a Westminster MP and also a member of the Scottish Parliament. After the sudden death of Donald Dewar, he became Scottish first minister, although enjoying only a brief tenure of office. Derk Schneider went on to have a fine career with Feyenoord and Go Ahead Eagles and won several full international caps. Despite the disappointment, it had been a memorable experience for Frank and the other young players – and at least they had done better than England, who bowed out with two defeats and a draw from their group games. Italy and hosts Yugoslavia drew 0-0 in the final and shared the trophy.

Attention then turned to another international football competition, this one taking place south o' the border during the summer of 1966 but I suspect Frank and his fellow Scots paid little heed to it. After all, it was only the World Cup finals. The Scots had a cunning idea – see who wins the competition, play them, beat them and then declare themselves world champions! Following his efforts in Yugoslavia during May, the Munro plan was to have some time off before getting back to pre-season training and then, in all probability, continuing to build on the progress of two seasons in the Dundee United first team. The best-laid schemes o' mice an' men gang aft agley, as a certain Scottish poet once wrote. Suddenly, Frank did not seem to be an automatic choice at the start of the 1966-67 campaign, which began with the Scottish League Cup group stage. And he was not happy about it.

He played in the opening League game, however, a 2-0 defeat at St Johnstone, but, to accommodate the return of Orjan Persson for the Tayside derby, he was relegated to substitute. He was unused as United lost 4-1 at home to their rivals from down the road. He was back a week later to help United win 7-0 at Ayr United but only because Tommy Neilson was sidelined. There were seven changes in the side, three positional, and, after a goalless first half, the re-jigged line-up really clicked, scoring seven times in the space of 27 minutes. For the next game, the visit of the mighty Rangers, Frank was again omitted while the other ten in the seven-goal romp kept their places. He spent a rainy afternoon as the unused sub as his team lost 3-2. That was probably the last straw for Frank. He was just short of his 19th birthday but he had broken into the first team at an early age and suddenly not being a first-choice selection irked him.

Instead of biding his time to see how things panned out, Frank put in a transfer request. It was more for the shock factor than anything else – call it the impetuosity of youth, if you like – and he never thought it would be granted. However, it was granted and he was in the news again with speculation all around as to which club had 'tapped him up.' In fact, there was no ulterior motive. It was just done on a whim. Indeed, one reporter commented: "It strikes me that his request to go comes with the impetuosity of his age and because he feels annoyed at being dropped." So, after 80 first-team games, which had been invaluable in terms of experience gained, Frank was open to offers. His short career at Dundee United had been full of highs and lows, bookings and fines, goals and gaffes, but he had enjoyed his time there, particularly because it was his home town and he had felt at ease there.

Chapter Two

Dons Come Calling

A statement from Dundee United manager Jerry Kerr after Frank's shock transfer request, read: "We are letting him go with reluctance. I think he is a wonderful player but he is obviously dissatisfied." The same report quoted Frank: "I don't really care where I go. Scotland or England, it's all the same to me." The Scottish newspapers were full of it –

"United will sell Munro"

"Tannadice shock – Munro wants away"

"Munro shock for United"

"United reluctantly agree – Munro for transfer"

Initial reports indicated several English clubs were interested in Frank, among them Newcastle, Huddersfield and Blackpool. Huddersfield boss Tom Johnston and Newcastle's Stan Seymour were said to have run the rule over him but, when the inevitable move came, the direction was north, not south. Aberdeen had money to spend, having sold half-back Dave Smith to Rangers for £45,000 in August, 1966. So, for a fee of £10,000 – some sources said £12,000 – Francis Munro joined Aberdeen on October 13, 1966. The details were finalised at an Arbroath hotel and Frank said after signing: "This is really marvellous. I have enjoyed my football at Tannadice but felt for some time that I can better myself with a change of club." If he thought he might have things easier, though, little did he know what was in store for him.

Not long before he moved, a newspaper report read: "What a controversial lump of a laddie he is. So full of natural football know-how, so difficult to direct in the matter of containing his weight." A story went round that while Frank was watching a game one day, he wolfed down eight pies at half-time. Now, as to whether the story was true or exaggerated, I can only say that I knew Frank for an awful long time and I cannot imagine this to have been the case. He might have had two or three but I could never see him eating eight. He told me he really could not remember. An Aberdeen fan said when he heard of Frank's transfer: "Well, he's coming to the right place to get his weight down. Just watch how Eddie

Turnbull takes it all off him." A former Scotland inside-forward, Turnbull was Aberdeen manager and had the reputation as a tough taskmaster. He had been a member of the fine Hibernian side who were Scottish champions three times in five seasons just after the Second World War. He was part of the Famous Five forward line with Gordon Smith, Bobby Johnstone, Lawrie Reilly and Willie Ormond. Turnbull could also boast being the first British player to score in European competition. Although Aberdeen were champions in 1955, they declined to enter the inaugural European Cup and Hibernian took their place. When Hibs won the first leg of their first-round tie with RotWeiss Essen 4-0, Turnbull opened the scoring to claim his place in history.

Turnbull was not a man to let Frank get away with carrying too much weight or not looking after himself. However, it must be said that once a player gets a reputation, the stories abound and most of them are exaggerated. Just look at the tales about Scottish legend Jim Baxter – although maybe 90 per cent of those were true! "You'll be sorry you joined us by the time we've finished with you" was what, in effect, Turnbull told Frank a fortnight after he signed for Aberdeen. He reckoned Frank was 2st overweight and put him on a crash programme to get rid of the surplus in double quick time. It meant a strict adherence to a diet sheet and a course of strenuous weight training, steam baths and hard labour track work. Afternoons were spent without respite on exercises planned by experts at an Aberdeen health studio. He spent an unhappy 19th birthday sweating off the ounces in the steam baths and declared "I feel great" after losing 5lbs – but he was lying through his teeth!

Let us turn to Eddie Turnbull for his side of the story. Eddie wrote about it at length in his autobiography, Having a Ball, and said Frank's move came about because of the need for a successor to Dave Smith. "I had already identified a possible replacement elsewhere and that was Francis Munro," he said. "I had spotted him as a youngster playing with the Scottish international youth team that I had briefly coached and had waited to see him make his breakthrough with Dundee United. I would check their team line-ups to see if their then manager Jerry Kerr was giving Munro a run in the team but I rarely saw his name and I wondered what was wrong. One of my friends in the press was Tommy Gallacher of the Dundee Courier. I called him and asked about Munro and he told me that Munro was not getting on with his manager. I took the plunge and called Jerry Kerr. 'I was wondering about Francis Munro, Jerry, as I had him with me in the youth team.' Jerry replied that Francis was not yet fulfilling his promise and, suspecting there was more to that remark than met the ear, I left things a few weeks and made some discreet inquiries. It turned out there had been some family difficulties, so I twisted Jerry Kerr's arm and said: 'Let me talk to him.'

"I could see immediately I was dealing with an unhappy young man, who was also carrying some excess weight. But I was sure that I could get the best out of this skilful footballer, so I persuaded the board to stump up £12,000 for him and talked Francis into coming to Pittodrie. 'You're a big lad, son, but you're carrying some excess weight. I'll get that off you and I know you can play, so come and join Aberdeen because we're going places,' I told him. How could he turn down such an approach? I made sure he went into good digs with a caring landlady and then got to work on his weight problems. The excess flab did not last long, especially after I gave him the 'hothouse' treatment. Poor Francis would spend hours in the stadium's boiler room wreathed in tracksuit and jerseys until he had lost sufficient weight to allow him to take a full part in training. And to encourage him, I joined him in the hothouse – I was soon wasting away to a shadow. I also enrolled Francis with a local fitness trainer and, as he got fitter, it was gratifying to see this young man blossom as a footballer. Indeed, I would say that once he gained full fitness, he was possibly the best all-round player I worked with."

It is worth stopping to re-read that last sentence. Eddie Turnbull's assessment of Frank bears out what we at Molineux came to appreciate – that Francis Munro was one of the game's truly naturally gifted players. Many years later, Frank did admit that Turnbull's tough fitness regime and insistence on discipline probably did him a lot of good. In an article in the Topical Times annual, Frank said: "I'd had the reputation at Tannadice Park of being a bit of a bad lad. I was young and impressionable and thought I could get away with doing all the wrong things." There was no chance of getting away with much at Aberdeen and Frank added that Turnbull was the only man he was ever scared of. "I was frightened to death of him. With United, I was Jack the Lad. In the side at 16 and a half, captain of the Scotland youth team, a regular in the United first team. I used to eat fish and chips every night, drink too much beer and generally let myself go. By the time I asked for a transfer from Tannadice, my weight had reached 15st 9lb."

Frank made his Aberdeen debut, two days after being signed, against Ayr United, in a 2-0 victory at Pittodrie made possible thanks to second-half goals from Jimmy Smith and Ernie Winchester. There were fewer than 5,000 there to see what was a welcome win for the Dons as they had won only one of their first five League games. Frank delighted the meagre home crowd with a sound display at left-half. A newspaper report headlined "Francie pleases Dons fans" gave an encouraging verdict: "Fans were very impressed with Francie's intelligent play at left-half. His passing was immaculate and he timed his tackles to perfection. If the big youth international can keep up this form – and lose about a stone in weight – the Dons boss Eddie Turnbull will have more than filled the gap left by the waygoing of Dave Smith to Rangers."

Making his debut the previous week was 17-year-old Martin Buchan, who would later skipper Aberdeen before going on to have a fine career with Manchester United and Scotland. It was he who made way for Frank and he was restricted to just four League appearances that season. But his time would soon come. Another Aberdeen new boy against Ayr was 19-year-old full-back Jim Hermiston and he, like Frank, would end his playing days in Australia. Hermiston established himself in the Dons side within a few seasons before a fall-out with the club saw him quit to become a policeman. He eventually emigrated and resumed his football career Down Under. In the Ayr line-up for the first time was Bertie Black, who had been signed from Kilmarnock. The teams for Frank's Aberdeen debut on Saturday, October 15, 1966 were:

Aberdeen: Clark, Hermiston, Shewan, Millar, McMillan, Munro, Pat Wilson, Melrose, Winchester, Smith, Jimmy Wilson. Sub: Little. Ayr United: Millar, Malone, Murphy, Quinn, Moran, Mitchell, Grant, McMillan, Black, Ingram, Hawkshaw. Sub: Paterson.

Frank recalled in Topical Times: "After my debut, Eddie had me back on the Sunday morning on my own for extra training. He put me in a kit, a tracksuit, a sweat-suit, everything he could find. Then he made me do running work on the track for an hour and a half. When I stripped off, perspiration flowed. I was so weak that I actually fainted. I had lost 15lb in one session! After that, Eddie put me on the scales every single morning. The training and the fact I was frightened to eat anything brought me down to 13st 5lb. If ever I tipped over that limit, I would be back on the track. I believe if I'd gone my old way, I'd have been out of the game in six months."

Those efforts at Pittodrie must have stood Frank in good stead because he managed to keep himself relatively trim while at Wolves. At the start of each season, the match programme would list our height and weight and, for 1969-70, Frank's weight was given as 13st 6lbs. Mind you, that still made him our heaviest player, apart from goalkeeper Phil Parkes.

While Davie Millar was at right-half in that Aberdeen game against Ayr, Frank soon took over that position and played there for virtually the rest of the season, with the Dane Jens Petersen at left-half. Turnbull had built a useful side with a blend of youth and experience and, after the Ayr victory, the Dons reeled off another seven successive wins, including one that would have warmed Frank's heart – a 3-1 away success over his old club Dundee United. He was cup-tied for Aberdeen's Scottish League Cup semi-final with Rangers, which took place during that successful League run, and could only watch as his new club lost 2-0 in a replay after a 2-2 draw.

Celtic were at the height of their powers at the time, so Frank could be pleased with his display when Aberdeen held them 1-1 at Pittodrie on Christmas Eve. On a cold windy day which saw a flurry of snow, Frank nearly won the game, too, when, five minutes from time, he shot from 12 yards, only for Ronnie Simpson to push it over the bar. It was the last of a series of fine saves by the 36-year-old goalkeeper. Bobby Lennox struck for Celtic on 25 minutes and it was Frank who created the Aberdeen equaliser for Harry Melrose five minutes later. Soon after, Frank sent a flying header narrowly past the post. The Glasgow Herald report of the game noted: "Once again, Munro showed that it was a shrewd move by Mr E Turnbull, the manager, to sign him from Dundee United." And this is how the Herald described the equaliser: "Taylor slipped the ball back to Shewan, whose cross to the far side of the goal was made to measure for Munro. The right-half headed the ball back across goal and Melrose's header found the net. Even then, Simpson got a hand to the ball but could not stop it." Simpson's display took some of the limelight away from Frank's sparkling performance. The keeper, who had collected FA Cup winner's medals with Newcastle in 1952 and 1955, was enjoying a second lease of life in a career that had begun with Queen's Park 20 years earlier. The following April, he became Scotland's oldest debutant when he helped them beat World Cup holders England 3-2 at Wembley.

Frank's first goal for the Dons came a week after the Celtic game in a 4-0 home win over Kilmarnock. The first half was goalless but the Dons took the lead through Harry Melrose ten minutes after the break and scored three times in the last 15 minutes, with Frank collecting the final goal. Two days later, he was on target twice as Aberdeen celebrated the new year with a 5-2 home win over Dundee. That put them second behind Celtic in the top flight. Any hopes of giving the Glasgow giants a run for their money quickly disappeared, however. Next day, Aberdeen lost 1-0 to St Johnstone in Perth at the start of a run that brought three defeats and a draw. Nevertheless, it was a decent start to Frank's Aberdeen career and, although it was against his principles, he did work at getting his weight down and trained hard to get himself fit. It helped that the manager kept him in a settled position at right-half and did not ask him to play in a different position every week. Training was different, too, especially the sessions played on the three-quarter pitch with four sets of goals. This was designed to switch from defence to attack and vice versa as quickly as possible. Frank enjoyed this because it was different and, most of all, it was with a ball at his feet instead of the mundane drudge of running round a track. The system was not that different from the one used by Arsene Wenger in his early days at Arsenal.

One of the first things Eddie Turnbull had done on being given the job at Pittodrie was to change the training methods. He had spent time at Chelsea, observing what Tommy Docherty did, and was amazed to find that, at Aberdeen, there were only six footballs for use during training. One of his first actions as manager was to send out for more, so each player could train with a ball. It was an indication of Turnbull's philosophy – training was about honing skill as well as fitness. Frank was still not keen on the manager despite admiring the way he did things, and thought he was a miserable so-and-so who ran the club like a sergeant major. I think this came from the fact he made the team have a cold shower before every match. Frank hated this but did not say no to the brandy he was given after it. Turnbull was proud of having served in the Royal Navy and believed that the sort of discipline he learned there had a role to play in building a successful football club. He was never one to mince his words and not unknown to come out with a Shankly-like comment. When he later managed Hibernian, he told striker Alan Gordon, who was a qualified accountant: "The trouble wi you, Gordon, is that yer brains are aw in yer heid."

The players may have viewed Turnbull with grudging respect rather than affection but on-field results were what mattered and his team threatened at one stage to finish League runners-up to the all-conquering Celtic. The dip in their League form at the start of 1967 came as they embarked on a successful run in the Scottish Cup. They breezed through the first two rounds by 5-0 scorelines, first away to Dundee, then at home to St Johnstone, the latter after a goalless first half. They had a tough quarter-final against Hibernian with Easter Road heaving under a 37,000 crowd but managed a 1-1 draw thanks to a Jimmy Smith header from a Harry Melrose corner four minutes before time. There was an even bigger gate at Pittodrie – 44,000, a midweek record for the ground – as the Dons won the replay 3-0. Ernie Winchester was brought back at centre-forward and scored after only three minutes. Jimmy Storrie made it two and he laid on the third 12 minutes into the second half, centring from the left for Winchester to head home.

It was an astute bit of management by Eddie Turnbull to recall Winchester with Jimmy Smith sidelined by injury. Winchester was no longer a first choice but the boss remembered he had in the past given the run-around to Hibs centre-half John

Madsen. Turnbull pointed out to Winchester that a good display would not only serve Aberdeen well but could impress clubs who might want to sign him. The selection certainly proved inspired, although it was reported the following day that Winchester had put in a transfer request. He left the club at the end of the season and signed for Kansas City Spurs.

That win over Hibs meant a semi-final to savour for Frank as it was another meeting with his old team Dundee United and in his old city. A week before the big match, the sides met at Pittodrie and Aberdeen lost 1-0, Jackie Graham scoring five minutes before half-time. The semi-final was a different story. It was a dour game before 41,500 fans jammed into Dens Park, the only goal falling to Aberdeen after just four minutes through United's Tommy Millar. Goalkeeper Sandy Davie dropped the ball from a Wilson corner and Jim Smith chipped back across goal where Millar, in trying to clear, put the ball into his own net. It should have been more comfortable for the Dons when they were awarded a first-half penalty after a foul by Lennart Wing on Harry Melrose. Frank had been delegated to take any spot-kicks after Jimmy Wilson had missed one against United at Pittodrie. However, when the moment came, Frank thought Sandy Davie, his old team-mate at United, might have an idea where he would send the ball, so he asked Jim Storrie to do the honours. Storrie promptly shot two yards wide. It was another lesson for Frank – that is what happens when you think too much!

Nevertheless, Aberdeen were rarely troubled as they clinched their place in the final. There was one moment of worry when Dennis Gillespie went down as he was tackled by Frank and United yelled for a penalty. Referee Tom Wharton ignored the claims and was not an official you would argue with. The man they called 'Tiny' stood 6ft 4in and was a refereeing legend. Frank said: "I know it may sound phoney but I'm sorry our appearance in the final at Hampden has to be at the expense of my old pals. I've a lot of sympathy for United, especially Tommy Millar." Looking ahead to the big day, a report in the Glasgow Herald reckoned Aberdeen would have to find more strength and sharpness in attack if they were to have their name engraved on the trophy for only a second time. There was no criticism of the defence, though, and special praise came for Frank. "Aberdeen have few worries in defence," reported the Herald. "They hardly put a foot wrong, particularly Munro, whose accurate passing was a feature of the game."

Three days after the semi-final win, there was a glimpse into the future when Frank donned the no 5 shirt with regular pivot Tommy McMillan sidelined. He did all right at Motherwell before blotting his copybook in the final minute. He under-hit a ball to Bobby Clark – keepers could handle back passes in those days

– and Hunter nipped in amid the resulting collision to give the home side a 3-2 win. In his familiar midfield role four days later, Frank got back on track by scoring twice in a 6-1 home win over Falkirk. His display brought a glowing report in the Aberdeen Press and Journal. "With a superb blend of power and football intelligence, this big lad really made the whole of the midfield his own and yet still had time to come away with a couple of goals," their correspondent wrote.

By then, Aberdeen knew their opponents in the Scottish Cup final would be Celtic, whose two first-half goals, from Bobby Lennox and Bertie Auld, had been enough to see off Clyde in the semi-final replay at Hampden after a surprise 0-0 draw in front of 57,000 at the same venue in the first meeting. Ten days before the final, the sides met in the League on a wet and windy night at Parkhead and Aberdeen gave their confidence a boost by blunting the much-vaunted Celtic attack to earn a goalless draw. A preview of the final noted: "Aberdeen have an excellent defence centred around twin centre-halves McMillan and Petersen, and a powerful midfield player in Munro. But they have not the attacking power of Celtic, who will have a big advantage on the wings. Johnstone and Lennox could be the Celtic match-winners." That proved a prophetic preview as each Celtic winger made a goal.

There were 126,102 fans at Hampden Park to see the final, which Aberdeen lost 2-0. Both goals were scored by Willie Wallace, one just before half-time and one just after. He fired home a cross from Lennox on the left to open the score and added his second by driving home a centre from the right by Jimmy Johnstone. It was no shame to lose to the wonderful Celtic side who ended up with all three Scottish domestic trophies that season before becoming the first British team to win the European Cup when they beat Inter Milan in Lisbon. Young Frank was not disgraced in the final as newspaper cuttings show. He was picked as the star man for his team with the comment "a tireless worker throughout, never gave up the fight." The teams on Saturday, April 29, 1967 were:

Celtic: Simpson, Craig, Gemmell, Murdoch, McNeill, Clark, Johnstone, Wallace, Chalmers, Auld, Lennox. Aberdeen: Clark, Whyte, Shewan, Munro, McMillan, Petersen, Wilson, Smith, Storrie, Melrose, Johnston.

One thing that helps if you are in a cup final is to have an untroubled build-up and for everything to go smoothly on the day. Aberdeen were unlucky on both counts. Manager Turnbull was ill during the week before the game and missed training. He was diagnosed with hepatitis and was far from well when he joined the squad at the Gleneagles Hotel. Despite his determination to be there on the big day, he was too ill to travel to Hampden. He had to listen to the game on the radio in his hotel room. So the team were without their mentor and, on the way to the ground, there was more disruption. Their coach was involved in an accident and the team arrived late. There was no chance of a measured pre-match preparation as the players hurriedly got changed in time for kick-off. Even the usually nerveless Frank must have been upset by the way things had gone before they had even kicked a ball. It was hardly the way to prepare to face Europe's top team.

A few hundred miles away on the same day, I was in the Wolves side fighting out an epic Second Division game with our top-of-the-table rivals Coventry City at a packed Highfield Road. Frank probably never gave that game a second thought as the Sky Blues, trailing to a Peter Knowles goal at half-time, came back to beat us 3-1. Little could he have guessed that the bulk of his football career would be with the team wearing all gold that afternoon. Celtic expected four days later to add the League title to the League Cup and Scottish Cup but were surprisingly beaten 3-2 at home by Frank's old club, Dundee United, despite twice being ahead. It was only delaying the inevitable and Celtic had the extreme satisfaction of clinching the championship at the home of their arch rivals Rangers with a 2-2 draw before 78,000 at Ibrox.

Despite the disappointment of losing the Scottish Cup final, the Dons had enjoyed a good campaign, finishing fourth behind Celtic in a Scottish First Division which in those days consisted of 18 clubs. It was the Dons' highest finish for 11 years, another measure of their progress being that they had reached the knockout stages of the League Cup for the first time since 1958. The final League game was a 1-1 draw at Kilmarnock and ended on a low note for Frank as his hand-ball 12 minutes from time enabled 19-year-old wing star Tommy McLean to level from the resultant penalty. Frank had appeared in all but five of the team's 34 League games and hit six goals. It had been a long hard season for Aberdeen but it was not over yet. A tour of America was still in front of them in a competition involving a Brazilian team (Bangu), one Italian (Cagliari), one Uruguayan (Cerro), one from Northern Ireland (Glentoran), one from the Irish Republic (Shamrock Rovers), three English (Wolves, Stoke and Sunderland), one Dutch (ADO den Haag) and three Scottish (Aberdeen, Dundee United and Hibernian). On tours like this, some teams treat the games like an afternoon stroll but others really want to win – and that was the case with Aberdeen, as, indeed, it was with us at Wolves. The two teams with the most points after facing all the other sides would contest the final in the Coliseum in Los Angeles.

It would prove a memorable experience for Frank, still only 19, and the rest of the squad. Aberdeen were based in Washington and played under the name of Washington Whips in the Eastern Division. The party were given an official reception by President Lyndon Johnson that led manager Eddie Turnbull, still recovering from his illness, to recall: "We were treated a bit like royalty." Turnbull had found out just what considerate hosts the Americans were. Still not well enough to jet out with the main party, he was flown out a few days later by the tournament organisers with his doctor so he could be at the President's reception.

Although the teams were divided into two groups of six, all 12 teams played each other, which is why Aberdeen eventually met Wolves of the Western Division. The Dons had lost their opening game with Stoke (alias Cleveland Stokers) 2-1 but then beat Hibernian (Toronto City) 2-1. In that game, Frank played at centre-half despite not being fully fit through a knee injury. The Dons were then held 1-1 by Cagliari (Chicago Mustangs) and beat Cerro (New York Skyliners) 3-0. A couple of 2-2 draws followed – with Glentoran (Detroit Cougars) and Stoke. They had played the Potters a second time as the competition format required that each team met one of the others twice. Then came the first showdown with Wolves.

The match in Washington on June 20, 1967, was a bad-tempered affair which escalated when Wolves chairman John Ireland attempted to retrieve the ball after it had gone behind the bench on the touchline. Frank and our midfielder David Burnside had been feuding for some time, so tempers were already fraying. Ireland was not able to control the ball properly and seemed to take an age to throw it back to the Aberdeen players who, at this point, took exception to him and surrounded him. Of course, the Wolves players, trying to protect Ireland, also piled in and there was one almighty melee at the side of the pitch. Punches were thrown and it took ages for the officials to calm things down. During the melee, Frank had flattened somebody with a punch and decided to retire from the mob before the referee identified him. Unfortunately, I was the unlucky person on the end of the punch and I finished up at the local hospital with a broken rib. That was my first encounter with Francis Munro.

Frank did not finish the game either. He and Burnside were sent off 16 minutes from time by referee Mike Rougally. As Burnside was trying to take a throw-in, Frank impeded him. So Burnside threw the ball at Frank, who promptly flattened him. Both men got their marching orders. It was Burnside, five minutes before half-time, who equalised a 23rd minute goal by Aberdeen winger Jimmy Wilson. Frank's sending-off had its sequel when he got home as the Scottish FA referee committee fined him £10 but at least did not ban him. The match, before 7,487 fans, finished 1-1, which at the time made little difference to the league positions. But Wolves had used three substitutes, which, it transpired, was against the competition rules. Aberdeen officials protested and successfully applied for the game to be replayed as a win would get them into the final. They would have finished top anyway had they not unexpectedly lost their final group game 2-1 to Shamrock (Boston Rovers). Going into it on the back of a ten-game unbeaten run, the Dons were shocked by the result, especially as it came three days after the Irish side had lost 6-1 to Hibernian. Frank was on target against Shamrock, whose goals came from Billy Dixon and Frank O'Neill.

Frank's other goal in the tournament group games came after just 12 minutes in a 1-1 draw with Sunderland (Vancouver Royals). Allan Gauden cancelled it out after 48 minutes. That meant a fifth successive draw as the first Wolves match had been followed by a goalless draw with ADO of Holland (Golden Gate Gales). Wins over Frank's old club Dundee United (Dallas Tornado) and Bangu (Houston Stags) by 2-0 and 1-0 respectively put Aberdeen back on track. After the Shamrock setback, the Dons needed to win the re-match with us to deny Stoke a place in the final and they duly won 3-0 in Washington on Monday, July 10, with Jim Storrie (2) and Martin Buchan netting. It did not make any difference to us as we were already assured of a place in the final. But the result meant the Scots topped their group ahead of Stoke by 15 points to 14 and would face us again on July 14.

The final was played in the Coliseum and what a game it was! We went on to the pitch at about 7.30 and came off at approximately 11.45. Nearly 18,000 turned up for this climax to the United Soccer Association tournament, with the President's Cup as the prize for the winners. The gate (17,824) was not many when compared with English or Scottish football but quite a few as far as the Americans were concerned because in 1967 soccer was in its infancy there. The hosts had worked hard to make it a success and their efforts had paid off. The whole tournament had been well received and the final turned out to be the icing on the cake. Before the game, there was the usual razzmatazz, something the Americans attach to all sport, with the teams not going out together but each player being announced individually and walking on to the pitch through the ranks of a pipe band.

Eventually, the football got under way and Peter Knowles carried on the excitement with a goal after only two and a half minutes. It became a high-tempo exciting game with near misses at either end. As usual with a match like this, the adrenalin flows and something has to give. Consequently, in all this excitement, Jimmy Smith, the Aberdeen inside-forward, was sent off. However, his dismissal for a foul on yours truly just past the half-hour came after he had put Aberdeen level. With our opponents down to ten men, we were clear favourites – but not as far as Aberdeen were concerned. They defied the odds and took the lead through a goal from the penalty spot. Guess who the scorer was? Yes, Francis Munro.

There was a rush of second-half scoring, starting in the 63rd minute. Knowles's centre was nodded across goal by Ernie Hunt for Burnside to make it 2-2. Jim Storrie restored Aberdeen's lead, only for Burnside to score twice to complete his hat-trick and put us 4-3 up, first heading home from fully 18 yards and then turning in a Derek Dougan centre. That should have been the winning goal but the Dons would not lie down and up stepped Frank once more. Two minutes from time, he headed home a long free-kick thumped into the Wolves six-yard area from inside his own half by fellow half-back Jens Petersen and we were into extra-time. We soon made it 5-4 through The Doog and should have clinched the final only for Terry Wharton to miss from a penalty for the only time in his Wolves career. Bobby Clark saved his kick and there was still time for Aberdeen to attack and win another penalty. Frank showed no nerves as he placed the kick this time to complete his hat-trick. So we were then into sudden death extra-time – the first team to score would win. Both teams were going home next morning and the way it was going, we feared we might miss our flights.

The vital goal was not long coming, thank goodness, but, after the thrills and spills of what had gone before, it was something of an anti-climax, a speculative cross from Wolves full-back Bobby Thomson being turned into his own net by Aberdeen's long-serving full-back Ally Shewan. While everyone felt sorry for Ally, all the players were glad it was over to be honest. It had been an exhausting night summed up by Peter Knowles, who decided to crawl on hands and knees to collect his medal. Jack Kent Cooke, the American billionaire who sponsored Wolves, gave a great off-the-cuff speech and said not even a Hollywood script writer could have come up with anything more dramatic. He later described the game as 'the most exciting I have ever seen in any sport.' Teams that night were:

Aberdeen: Clark, Whyte, Shewan, Munro, McMillan, Petersen, Storrie, Smith, Johnston, Buchan, Wilson. Wolves: Parkes, Taylor, Thomson, Holsgrove, Woodfield, Burnside, Wharton, Hunt, Dougan, Knowles, Wagstaffe.

Recalling the winning goal many years later, Shewan said: "The ball came over from the Wolves left, Tommy McMillan went to head it but at the last moment left it to our keeper Bobby Clark. I was running back and it hit me and trundled over the line. I have never felt so bad in my life because it cost us a fortune in bonuses." In an interview with the Football Monthly magazine, Frank called the game 'the most thrilling of my life so far.' He added: "There had been little between us and, although there was a handsome trophy to be won, neither side seemed desperate to make it much more than an exhibition game for the benefit of the locals. Then came an explosive burst of four goals in four minutes in the second half which was to wipe away all that 'take it easy' atmosphere."

It had been a wonderful trip for Frank and the other Aberdeen lads, the team staying at the finest hotels and being welcomed warmly wherever they went. As manager Turnbull said: "It was a great experience for the players who not only played their hearts out but also got to see a lot of that great country while enjoying the best hotels and hospitality." Full-back Jim Whyte confirmed the special reception the Aberdeen squad had received. "We were treated like celebrities," he said. "Everywhere we went, we seemed to be well received. They also took us to Disneyland."

A footnote to the tournament . . . at the end of it, an All Star XI was selected. I don't know if it was by the Press or the tournament organisers but Frank was not included despite having been outstanding throughout. Aberdeen did have in it keeper Bobby Clark and defenders Pat Stanton and Tommy McMillan. Even more amazing, there was not one Wolves player selected and we won the damn thing! After six long weeks in North America, both Aberdeen and Wolves flew home tired but happy – and back to reality. That was certainly the case for Jimmy Smith, the man whose foul on me brought a sending-off. Within a day of arriving home, the Scottish Football Association handed him a 14-day ban and a £30 fine for collecting four bookings during the past season. The Dons' daring deeds in America had obviously been followed by their fans but Frank was still surprised to find there were about 200 of them at the airport to welcome the players back.

He had other matters to sort out when he returned. As I said earlier, Frank and cars were a dodgy combination and, while out of the country, his casual approach to the motoring laws caught up with him. It was reported in the Glasgow Herald that a warrant had been issued by Dundee Sherriff's Court for his arrest. The paper said: "Munro, of 72 Seaforth Road, Aberdeen, is alleged to have permitted another man to use his car without insurance cover. The man, David Palmer Strachan, of 14 Lyon Street, Dundee, was fined £5 for speeding and admonished for using the car without insurance." The solicitor representing Frank and the driver said the latter pleaded guilty but the solicitor added that he was withdrawing from representing Frank as he had been unable to get instruction. Because Frank failed to appear, a warrant for arrest was granted.

I assume the matter was sorted and Frank had to take his punishment –

probably a severe one – but it was typical of him to land himself in hot water unnecessarily. He was no criminal but his happy-go-lucky approach to life probably meant serious matters like the laws regarding motoring were too complicated to command his attention. It would not be the last time he found himself in trouble for such misdemeanours.

Chapter Three

Pittodrie Parting

Back in Aberdeen, there was not much time to relax. After landing on Monday, July, 17, 1967, following the long haul from Los Angeles, Frank and most of the Dons party hurried home, although skipper Harry Melrose made straight for the Queen's Cross Maternity Home, where his wife had given birth to their third child the night before. Full-back Jim Hermiston had also become a father while away on tour. The squad would soon be back in action again with a prestige pre-season friendly on Wednesday, August 2, against Chelsea.

The visit of the previous season's beaten FA Cup finalists to Pittodrie attracted a 29,000 attendance and was a chance for Frank to meet up again with Tommy Docherty, who had been a most considerate boss during their brief time together. The Doc was impressed by Frank and, indeed, the whole Dons team in a game that was sometimes more like a cup-tie than a friendly. He said afterwards: "Aberdeen will be one of the toughest teams to beat, particularly at Pittodrie." The Doc's prediction would not look so hot when the League season got going and the Dons lost two of their first three home games. Trailing to a Bobby Tambling goal just after half-time, Aberdeen hit back to beat Chelsea 2-1, Jimmy Wilson grabbing the winner eight minutes from time after Jim Storrie had equalised. The Londoners were not helped by an injury to their Scotland international full-back Eddie McCreadie, who had to soldier on as Dundee referee Bob Henderson would not allow more than two substitutes for each team. Chelsea had used theirs so the limping defender, who had been having treatment on the sidelines when Storrie scored, had to keep going. Docherty, however, did not make this an excuse, saying: "We were beaten by a better team on the night. Aberdeen played with tremendous zest and tremendous skill. They are quite a side."

Despite the lavish praise from the Doc, 1967-68 did not start well for Aberdeen, who were back in competitive action just over three weeks after arriving home from the United Soccer Association tournament. In the League Cup, they were in a tough section with Celtic, Rangers and Dundee United and would be without the suspended Jimmy Smith for the opening three games. They failed to win any of their League Cup matches and finished bottom of the group. With a shot that brought a spectacular leaping save from keeper Erik Sorensen, Frank soon made his presence felt in the opening fixture before a 36,000 crowd against Rangers at Pittodrie. He also sent a free-kick narrowly over in a game that ended 1-1. Frank must have thought they might get something out of the next League Cup match, away to his old team Dundee United, especially when the match remained goalless for the first 56 minutes. Then the Dons were hit by five goals without reply. Hopes of progress were as good as over when Aberdeen then lost 3-1 away to Celtic. In the return with United, Frank made the opening goal for Jim Storrie and then fired in a low shot to restore the lead in the second half but United would not lie down and levelled again.

The Dons ended the group stage with a 5-1 home defeat in the return with Celtic, despite Jimmy Smith giving them an eighth-minute lead. Frank got himself booked in that one, leading the protests after the referee awarded a penalty from which Tommy Gemmell equalised after a re-take, Bobby Clark saving his first effort. Trust Frank to be in the thick of things. At least the referee, John Gordon of Newport-on-Tay, received only a verbal assault from Frank. Far more serious was a physical attack from a fan who ran on to the pitch a few minutes later and threw himself at the official and knocked him to the ground. Six policemen dragged the man off and when the teams came out after half-time, during which there had been several arrests as trouble broke out behind one of the goals, the referee had to walk between two rows of six policemen to ensure his safe passage on to the pitch. All this and there was nothing really at stake as Celtic had already qualified for the knockout stage while Aberdeen had no chance of doing so.

Once the League season got under way, Frank's form remained fairly good but events would take a dramatic turn before the campaign ended. He loved Aberdeen and was really settled there, all the more so when he married Margaret Nicoll of Byron Street, Dundee, on Monday, September 4, 1967, at Saints Peter and Paul Church in her home city. Best man was Frank's brother James. Two days after the wedding, Frank was to spearhead Aberdeen on their very first foray into Europe against KR Reykjavik. The match, on the Wednesday before the League season began, was in the European Cup Winners' Cup, for which Aberdeen qualified as Scottish Cup runners-up, with winners Celtic going into the European Cup.

Frank had an injection in his knee before the game but this did not stop him becoming the first Aberdeen player to score a goal in Europe. He went on to net another two to complete his hat-trick in the 10-0 win over the Icelandic side at Pittodrie. The visitors held out for 19 minutes before Frank struck and Jimmy

Smith, Jimmy Storrie and Tommy McMillan added more before the break. It was a landmark for McMillan – his first senior goal for the club and it would prove to be half his career total for them. Seventeen minutes after half-time, it was 8-0 thanks to two more goals from Frank and others from Ian Taylor and Storrie. After Jens Petersen made it nine, double figures were reached through Smith with 12 minutes still left to play. So the ten goals had been scored in just under an hour's play. Aberdeen won the return 4-1, with Frank again a scorer. His feat of hitting a European hat-trick has been matched for Aberdeen only by Mark McGhee.

After the dismal League Cup campaign, at least the start to the League season was marked with a win, although it did not signal an upturn in the team's form. Frank was on target on the opening day when Dundee were beaten 4-2 at Pittodrie and the Glasgow Evening Times report named him the game's 'top man.' He also scored what proved to be his last goal for the Dons when Dundee United were brushed aside 6-0 but the wins over the Tayside teams were the only ones for Aberdeen in the first ten games of the League season. They lost 2-1 at Hearts and several players were struggling, Frank among them. It was not the best occasion to have an off-day as Liverpool boss Bill Shankly was running the rule over him and other possible targets. Wolves also had a representative at the game. Frank was a wanted man, it seemed. After that defeat, manager Turnbull clearly felt a shake-up was needed. Now under threat for a starting place from the blossoming talent of Martin Buchan, Frank could not take his selection for granted and was dropped for the trip to Partick Thistle. He was not alone as forwards Jim Storrie, Davie Robb and Ian Taylor were also axed from the team who earned a 2-2 draw after going a goal down and coming back to lead 2-1 at half-time.

A quick return was hardly on the cards for Frank when, a week later, an unchanged Aberdeen beat Raith Rovers 6-2. He was named substitute but was not used as the Dons rattled in five second-half goals, although the win still left them just in the bottom half of the table. Still at sub for the trip to Hibernian, Frank was back in action after only ten minutes when Robb sustained an eye injury and had to go to hospital to have stitches. Hibs won by the only goal but circumstances contrived to help Frank re-establish himself in the team. He was given another chance to show his potential as a central defender in the home game with Motherwell thanks to an injury to centre-half Tommy McMillan and still found time to send an effort against a post when he went up for a corner as the Dons won 2-1. Frank would probably have been relegated to sub again but Buchan was injured against Motherwell, so he kept his place for the next trip into Europe – to face Standard Liège in Belgium.

PITTODRIE PARTING

Aberdeen's hopes of progress in the Cup Winners' Cup were virtually finished after 12 minutes. They were two goals down in the first leg of the second-round clash, which ended 3-0, and only 11,000 turned up for the second leg at Pittodrie. The stay-aways missed a great attempt by the Dons to pull the tie out of the fire on a snow-bound pitch. Frank fired them ahead when he turned home a Billy Little centre after 20 minutes and Harry Melrose hit a second with 25 minutes left but the Dons just could not find another despite going close several times before bowing out 3-2. Frank was as disappointed as anyone but the defeat would soon be forgotten. Things were about to change in a big way for him.

On Saturday, December 30, 1967, he was in the side beaten 4-1 at home by table-topping Rangers in front of more than 20,000. The Glasgow giants were too good that day. Little did he know it but that would be his final game for The Dons. He was obviously fired up as an early paragraph in the report in the Glasgow Times confirmed – "Willoughby was sent crashing to the ground by Munro. He got up limping and with his face twisted in pain." Despite the rough treatment, Alex Willoughby had the last laugh by scoring the fourth goal. Frank nearly signed off with a goal but his shot was deflected on to a post. Jimmy Smith reduced the score to 2-1 from the resultant corner but two late goals put Rangers out of sight. Here are the line-ups in what proved to be Frank's last Aberdeen match:

Aberdeen: Clark, Whyte, Shewan, Petersen, McMillan, Munro, Little, Buchanan, Johnston, Smith, Craig. Sub: Pat Wilson. Rangers: Sorensen, Johansen, Greig, Watson, McKinnon, Dave Smith, Penman, Willoughby, Alex Smith, Johnston, Persson. Sub: Jardine.

As we have already mentioned, League football was still traditionally played on New Year's Day in Scotland and, on January 1, 1968, two days after the Rangers game, Aberdeen were scheduled to play Dundee at Dens Park in Frank's home town. As you can imagine, it was a notable day for him and consequently he had organised 35 complimentary tickets to accommodate friends and family for the big occasion. He was eagerly looking forward to the game. Alas, it was to be one of the most disappointing days of his career to that date and was the prelude to a major change in his football life. Early that morning, the team bus was ready to leave Pittodrie but was delayed for ten minutes, waiting for one of the players to arrive. Unfortunately, the player in question was Frank and he was totally embarrassed to step aboard, knowing he had held everybody up. Eddie Turnbull gave him a cursory glance as he walked past to take his seat at the rear but, surprisingly, he did not say a word.

A hotel in Montrose was the next stop on the road to Dundee – for a pre-match meal and team talk. On arrival at the hotel, though, Frank was taken to one side to have a private talk with Turnbull. He knew he was in for a rollicking and was grateful the boss had not embarrassed him by bawling him out in front of his colleagues. But he was totally unprepared for what he was to hear. "I'm not playing you today," said Eddie sternly. Frank was shell-shocked. He may not have been consistently the best player in the team that season but he had grabbed the chance to re-establish himself and was in good form. He could not think how the manager could contemplate leaving him out. "Why?" was all Frank could ask. "I believe you were drinking last night" was Turnbull's reply, "and the fact that you were ten minutes late this morning confirmed my beliefs." "I wasn't out drinking," Frank protested. "A pal came round with his wife and we let the new year in with a glass of sherry." "Nevertheless, I'm not playing you and that's the end of the matter," said Turnbull.

Frank was utterly deflated. He had looked forward to this game in his home city, with almost three dozen family members and friends going to watch him. So at 3pm, he was resigned to sitting on the bench, wrapped up against the cold, watching his team-mates master a snowy pitch, watched by a large crowd, Scotland manager Bobby Brown among them. He did not even have the prospect of getting a few minutes' action. There was only one substitute in those days and the no 12 shirt was given to Davie Robb. Aberdeen won 2-0, their first away League victory of the season, but that hardly mattered a jot to Frank. What should have been a great day back home had proved to be one to forget.

If Frank thought the final whistle signalled the end of his wretched day, he was wrong as there was more drama to unfold. After the game, Turnbull took him to one side and said: "Report to the ground at 2 o'clock tomorrow." He walked away before Frank could ask why. That night, he lay awake wondering why he had been told to be at Pittodrie. Was Turnbull going to fine him and discipline him because he believed he was drinking the night before a game? Was he going to put him through a rigid training session or did he merely want to clear the air? He just could not think why the manager wanted to see him – but he duly found out exactly why and, once again, there was a shock in store for him.

"Come in and take a seat," said Turnbull. Frank sat down, wondering what was coming next. "OK," said Turnbull, "I'll come right to the point. Wolves want to buy you." Frank was taken aback for a few moments because he never expected what he had just heard. Then, when it sank in, it was really good knowing he was wanted, especially in a team he felt he knew, having played against them three times in America a few months earlier. One thing that did not register with him at the time was the fact Turnbull must have known about the inquiry from Wolves when he left Frank out of the team. He never did get the real reason from Turnbull for his exclusion from the side who played Dundee. Could it have been that should Frank be injured in that game, then the interest could have gone cold? Anyway, he was pretty sure the Wolves offer was the reason for his omission.

"Would you be interested in joining Wolves?" Eddie Turnbull asked. "Well, I would like to talk to them," he answered. "OK," Turnbull continued, "the secretary will make the necessary travel arrangements for you, so I suggest you go home and inform Margaret of today's development." Next day, Margaret and Frank were given two tickets for the flight from Aberdeen to Birmingham with instructions that they would be met, not by Wolves boss Ronnie Allen but by a gentleman named Joe Gardiner. A reporter managed to grab hold of Frank as he changed planes at Glasgow and was told: "This one came out of the blue. I have already spoken to Mr Allen on the phone, so I know what sort of offer awaits me. But my wife Margaret and I want to look over the place and see about the housing."

Frank had never heard of Joe Gardiner but, in years to come, found him to be the perfect gentleman and completely devoted to Wolves. Gardiner had played for the club before the war, forming a fine half-back line with England internationals Stan Cullis and Tom Galley. When Cullis became boss and steered Wolves to their greatest triumphs, Gardiner was trainer and, in effect, second-in-command; a key man in all their success. On their journey from Birmingham Airport to Molineux, Frank realised the tickets he had were one way. This meant either he was not expected back or Aberdeen were too tight to pay the return fare.

Arriving at Molineux, they were met by Allen and shown to his office to talk terms. Chairman John Ireland joined them and his immediate reaction was to hold his hands up in a defensive manner. "Am I safe?" he asked, smiling, and Frank realised he was referring to the incident on the touchline in America. Preliminaries over, it was time to discuss wages and a signing-on fee but the negotiations became a non-event. When Frank was offered £60 a week, he nearly fell off his chair. He was on £28 a week at Aberdeen, so no haggling was needed. They shook hands and a deal was done at, according to Frank, £40,000, although most papers reported the fee as £55,000 and Turnbull referred to it as £50,000. Frank also received a £2,000 signing-on fee – less tax, of course, which was five per cent.

Allen sang Frank's praises to the Press: "He has a power, strength and presence that I am sure will do us a great deal of good." That sounded as though his new boss saw him as a key figure in his team. It did not work out like that but more of that later. At the same time that Frank signed, we said farewell to one of our stalwarts, goalkeeper Fred Davies, who moved to Cardiff City. Frank and Margaret went back to Aberdeen – paid for by Wolves – to tie things up at the other end and then returned to Wolverhampton to settle down to life in the Midlands. Their first home was in Grovelands Crescent in Fordhouses. A whole host of the lads chose to live in that area of town, simply because the houses were newish and on a lovely estate and the rent was quite low (25 shillings or £1.25 a week) – something that would come back to haunt Frank and me in a few years' time.

Turnbull reckoned Allen had been set on signing Frank ever since the American adventure and recalled: "During the tournament and especially in the final, Francis had played very well, showing the considerable skill he had for a big man. He was also one of the finest long passers I've ever seen and it was no wonder that Wolves wanted to sign him." The only brief stumbling block over the move was the fee, as Turnbull explained: "At first, they did not match our valuation but, nearly eight months later, when Allen made the very substantial offer of £50,000, we could not turn it down. It was four times more than we had paid for him just 18 months previously. It was also a chance for Francis to play in top-flight English football and earn considerably more than he was getting at Aberdeen."

From that, you can work out that Wolves' interest in Frank dated back to that summer in the USA and they must have made an early bid to get him to Molineux. It failed but Allen was determined to get his man and, fortunately for Frank and Wolves, his persistence paid off. He would prove to be one of Allen's best signings, right up there with the likes of Mike Bailey, Derek Parkin, Derek Dougan and Kenny Hibbitt. While it would fall to another gaffer to make us a trophy-winning side, the foundations were without any doubt laid by Ronnie Allen.

Pittodrie was busy as striker Jim Storrie had been signed by Tommy Docherty, who was by now managing Rotherham, and winger Jimmy Wilson had joined Motherwell in a swop deal with George Murray. Turnbull's willingness to sell Frank no doubt had a lot to do with the fact he had a ready-made replacement in Martin Buchan. Jens Petersen was virtually an automatic choice for one of the two half-back positions, which were still traditional in a 1960s line-up, so Frank and Martin were rivals for the other one and Frank faced a battle to get in. Little did he know but he would have a harder job getting first-team football at Wolves.

Chapter Four

Molineux Struggles

Frank made an early debut for Wolves but there was a threat to him having an extended initial run with his new club. It came via the Scottish FA. He had received three bookings while with Aberdeen and could have been suspended. Ronnie Allen said: "He may be suspended, he may not, I had to take the chance." Frank said after signing: "It has been a great day. I only hope Monday won't spoil it." Happily, when the disciplinary body, the SFA referee committee, met on the Monday after his debut, they took a lenient view and fined him £100. Frank did not have to appear before the committee and was all set to build a new career in the famous gold and black of Wolverhampton Wanderers. I say gold and black but should point out that our colours were then virtually all gold, with just black trimmings, as we were still wearing gold shorts at the time. The new strip had been introduced for an FA Cup replay at Molineux in February, 1965, and Wolves stuck with it for a couple of seasons or so. I do not think the fans ever really warmed to the colours, preferring to see us in gold shirts and black shorts.

Saturday, January 6, 1968, was the day Francis Munro made his Wolves debut. He was to play a gigantic role for us in more ways than one but it nearly did not turn out that way. From being one of the mainstays of the Aberdeen team, Frank found he was just another player as far as Wolves were concerned and he had to earn his place in the team. In his first game, against Everton at Molineux, he played in the no 7 shirt in a position completely foreign to him. The result was 3-1 to the visitors thanks to first-half goals from Joe Royle and Mike Trebilcock and another from Royle in the final minute after Peter Knowles had given us some hope with just over 20 minutes left. Frank did have his moments during his tough baptism and he found me with a lovely long pass which enabled me to put the ball through for Peter to score our goal.

In the Express & Star, long-serving Wolves correspondent Phil Morgan wrote that after our goal "this is where new boy Frank Munro came into the picture, as he did frequently and often impressively." However, it was an eye-opening debut for the young Scot, what with the pace of the game, the unusual position he played in and the new players. Frank was totally confused. The teams that day were:

Wolves: Williams, Les Wilson, Thomson, Bailey (Ross 75), Woodfield, Holsgrove, Munro, Knowles, Dougan, Evans, Wagstaffe. Everton: West, Wright (Brown 77), Wilson, Kenyon, Labone, Harvey, Hunt, Ball, Royle, Hurst, Trebilcock.

The next game was at Leicester and at least Frank was picked in a familiar position, wearing no 4 and playing in midfield as deputy for injured skipper Mike Bailey. I was sidelined with Bobby Thomson, so it was a makeshift side at Filbert Street with The Doog as skipper. On a snowy day which saw many games called off, there was another new face in our side – winger Mike Kenning, signed from Norwich the previous day. He opened the scoring but we again lost 3-1. These were busy times on the transfer front as winger Pat Buckley was sold to Sheffield United and centre-half Graham Hawkins to Preston. Again, Frank got a favourable note from Phil Morgan – "Frank Munro tried from the midfield area but with the attack generally firmly held, it was of little use." Mike Bailey was fit for the next game, so Frank had to move again, this time to inside-left, wearing no 10. West Ham, with their World Cup trio of Bobby Moore, Martin Peters and Geoff Hurst, were the opposition at Molineux and we lost 2-1 thanks to goals from Brian Dear and Hurst. Derek Dougan, on his 30th birthday, scored a late reply for us. This time Phil Morgan's Monday verdict in the Express & Star hinted that Frank was finding the pace of English football a bit different from the Scottish game. Phil wrote: "The persistent and brisk tap-tap of the Hammers exposed the sluggishness of Frank Munro, good though he was with the ball at his feet."

It was not easy for Frank and he was beginning to think he had made the wrong move. Three games, two at home, three losses. The next match was a good one to miss as it brought yet another defeat, this time in a third-round FA Cup tie at Tommy Docherty's Rotherham. Frank could not play because he was suffering from tonsillitis, so David Burnside took his place. The Doc pulled off a big surprise by guiding his Second Division team to a 1-0 victory, the goal coming from Frank's former Aberdeen team-mate Jim Storrie. This meant we had lost seven successive matches. The trip to Millmoor was significant in another way. It also proved to be the final Wolves appearance for Burnside, who eventually left us for Plymouth. Rotherham beat Aston Villa in the following round but their run was a brief diversion on their way to relegation.

Burnley were next for us in the League and Ronnie Allen decided to give a quick recall to the well-again Frank and make him feel more at home in his normal position of right-half. The manager moved Mike Bailey to no 10 to accommodate

Frank and the tactics half-worked because we drew 1-1 at Turf Moor. In the Express & Star, Phil Morgan noted: "The return of Frank Munro, improving as the game went on, undoubtedly added strength." The other side of a three-week break in fixtures, it was virtually the same team for a 2-0 defeat at Newcastle. But there was one notable change to the line-up because coming in at right-back was Derek Parkin, a highly-rated young defender signed from Huddersfield. He would go on to become a Wolves legend and set a club record number of appearances. His fee of £80,000 was at the time a British record for a full-back.

By this time, Frank was getting very depressed and anxious. Not only were the results not forthcoming but his own game was suffering. How he wished then that he had not made the move from Aberdeen. He was left out for the next game but then Allen gave him the no 10 shirt for the visit of Sunderland as Alun Evans was dropped and Peter Knowles suspended. There was yet another new face, Frank Wignall, bought from Nottingham Forest for £50,000. At last there was a win, Frank's first in a Wolves shirt, as the visitors were beaten 2-1. Derek Dougan struck nine minutes from half-time and Mike Kenning doubled the lead from the penalty spot before George Herd got a late goal back. It was a very relieved Frank Munro who went home that night.

With the arrival of Wignall and with Knowles available again, there was a lapse of three games before Frank had another first-team outing. That came against Coventry City at Highfield Road, where Mike Bailey again moved up to wear no 10. We lost 1-0 thanks to a penalty by Neil Martin eight minutes from time, so Frank – probably worse than the rest of us – was back to feeling depressed. Some indication of how he had found the transition to the English game was revealed when he told the Wolverhampton Chronicle: "The pace in the First Division is a lot faster than in Scotland and it is like playing against Celtic every match. Every game I play is hard and there are no easy games. But I like this as I think it is much better all-round football."

Wignall proved a good acquisition by Allen in the bid to stave off the threat of relegation and scored nine goals in 12 games. The week after the Coventry defeat, with Frank dropped to sub, Dougan hit a hat-trick as Nottingham Forest lost 6-1 at Molineux. Frank did get 18 minutes of action when the two-goal Wignall went off but that would be his last taste of First Division football for months. He was relegated to the reserves for the rest of the season, apart from being the unused substitute in a 0-0 home draw with Manchester City. The lack of action only added to his mood of depression and his feelings were brought home to me during a chat at our Fordhouses 'local', The Moreton, a pub these days but back then a private club where most of the players went for a drink. I remember sitting at the bar on one of those high stools chatting to Frank about his inaugural half season in English football. He could not understand why he had not got the pace of the game. He was a star in Scotland, an established player, one to be feared, but down here he was just another bit-part player. It had not helped that he had been played in three different positions and had not been given an extended run in any.

During the close season, Frank went back to Scotland for a holiday and to put the feelers out about a possible transfer back to his homeland. He told the Scottish newspapers: "Margaret is a Dundee girl and is homesick while I haven't settled down to English football and would love to be back." While in Scotland, he kept fit by training with his old club Dundee United. "I definitely want a move," he told Dundee Courier reporter Tommy Gallacher. "It is not because I dislike playing in English football. In fact I enjoy it, although I think it is tougher and faster than the Scottish game. But between January and the end of this season, I only played 13 games in the League side. I thought I was playing well, too, but I was dropped just the same. The trouble is that manager Ronnie Allen and I don't seem to see eye to eye, so, in these circumstances, there isn't much point in my remaining at Molineux."

The problem was that a move back to Scotland for the price Wolves had paid left only two clubs being able to afford him – Rangers and Celtic. That was unless Wolves were prepared to take a loss, which was highly unlikely. Eventually, he decided that the best thing to do was to go back to England and get his head down, train hard in pre-season and get where he felt he belonged – in the team. He became agitated again when he could see in pre-season friendlies he was not going to be included in any short-term team plans. Why had Allen bought him if he was not going to play him? It was not until Wolves' eighth game of 1968-69 that Frank finally got a chance. After a 1-1 home draw with Stoke, Ronnie decided to drop fans' favourite Peter Knowles in favour of Frank for the trip to Leeds, then nearing the height of their powers under Don Revie. At last a chance and the headline in the Daily Mirror reflected that, proclaiming "Forgotten man Munro returns for Wolves". In the report underneath, Frank told Peter Ingall: "I found it difficult to settle down last season. The pace is much faster in England and it has taken me much longer to settle into the club's style than I thought. I hope this proves the turning point, although I couldn't have a tougher comeback than Leeds."

It was a shock move to drop Knowles but Frank quickly made the most of his call-up by scoring his first goal for the club – one set up by a fine solo run by Mike Bailey. Terry Cooper equalised on 68 minutes and Jack Charlton grabbed a late winner to deny the visitors a deserved point. Frank received a vote of confidence from Phil Morgan in the Express & Star – "Leeds are still one of the best four teams in the country and it was as well, in my view, to have Frank Munro around. His usefulness was two-fold. He not only scored a fine goal to give Wolves their eighth-minute lead but did as much as anybody to try to retain it."

Sadly, it was a false dawn for Frank. Another three games and he was out of the team again. Of his four games, the team had lost at Leeds, drawn 1-1 at home to Sunderland, drawn 0-0 at Albion and then lost 6-0 at home to Liverpool on the day £100,000 teenager Alun Evans returned to Molineux to score twice for Bill Shankly's side. It was from Frank's centre seven minutes from time that Wignall had grabbed the equaliser against Sunderland on the day Wolves fielded yet another new signing, goalkeeper Alan Boswell, bought from Shrewsbury. After the Sunderland match, Frank played against Millwall in a League Cup tie and scored one of the goals in a 5-1 win at Molineux. Ten minutes after half-time, Eamon Dunphy had cancelled out Derek Dougan's first-minute goal. However, Frank restored the lead within three minutes, sliding the ball home after The Doog had headed on a long throw by Mike Bailey. In the Express & Star, Phil Morgan reported that there had been some "excellent bits of individual football" from Peter Knowles and Frank.

That hammering by Liverpool would have extra significance. The writing was on the wall for Ronnie Allen because rumour had it that for some time the Wolves directors had had their eyes on Bill McGarry, the Ipswich manager. They were waiting for a day like this to set the wheels in motion for him to take over. Even though he was by then not in the team, Frank felt rather sorry for Allen. He did not see eye to eye with him but this did not stop him admiring his methods. There was no long-slog running but plenty of interesting ideas to make training fun – if ever training can be fun. Although our results had been reasonable following the Liverpool debacle, with three victories, three draws and three defeats, Allen was sacked after we drew 1-1 at Burnley on November 16, 1968. Frank got some action as substitute that day and must have thought the team were showing signs of improvement but Ronnie was clearly on borrowed time. He revealed that chairman John Ireland had asked him to resign after the Liverpool defeat but Ronnie said he would only consider it if it was the unanimous decision of the board – and it was not. It proved a brief reprieve and now he left, saying: "I am certain that the club is in a better position than at any time since I became coach in April, 1965. Yet, apparently, the board feel they can find someone who can do a better job." That 'someone' was McGarry, who officially took over nine days after the sacking and brought with him his second-in-command Sammy Chung.

Frank had never heard of McGarry and thought the change of manager might be to his advantage. Wrong! McGarry would prove to be the sergeant major of all managers. With one of Allen's 'lieutenants', Gerry Summers, picking the team before McGarry officially took over, we said farewell to Ronnie in some style with a 5-0 win over Newcastle at Molineux. That put us 13th in the table, which was not a bad starting point for the new boss. We had been 17th after the Liverpool hammering. On day one of his reign at Molineux, McGarry told Peter Ingall of the Daily Mirror: "I have no hard and fast philosophy about managership except that I don't want the players to like me, so long as they respect me. Once players start liking a manager, he can find himself out of a job. Managers cannot afford to get too close to them. I prefer to train and then finish with my players until the next training session." Well, as far as Frank and I were concerned, the new boss would over the next few years easily fulfil his wish not to be liked.

Under Ronnie Allen, Frank's record had not been very successful – one win, three draws and seven losses in his 11 starts. Could his fortunes change under a new manager? The answer was no. It was to be almost two months before Frank got a game – at no 10 – under the McGarry regime and it was a losing one, 4-0 at Everton. He was substitute for the next game, at home to Burnley, and went on for right-winger John Farrington after an hour on the day Hugh Curran, a striker signed from Norwich, made his debut in a 1-1 draw. As an unused sub when we made the long trip north to face Hull in the third round of the FA Cup, Frank was able to witness at first hand McGarry at his most autocratic. This was one of those trips where an overnight stay was deemed necessary and, the evening before the game, we were sat down ready for our evening meal when John Holsgrove told the waiter he would like prawn cocktail for his starter. McGarry, sitting with the directors and backroom staff at another table, overheard and went crazy.

He rose to his feet and bellowed at John: "Fucking prawn cocktail, what do you think this is? Fucking Butlin's!" He walked over and stood at the end of our table before growling: "I'll tell you what you can fucking eat – soup to start, steak or chicken for the main course and fruit salad for dessert." The place had gone deadly quiet, apart from McGarry's ranting, and Frank, me and the rest of the lads just sat there like chastised school kids. It was a sort of Oliver Twist moment for John Holsgrove and it always brings a smile to our faces when anybody recalls it. What's more, that menu laid down by McGarry – soup, steak or chicken, then fruit salad – applied wherever we went, home or abroad, for the rest of his reign as manager.

We won the Cup game 3-1, no doubt due to a large extent, in McGarry's opinion, to preparing by eating the right kind of food the night before. It mattered little to Frank as he spent the afternoon at Boothferry Park sitting on the bench, not being called into the action as we recovered well from trailing to a Chris Chilton header as a couple of goals from Derek Dougan and one from Frank Wignall saw us through. For seven League games, Frank had to take a back seat and thoughts of a move must have been on his mind once more, especially as McGarry seemed to be starting to make changes to his squad. Somewhat surprisingly, he had sold England international full-back Bobby Thomson to Birmingham, then being managed by the former master of Molineux, Stan Cullis. Winger Mike Kenning had rejoined Charlton and maybe Frank thought he did not rate highly with McGarry and it was time to look elsewhere. Confirmation of this came via long-serving Midland freelance sportswriter Brian Marshall in his regular column in Soccer Star, the weekly football magazine. Wrote Marshall: "Another to be on the move could be Frank Munro, who has failed to win a regular place since his move from Aberdeen. Munro himself asked for a move a few weeks ago but no firm decision has been made in his case."

It was a frustrating time and Frank could so easily have left if the right offer had come along. Fortunately for him – and Wolves – it did not and finally he got some first-team action again thanks to me. I was sidelined with a thigh injury and after McGarry had tried young Derek Clarke and then John Farrington in the no 11 shirt, he turned to Frank for a run of three games. He did well in a side who fought out a goalless draw at Molineux with Leeds, who were on their way to becoming champions with what was then a record 67 points. Next, we lost 1-0 to Liverpool at Anfield, where England World Cup hero Roger Hunt hit the 300th goal of his career. A 25-yard shot from Frank into the side-netting was the closest we went to an equaliser. Then, on Easter Monday, we lost 3-1 at Arsenal, where one of Frank's well-timed through passes almost led to a goal for sub Derek Clarke, one of the five footballing brothers from Willenhall. Frank was definitely starting to assert himself in the side now he was getting some regular action.

We were again close to the relegation zone and urgently needed a win. It came the following evening with a fine 3-1 home victory over Manchester City despite the setback of Franny Lee giving them the lead after 30 seconds. Irish youngster Bertie Lutton was given his debut and played on the left, enabling Frank to wear the no 10 shirt and play a midfield role. It was Lutton who paved the way for Frank to get on the score-sheet seven minutes from time. He brought the ball out of defence and fed Peter Knowles, whose perfect through pass put Frank clear to fire home. Knowles had headed us level two minutes after the break and Derek Dougan put us in front on the hour. Frank had done well and proved to the home crowd that he really had what it took to do well in the top flight of English football. Phil Morgan in the Express & Star said that Frank's goal was "a worthy effort with which to round off a thoroughly worthy performance."

This was a vital win and all the more notable as it came against a City side who had been League champions the season before and had now reached the FA Cup final. In fact, the side at Molineux that night were the same as the team who would beat Leicester 1-0 at Wembley a few weeks later. Another game for Frank at no 10, as we came down to earth with a 1-0 home defeat to Albion, was followed by a substitute appearance in a 1-1 home draw with Coventry when he went on for injured full-back Gerry Taylor. Then came two games in the no 8 shirt for Frank as we finished the season with defeats, 2-0 at Sunderland, where his departure after 66 minutes enabled Paul Walker to get his first taste of First Division football, and 4-1 at Newcastle. Frank, had made a mere 12 League starts over the season, plus four appearances as sub. He certainly had been shifted around and it did not seem fair to him that he was not given an extended run in any of the positions. Basically, all he wanted to do was to play football.

However, one of those injury pile-ups which often happen to clubs had enabled him to figure in each of the last eight games of the season. Mike Bailey, Hughie Curran, Peter Knowles and I were among those sidelined at various times in those last few weeks, so Frank was in the team by accident rather than design but at least he had been given the chance to show what he could do. He was again wearing no 8 when we took a team to Ipswich for Ray Crawford's testimonial. Frank was replaced by Peter Knowles in the second half and we were on the wrong end of a 6-0 scoreline. That defeat, if a lot heavier than we would have liked, was of little consequence....forget East Anglia, it was next stop USA!

Chapter Five

His True Role

Let me remind you of that quote from Scotland youth team manager Roy Small: "Frank Munro is a natural at CENTRE-HALF." Frank was 16 at the time the comment was made. By the start of the 1969-70 season, he was 21 and nobody had given him a chance in that position. Roy Small could see it but, four managers and numerous coaches later, nobody else apparently could. However, fate would give Frank his chance and he would make the most of it. During our tour of America in the summer of 1969, he played at centre-half out of necessity and at last the penny dropped with Bill McGarry. Echoing the words of Roy Small, he was heard to say "This lad's a natural at centre-half" – although he did not say it too loudly in case he was wrong! But he was not wrong and Frank was about to find his natural position at last.

For Frank, this did not matter one bit because, as long as he was in the team, he would play anywhere. As I have said before, he just loved football and if playing centre-half meant he was going to be in the team every week, this was his position. He hated training, particularly the running aspect, but would play with a ball all day if necessary. For a big man, his balance was unbelievable and he loved matches on frozen grounds – well, he would coming from Scotland, wouldn't he? The tour we were on was to be a key one in the making of him. Dave Woodfield, then our regular no 5, was injured in our opening game, a 3-2 defeat in Baltimore to a West Ham side featuring a promising 20-year-old by the name of Trevor Brooking at centre-forward and a right-winger called Harry Redknapp. So Frank teamed up with John Holsgrove as twin central defenders. Of all the teams to face, it was Dundee United in the first 'home' match at our Kansas City base. It may only have been one game, which we won 4-2, but he did more than enough to show he could make the position his despite Woodfield, Holsgrove and John McAlle also being candidates. I am sure McGarry must have seen how well Frank did and the seed was sown in the back of the manager's mind that he had the ability to be a top-class centre-half.

Any one of the players Frank played with will tell you he was the most skilful centre-half they had ever seen; ball control, heading ability, a fearsome shot – you name it, he had it. The only department in which he lacked a little was speed but he more than made up for this with his reading of the game. For such an immensely-built man, Frank could do the most delicate of things. One of his favourite tricks was to lean back, throw a coin in the air, catch it on his forehead, lean forward and let it slide off his head and into his top pocket. He was quite a joker, too, even in the most serious of situations. He used to frighten our goalkeeper Phil Parkes to death. A ball would come down the middle of the pitch at about chest-high, with the opposition centre-forward chasing it, and Frank would stand there as if to take it down on his chest. However, at the very last second, he would move to one side and shout "Yours, Lofty" and the ball would skid off the turf to Phil. This was okay if Phil knew when Frank was going to do it but it could be any one of 20 times that the ball would come down the middle, so Phil had to be on his toes.

An example of this was picked up by Express & Star man Phil Morgan in his report of our 1-0 win over West Ham in October, 1969. He wrote: "One of Phil Parkes's best saves, by the way, was from Frank Munro, whose short surprise back passes and headers show a tremendous faith in the goalkeeper's alertness." You see, his various tricks had not gone unnoticed. Perhaps if Frank's bits of nonsense had ever resulted in a goal, he might have stopped doing it but, amazingly, it never did, which says much for Lofty's awareness. Another thing about Frank was that he appeared to have no nerves at all as far as football was concerned. In fact, he used to laugh at me for being so anxious before a game. He did not understand, never having been in that situation. It's a great way to be but few people have that sort of approach and Frank was so fortunate in being able to take every game in his stride. We found a Press cutting among his collection in which he explained his fortunate pre-match demeanour. "I've never been bothered by nerves," he said. "Even as an 18-year-old playing against Celtic in the Scottish Cup final, I never had a twinge. It's not that I lack determination or that I've a couldn't-care-less attitude, it's just that I don't get wound up as others seem to do." He was so lucky in being like that.

We again won the tournament in the USA but, unlike the one two years earlier, it was decided on a league basis with no final to add extra drama. Six points were awarded for a win and a bonus point per goal up to three. There were only four other teams involved this time and we all had American names to play under – West Ham (Baltimore Bays), Aston Villa (Atlanta Chiefs), Dundee United (Dallas Tornado) and Kilmarnock (St Louis Stars). We had to play under the name

"Kansas City Spurs". We would have preferred it to be Kansas City Wolves but had no choice.

After losing that opening game to West Ham and then beating Dundee United, we got our revenge over West Ham 4-2 in Kansas, with Frank playing in midfield once more. He would be used there for the rest of tournament, with the two central defensive positions shared by Holsgrove, Woodfield and McAlle. After the Dundee game, we won the next five to make it six in a row. That was enough for us to clinch the title with a game to spare, so it made no difference when we ended by losing the return with Dundee United 3-2. We were top with 57 points, followed by West Ham (52), Dundee United (31), Villa (28) and Kilmarnock (26). Our biggest win was 5-0 against Villa, who included former Molineux maestro Peter Broadbent. He had just celebrated his 36th birthday but still looked a class player. Frank was replaced in the second half by Duggie Woodfield, who was well pleased when he slammed in our final goal in the last minute. That victory, in Kansas, clinched the title for us.

So Frank Munro had posted the signals and it was going to be very interesting to see whether he could use the following season to establish himself in a new position. Although the pre-season programme was not as extensive as today, we still played a few games leading into the campaign and they were enough for Frank to show that central defence was the area where he was most likely to emerge as a regular. For the game at Oxford, which we won 5-1, the central pairing were John Holsgrove and John McAlle. During the match, they were replaced by Duggie and Frank. In a 1-1 draw at Bristol City, it was Woodfield and Les Wilson, with McAlle going on for Les. Frank began in midfield but was replaced by Peter Knowles, who scored Wolves' goal with a late penalty. The next day, there was an addition to the Molineux Scottish clan as Bill McGarry signed Jimmy McCalliog from Sheffield Wednesday for £70,000.

McCalliog was on parade in the final game of our warm-up, in which we beat Kilmarnock 1-0 at Molineux. For this game, having looked at five central defenders, McGarry significantly decided on Frank and John Holsgrove in the middle of our back four. In his report of the game in the Express & Star, Phil Morgan wrote: "It was perhaps appropriate that much of the limelight should be taken against a team of Scots by Wolves' own trio from beyond the border, Hugh Curran, Frank Munro and Jim McCalliog." Had Frank done enough to convince McGarry that he deserved a run in his new role? The answer was yes as the boss decided to start the League season with the Munro-Holsgrove partnership. This was it – the chance for Frank to carve out a new career and he certainly made the most of it as we began with four successive wins. Frank was played as the more central of the two.

The second of those victories came against Southampton at Molineux and Frank hit the winner. Derek Parkin put through his own goal after 24 minutes, only for Peter Knowles to equalise almost immediately. Around ten minutes from half-time came Frank's big moment. A Mike Bailey throw was deflected into his path as he ran into the penalty area thanks to a flick-on by Derek Dougan and he fired home via a post. I was out injured for that game and for the next one, a 3-2 win over Sheffield Wednesday at Hillsborough, where there was a glimpse of the future, not that many realised it. John Holsgrove was injured early on and John McAlle went on to partner Frank. Phil Morgan noted: "John McAlle, substitute when John Holsgrove left after 12 minutes, did well alongside Frank Munro, who commanded the middle." This was the first time they had been paired together in the centre of our defence and clearly they had done well. 'Scouse' would have to wait over a year for a chance to start alongside Frank and he, too, made the most of his opportunity when it came.

Wolves' winning start to the season was ended by Manchester United before a crowd of well over 50,000 at Molineux when Ian Ure, another centre-half who had come to prominence in the city of Dundee, made his debut for the visitors. He had been bought two days earlier from Arsenal for £80,000, the only major signing by Wilf McGuinness during his brief spell as United boss. United's start to the season was in stark contrast to that of Wolves – they began with a draw and three defeats. No wonder they had moved quickly to sign Ure to bolster them. Although the spotlight was on the ex-Dundee man, it was the ex-Dundee United one, Frank, who looked the better centre-half in a game which ended goalless. George Best looked like winning it late on when he burst past three defenders but it was Frank who stopped him in his tracks.

No doubt about it, Frank was settling down well in his new role, not that this attracted as much attention as it might have done. All eyes were on Peter Knowles, seen by many as the most naturally gifted Wolves player since Peter Broadbent. Early in 1969-70, Knowles sensationally quit the game because he felt it was contrary to his beliefs as a Jehovah's Witness. It was a decision which many could not understand but which Peter says he has never regretted. Knowles and Munro had been good pals in Frank's early times at Molineux, as Frank recalled in Clive Corbett's book Those Were The Days: "I was very close to Peter. We used to go out for a drink in Birmingham.....two halves and he'd be drunk. We used to go to the same barber for haircuts. It was about being the best looking bloke in the programme. He started reading the Bible on the coach. I think it was his wife who got him into it. We honestly thought he'd be back within six weeks." Frank also felt Knowles might have been a great asset to us as we proved to be a more than useful team. "If Peter had continued, we would have won more," he said. "I'm convinced. I think he was so good, he would probably have gone on to become the second best Wolves player ever, after Peter Broadbent. He was exactly the same. They both had tremendous feet."

While one career was about to be brought to an abrupt end under great media attention, the foundations for another one, Frank's, were being laid. His place in the side may only recently have been cemented but he was no shrinking violet as he showed when we drew 1-1 at Ipswich. We were ahead through Derek Dougan's first-half goal and looked set for a win until Phil Parkes missed a Mick Mills centre and Derek Parkin used his hand to keep the ball out at the far post. Phil saved the resultant penalty from Town sub Peter Morris and the referee seemed happy until a linesman flagged and told him he thought Lofty had moved early. A re-take was ordered, although our keeper seemed only to have leaned slightly to his right as the kick was taken. Frank really lost his rag, so much so that he got himself booked as he told Peter Walters, the ref, what he thought of the decision. To add insult to injury, Colin Viljoen then took the spot-kick and made no mistake.

What an opening to 1969-70 it was! We lost only one of the first 12 matches, which was the best start since the days of Stan Cullis's managership, even though too many of the games were draws. Unlucky 13? It was in the 13th game, at home to Everton, that Doog was sent off after 60 minutes for arguing with a linesman and that Frank injured his leg and was replaced by Paul Walker. Scotland national manager Bobby Brown was at the game, mainly to run the rule over Hughie Curran, but he must have also been impressed by Frank before injury curtailed his afternoon. Despite the reorganisation, we were beaten only 3-2 but Bill McGarry was not very pleased about it. What is it with managers that they think you should win every game?

Confirmation that Frank had caught Bobby Brown's eye came from Tommy Gallacher in the Dundee Courier. He reported that the manager was 'practically raving about the former Dundee United and Aberdeen player.' Brown told him: "He has lost a lot of weight and he is a 95 per cent better player than he has ever been. Wolves are playing him as a sweeper and he reads the game very well. He stood out as one of the most intelligent players on the field." Frank's injury was not as bad as he thought, or so he said, and he played the next five games with it, although probably not 100 per cent fit. That was typical of him. He hated not playing unless it was absolutely necessary. The five matches included a 3-1 League Cup defeat at QPR and ended with a 1-0 defeat at Manchester City, where Frank came off after 68 minutes suffering from the effects of 'flu. He was booked for a foul on winger Clive Clark in the QPR game and had also picked up a caution in the previous round when we won 3-2 at Brighton. Three bookings in the space of a month would take their toll.

If he missed a game, Frank feared he would not get back in again and was proved right. However, it was not injury or illness that lost him his place. Those bookings had landed him in trouble and he was given a 28-day suspension as well as a £50 fine. Dave Woodfield took Frank's place and this coincided with a run of good results, so, even when Frank was available once more, Bill McGarry stuck with Duggie at centre-half. It was a blow to Frank's progress after 17 games when the team had lost only three times. However, this was McGarry picking the team and he was somebody you did not argue with. Earlier in the season, Duggie had asked for a transfer when he suddenly found himself out of favour after being virtually an automatic choice for four seasons. His old boss Stan Cullis was reported to be interested in signing him but Birmingham were a Second Division side and Dave preferred to await his opportunity at Molineux. It duly came.

While Frank's suspension was bad enough, Derek Dougan, sent off for a second time that season, incurred a ban twice as long. That paved the way for a recall for Frank in a new role. In Dougan's place, McGarry tried Paul Walker for a couple of games and then Bertie Lutton. They were not really centre-forwards, so, for the home game against Sunderland, he turned to Frank as he was available again. We won 1-0 thanks to a Hugh Curran goal and Frank showed some promise up front. On a frosty pitch, he went close to scoring several times and saw one shot hit a post and rebound into the arms of a grateful Jim Montgomery. In the Express & Star, Phil Morgan noted: "Munro did not do at all badly in his latest role and in the hectic opening spells he and the rest of the forwards looked really menacing."

An injury meant Frank had to come off against Sunderland but he was fit for a significant step in his career four days later when he donned the Scotland shirt for the first time since his youth international days. It was just before his forward stint against Sunderland that he received a boost to his morale when chosen by Bobby Brown for Scotland under-23s. He was in a squad of 16 to face France at Hampden Park and the Glasgow Herald reported: "Frank Munro has made such a strong impression on Mr Brown that it isn't surprising he is one of five half-backs listed for the game. Nor is young Kenny Dalglish's inclusion entirely unexpected.

He has been outstanding in his first-team appearances for Celtic." Dalglish was still only 18.

We could have been forgiven for assuming that news of Frank's impressive transformation into a central defender had been noted north o' the border, particularly in view of Brown's remarks to Tommy Gallacher. Despite recognising that Frank was now a defender, though, the manager named him in midfield. He was also given the honour of captaining the side, the original choice of skipper, Eddie Gray of Leeds, having had to withdraw. It was not the first time his leadership qualities had been recognised, of course, as he had captained the Scotland youth team. Manager Brown said he had given a great deal of thought to his second choice as captain. He had had a talk with Frank before he took the party to Inverclyde House for training and announced just before they returned from an evening stint that Frank would be the on-field boss. Brown said: "The boy has impressed me greatly. I saw him play for Wolves against Newcastle on a day that I hadn't gone particularly to watch him but his name went into my notebook there and then. I made a point of seeing him against Everton and he is just the type we need." One newspaper noted in its preview that home fans would see "a slimmed down version of the powerhouse that moved from Aberdeen to Wolves two and a half years ago."

Eddie Thomson and John Blackley were the men in the middle of the back four when, on Wednesday, December 3, 1969, the young Scots beat their French counterparts 4-0. A meagre 5,004 turned up on a cold evening on which Derby centre-forward John O'Hare and Leeds winger Peter Lorimer each scored twice as Frank had a comfortable and competent debut. The Scots were kept waiting 26 minutes for their first goal, O'Hare grabbing it with a diving header to Lorimer's centre. O'Hare looked certain to score again two minutes from half-time when he was pulled down from behind by Rostagni. "Hot shot" Lorimer made no mistake from the penalty. There was a French revival after the break but Raymond Jacobs reported in the Glasgow Herald that the Scots "were too sure, quick and sophisticated in midfield to allow their grip on the struggle to slip. Munro and (Willie) Carr saw to that." From that, it would seem Frank did well in his old role as a midfielder and Herald man Jacobs confirmed that "the promise shown by several of the players new to international football must have been as encouraging to the team's manager, Mr Bobby Brown, as the result was satisfactory."

Goal no 3 came ten minutes into the second half when Robb beat three men and had his shot parried by Baratelli, only for Lorimer to put home the rebound. Lorimer made the final goal, rounding the keeper and then laying the chance on a plate for O'Hare. Gair Henderson was even more enthusiastic in his report in the Glasgow Evening Times. "This was a night in which every young Scot shared in the glory that was going," he wrote. "There were no failures on the Hampden field for the very good reason that every player was out there fighting for his future."

While Frank was with his country, the rest of us from Wolves made a trip to Scotland the day before. And, when he heard about the goings-on, he was highly amused. This brief respite from the pressures of First Division football saw the team honour a commitment to Dunfermline, who some years earlier had sold us wing-half George Miller, with a match at East End Park as part of the deal. McGarry should have consulted Frank, or one of our other Scots, because he got his geography all wrong, apparently thinking you could do Dunfermline in a day, play the game and come home again. He was totally wrong. He had not organised a pre-match meal or even a hotel to stay the night. Consequently, we stopped at a transport café, had a pie and a cup of tea, then played. One consolation was that we won 4-0 on a really muddy pitch (it had rained all day). We arrived home in the not so early hours but McGarry still had us training next day. Frank claimed he did not know who did it but, for the next away game, there was a road atlas on the manager's seat – much to everyone's amusement, though not his, of course.

For our trip to Leeds, McGarry decided Les Wilson would be the latest deputy for The Doog and he scored in our 3-1 defeat. Frank was named sub after his midweek efforts in Glasgow and he had to play the whole of the second half after I picked up a knock. An injury to Mike Bailey then meant Les moved back into midfield, enabling Frank to do his centre-forward impression for three more games. In the wake of his football ban, Frank then collected a driving one when once again his apparent reluctance to acknowledge the basic requirements of the motoring laws caught up with him. At the Dundee Sheriff Court, he was fined £10 and disqualified from going behind the wheel for three months. He had admitted the offence – driving without L plates – by letter at a hearing a couple of weeks before, on the day he captained Scotland under-23s at Hampden.

The case had been adjourned for Frank to appear in court and give reasons why he should not be disqualified. He instead sent a letter but got a shock when he saw a copy of the evening paper on Thursday, December 18. On the front page of the Express & Star was a report headlined 'Warrant out for Wolves player.' His letter had not reached the court and suddenly Francis Munro was a wanted man. Next day, Frank explained to the paper: "It was a real shock when I read they had issued a warrant for my arrest. I immediately got on the phone and cleared up the situation. I suppose the letter must have been delayed in the Christmas post."

When told the facts, the court withdrew the warrant and the letter was indeed found in the court's post. Sheriff Graham Cox read it before passing sentence but it did not persuade him not to ban Frank, the court having been told he had a previous motoring conviction. That probably related to the spot of motoring bother that happened when he was with Aberdeen a couple of years earlier. In view of the nature of this second offence and time of year, I suppose you could say it was 'the first no L' for Frank. Apparently, the driving offence had been committed in Dundee during July, so he must have been on a visit home and maybe thought the Scots police would not know he had yet to pass his test – or, more likely, knowing Frank, he just did not think at all.

When Dougan returned to the side, Frank was the player to drop out as we went meekly out of the FA Cup 3-0 at Burnley. A week later, we were back at Turf Moor for a League match and this time Frank got the nod for the no 10 shirt ahead of Les Wilson and we won 3-1, goalkeeper John Oldfield, newly-signed from Huddersfield, making his debut. I remember Jim McCalliog missed a penalty when we were leading 2-1. Steve Kindon, then with Burnley, was injured and Jim had to wait while Kindo was carried off on a stretcher. Peter Mellor then saved the spot-kick, only for the ball to be crossed back into the middle, where Mike Bailey hammered it home.

Four days after the Burnley game, another under-23 cap came Frank's way as substitute back at his old stamping ground, Pittodrie, in January, 1970, when the Scots were held 1-1 on a windswept and rainy night by the Welsh. His place in the starting line-up went to Alan Campbell but the Charlton man and West Brom's Asa Hartford struggled to make any impact in midfield and half-way through the second half they were replaced by Frank and Joe Harper, the Aberdeen left-winger. Wales had taken the lead after only 11 minutes when Dick Krzywicki sent in a low cross which Dennis Hawkins flicked home. The subs made a big difference and helped inspire a late rally. Harper, later to switch to striker with his club to great effect, sent over a corner which John O'Hare fired home with ten minutes to go. With the very last kick, the Scottish lads nearly snatched an unlikely victory when Peter Lorimer's shot struck a post. According to reports, the only Scot to emerge with any credit was Willie Carr, a Coventry player then but destined to join us five years later. "Too many players from whom so much was expected just didn't live up to reports and reputations from South of the Border," wrote Gair Henderson in the Glasgow Times, referring to the six Anglo-Scots in the starting line-up. That theme of knocking the Anglos was hardly unfamiliar.

What Frank dearly wanted was more opportunities to further his progress as a central defender but it seemed the way back was blocked. We at Wolves had quite a few injury problems and, when Dave Woodfield and Bertie Lutton joined the casualty list, Frank thought his chance would come. He was indeed recalled for our trip to Stoke, where we drew 1-1, but it was as Lutton's deputy in midfield while John McAlle played alongside John Holsgrove. Significantly, Phil Morgan noted in his match report: "Frank Munro came back to make a notable impression in defence when the Peter Dobing-inspired home attack really got going." For the next game, Les Wilson partnered Holsgrove and scored in our 3-1 home defeat by Manchester City but a bit of unbelievable foolishness by Les unexpectedly paved the way for Frank's return to central defence for the rest of his career.

It all came about because McGarry sent on Paul Walker in place of Les with about 20 minutes to go – a decision Les was not happy about. As he left the field, he made what the Express & Star coyly described as 'a very obvious gesture' towards the manager, who was sitting in the directors' box, and then stomped down the tunnel. Phil Morgan's report of the incident quoted McGarry, who said it was an internal matter. In those days, the paper's relationship with Wolves was very different and Phil, who often travelled on our coach to games, felt a loyalty to the club so went along with playing down the incident. You can imagine how such a story would be treated nowadays. A player at a top-flight club giving the V-sign to his boss would be back page news – possibly front page. Les had done a good man-marking job on City's Colin Bell when we won 3-1 at Molineux the previous April and had done the same earlier in the season even though we lost that one. He felt he was doing well again in this latest encounter with Bell, which was why he was angry about being taken off. He was kind enough to tell us his version of this incident and its consequences:

"I was one of Wolves' fittest and quickest players, so I could get the other side of Colin Bell when we were attacking and also get behind the ball when we lost possession," he recalled. "To the best of my recollection, it was a very tight game. City had taken the lead when, would you believe, I outran Colin and received a quality pass from, I believe, Jim McCalliog to make it 1-1. Of the eight goals I scored for Wolves, this was the only one I managed at Molineux. Within minutes of City scoring their second goal, Sammy Chung, yelled at me 'Reverend (my nickname), you will be coming off for Paul Walker' and my reply was 'Sam, you must be fucking joking, I am enjoying this challenge.' I was very frustrated and furious at being the one taken off. As I was leaving the pitch, I jogged over to the Waterloo Road Stand, where Bill McGarry was sitting alongside the Wolves directors. I was so infuriated that I put my two fingers up to him and walked straight to the tunnel and then to the dressing room, where I showered and got dressed.

"It was very unprofessional of me and out of character. I had no excuses; I was bang out of order. I heard a roar as City scored their third goal and all our players came into the dressing room, heads down. Needless to say, McGarry was not pleased and blasted a few players for under-performing. After his rant, I walked out of the dressing room, ignored the boss and drove home to Penn, devastated at what I had done in front of a very supportive crowd of 32,000. I stewed for nearly two days. This incident in front of the Waterloo Road Stand was my 'Waterloo' in my career at the wonderful Wolves. Derek Dougan called me on the Sunday and said he and the other players could not believe what I did when I left the pitch but did say it was totally out of character and contrary to my temperament.

"The first team did not have to report for training until the Tuesday, so it was to be the longest weekend in my young career. I did not sleep, did not eat and was still very angry at McGarry and Chung at being taken off. On the Tuesday, as soon as I walked into the dressing room, Sammy said: 'The gaffer, wants to see you in his office immediately. Don't get changed for training.' It was a long walk down corridor to the manager's office and getting there seemed to take an eternity. McGarry looked at his desk when he spoke to me; he never, ever seemed to look people straight in their eyes. He was blunt and his words were short, sharp and extremely clear: 'Reverend, I could have taken off any one of six players on Saturday. The reason I changed you for Paul Walker was simple; we needed another goal quickly and I sacrificed you for Paul, who is a forward. You certainly did not play badly at all, in fact you did extremely well and gave your all. Some more talented players than yourself went through the motions and played poorly.'

"McGarry went on: 'Of all the players here, you were the very last one I thought would embarrass me in front of the directors and fans. I still cannot believe it, coming from you. You will not be with the Wolves first team for as long as I see fit, you will be fined two weeks' wages and you will play in the third team some time this week. This will never happen again under my watch. Les, you have been a great example of the complete Wolves team player, you have been an excellent professional and you have done well for me – but I, the club and, most importantly, the Wolves directors cannot tolerate this sort of behaviour from you or any other player. You will pay the price for what you did and you will pay big. You will be training with the third team and youth players today and for the rest of the next two weeks and Phil Shaw will take away your wages.'

"I was segregated from the Wolves first team for two weeks and played in the third and reserve teams for the next three games and went without my wages and more importantly the bonus money and crowd bonus money that all of the Wolves players were on as incentives. I missed the next three first-team games but I got on with my training and in three weeks I returned to first team duty on March 21 and faced Leeds, playing at right-back and marking the gifted Peter Lorimer. It was all a great lesson for me in my future coaching and management positions – the gaffer has to be right or wrong and makes all the bold decisions and players have to accept them."

I am sure Frank's opportunity to resume his central defensive position would have eventually come but now it had happened earlier than he might have hoped. Thanks to Les's moment of madness, the door was open again to Frank for the role he now saw as his future. For our trip to The Hawthorns to face West Brom, Frank wore the no 6 shirt and made the most of his chance. I may be biased but I believe his displays in the seasons that followed earned him the right to be mentioned in the same breath as the truly great centre-halves in Wolves history, namely Stan Cullis, Billy Wright and Bill Slater. Frank's return to central defence saw us draw 3-3 with Albion after three times taking the lead. Little did we know it but the game also saw the start of another great Wolves career – a 19-year-old John Richards made his debut as deputy for the injured Dougan.

He may have been temporarily unable to take control of a car but Frank was certainly motoring on the football field and it was no surprise when he collected a third under-23 cap – against England at Roker Park, home of Sunderland. After the poor display against the Welsh, there were seven changes but Frank was still not chosen as a central defender, skipper John Blackley being again paired with Thomson. Those two had their hands full marking Peter Osgood and Brian Kidd. Two goals from Osgood and one from Kidd put England 3-1 up before the game was abandoned after just over an hour because of a heavy snow storm. Frank was not the only Wolves man on duty that night as Derek Parkin was in the England line-up, winning his third cap at that level. Although trailing when the game was halted, the Scotland lads had, according to the Glasgow Herald report, not done badly. In particular it mentioned keeper Tommy Hughes and full-backs David Clunie and Billy Dickson but added "Francis Munro and George Connelly, although restricted to a midfield role, also emerged with credit." England went three up before Colin Todd put through his own goal with a header to a free-kick by Frank to give some hope to the Scots just before the snow began. Playing in his old role, he had done all right and Jim Blair in the Glasgow Evening Times wrote that he "got pass marks in midfield." That was fine but Frank wanted to be

'Francie' Munro, as he was often known north of the border, cuts a sturdy figure as the biggest lad in the team, even in his formative days in the game. The football-mad youngster is pictured one in from the left on the front row of this line-up from St Vincent de Paul School. Left: A young man seeking his fame and fortune - with Molineux as his destiny.

The budding international...Frank watches his keeper Dennis Devlin collect the ball safely during the 1966 UEFA youth tournament clash with West Germany. Right: Proudly showing off his Scotland blazer prior to another trip with his country. The trail was to lead all the way up to the senior team, although his admirers insist he was capped nothing like as many times as he should have been.

Frank sparked a family feud by joining Dundee United rather than the rivals down the road. He cut his teeth at Tannadice before switching north to Aberdeen (left), where he continued to come good despite a setback in a game against his future employers during the 1967 tournament in the United States. There was some time on the bench (bottom photo) but he did plenty to catch the eye of Wolves manager Ronnie Allen.

Francie Munro Sent Off v. Wolves

Munro sent off as Dons hold Wolves

Dons give Munro a late test

The "new" Munro's return to Tannadice

Above: Unfortunately, Frank's licence was nothing like as clean as his car. Below: With Margaret Nicoll, who became his wife.

£70,000 BID FOR DONS ACE MUNRO

FRANCIS MUNRO, Aberdeen's 20-year-old right half, is set to sign for Wolves today for a fee of about £70,000.

The shock deal was revealed by Aberdeen manager Eddie Turnbull who said last night:

"The clubs have agreed on a substantial fee.

"Munro spoke to Wolves' boss, Ronnie Allen, and the player and his wife have flown south to meet officials.

"The deal is expected to be completed on Friday morning."

Munro, who joined Dons from Dundee United for £10,000 in October, 1966, was ordered off while playing AGAINST Wolves in America during the close-season.

Fined

He was fined £10 by the Referees' Committee for that offence only last month.

And he will be on the mat again on Monday for collecting THREE CAUTIONS.

Now the former Youth cap may make his debut FOR Wolves against Everton at Molineux tomorrow.

Munro is the THIRD Pittodrie player to be transferred

A £70,000 catch . . . that's what Margaret Munro got when she married Dons star Francis in September. For the big wing-half is set to join Wolves for that fee today.

DONS CRASH AGAIN TO

Remember . . . ?

SAID Francis Munro, of Wolves, the other day — "It's going to be great for me going back to Dens Park. I played my first big game for Dundee United there — on my 16th birthday — and scored the winner. It was a 1964 League Cup tie — and United got through by 3-2. The funny thing is if I hadn't signed and played for United, I'd have been in the crowd as a Dundee supporter."

The Midlanders' other Scots, Munro and McCalliog, did their Scotland chances no harm either.

Hearts made things so easy for big Frannie. It was unbelievable. Here was a centre-half at least eight inches taller than Donald Ford. Yet they continually pumped high balls down the middle.

It's hero Munro

WOLVES marched into the U.E.F.A. Cup final with a 2—1 win, 4—3 on aggregate, against Hungarians Ferencvaros at Molineux last night.

And Scottish international Francis Munro, the man who scored Wolves' equaliser in Budapest in the first leg, and keeper Phil Parkes were once again the heroes.

The English club were given a great start when 18-year-old Steve Daley, making his European debut, scored after only 30 seconds.

Then, a minute before the interval, Munro added a

Meanwhile, Wolves' centre-half FRANCIS MUNRO is making a desperate effort to be fit for the Pittodrie national. The former Dundee United and Aberdeen player, who was also on the Doc's staff at Chelsea, has a groin injury which has kept him out of Wolves' last three games.

He was home in Dundee at the week-end and told me, "I think I've got a good chance of being fit if I'm chosen. I've been at Tannadice for treatment from ANDY DICKSON, reckon he's one of the best physiotherapists in the business.

Francis Munro, signed by Wolves for £60,000 on Friday, could not be blamed for their home slump against Everton. The former Aberdeen boy looked a fine prospect, though he lacks pace.

Frank Munro, of Wolves, will appeal against his third booking of the season, received in Saturday's game with West Ham. He will call on the evidence of the TV recording as part of his defence.

Above: The newspaper coverage surrounding Frank's switch to Anglo Scot status in the middle of 1967-68. He was delighted to meet up again with Ronnie Allen (right), this time at Molineux, although the former Albion forward's successor in the hot seat, Bill McGarry (pictured below right with his assistant Sammy Chung), often drove him to distraction. Through his grumbles, though, the style was always there, as shown in this clash with his first club Chelsea (below).

Twin towers at work.......Frank Munro and John McAlle, partners for almost six years, deny former Wolves man Frank Wignall in a stirring 2-1 win at Derby in January, 1971. The black arm bands are being worn because of the Ibrox disaster shortly before. Below: Slow down, I hate training! Alan Sunderland and Steve Kindon provide the company in a few laps of the Molineux pitch.

You keep a proper eye on Ray Kennedy and John Radford for once and a pesky defender pops up to score! Munro has anguish written over his face as Peter Simpson, rather than his and John McAlle's least favourite foes nets at Wolves' expense at Highbury. Below: A watching brief, along with McAlle, Mike Bailey and Jim McCalliog, in a 2-1 win at Huddersfield in April, 1971.

Pride is etched on the unmistakable Munro features (left) as he strides out at Wembley in 1975 on the occasion of one of his nine senior Scottish caps. It rankled with many at Molineux that he missed out on a place in his country's squad at the 1974 World Cup finals in West Germany. Below: Oops, sorry, lads! A rare blunder results in a costly own goal in a draw at Southampton that ensured Frank received a few words of rebuke from Bill McGarry.

recognised as a central defender. He hoped his midfield days were behind him.

When he returned to central defence in that draw at The Hawthorns, it was in partnership with Dave Woodfield and they stayed together for the next two games. Then John Holsgrove unexpectedly returned as Frank's partner, courtesy of an unusual but brave decision by Dave – he asked to be dropped for the home game with Leeds. Bill McGarry told the Daily Mirror: "I had named Woodfield in the party of 13 but he asked me if he could play in the reserves. He felt he is going through a bad patch and he is big enough to admit it." So it was back to the Holsgrove-Munro partnership against Leeds, who won 2-1 at Molineux. Frank stayed in the team for seven of the last eight games that season. On Easter Saturday – the next fixture after Leeds – we drew 2-2 with Arsenal at Highbury, where we were two up with 19 minutes to go, only for George Graham to score twice for the Gunners. In his Sporting Star verdict, Phil Morgan wrote: "When the home side gained the initiative, it was the turn of the defenders to shine. There was magnificent work from Munro and Holsgrove." That was more proof that Frank was in the position on the field that nature had intended.

The game Frank missed in the run-in was the final one in an Easter programme that saw us play three games in four days, which was par for the course back then. For the trip to West Ham, McGarry decided to play Bernard Shaw instead of Frank, who was an unused sub. Maybe the plan was for Shaw to do a man-marking job on Jimmy Greaves. The former England striker may have been past his best by then but he was still capable of living up to what was so often said about him – "he did nothing all game apart from score two goals." That's what he almost did against us that night despite Bernard keeping a pretty tight rein on him. Greavesie scored a rare headed goal after two minutes and early in the second half seemed to help a Billy Bonds header into the net, although the goal was credited to Bonds.

Frank was quickly restored to the starting line-up for the final two games, at Derby and at home to Coventry, both of which we lost. That meant that a campaign that had begun with four straight wins ended in four straight defeats. In fact, we did not win once in our final 13 matches, so it was a good job we had made that superb start. It turned out it was Wolves' worst ever finish to a League season. It was hardly the way we wanted to go into the history books. With 32 appearances, 25 of them as a central defender, it had at least been a season of considerable progress for Frank, if a disappointing one for the team. Because of the World Cup in Mexico that summer, our League season ended early. Our last match was on April 10, not that there was any chance of having a longer-than-usual break – the club had seven more matches lined up for us.

I was injured, so I missed the three-match tour to Yugoslavia, as that part of the world was then known. Five days after our last League game, the lads were in Sarajevo and beat Zeljeznicar 1-0 thanks to a Jim McCalliog goal. That was the first time Zeljeznicar had lost to foreign opposition in 25 years. It was a false omen, however, as we then lost 3-1 to Sloboda in Tuzla and 5-2 to Skopje. The trip was beset by injuries and there was a strange incident involving John Richards against Sloboda. He had to go off with a back strain and Derek Clarke replaced him. Then Kenny Hibbitt was injured, so McGarry sent John back on. That has to be some sort of record. In the Skopje game, Hugh Curran gave us the lead from the penalty spot but the home team came back to lead 3-1 before Jim McCalliog reduced the arrears. As Skopje sewed the game up, there were more casualties and because we were so short of players, Sammy Chung went on to replace Derek Clarke.

There may have been mixed fortunes for Wolves but it was all good experience for Frank in his new role and there was still no time to put his feet up as nine days after the final game in Yugoslavia, we embarked on a new competition in the shape of the Anglo-Italian Cup. Six English teams took part – Swindon, Sheffield Wednesday, Middlesbrough, Albion, Sunderland and Wolves, and six Italian teams, Napoli, Juventus, Roma, Fiorentina, Lazio and Vicenza. We were divided into three leagues of four but you did not play against teams from your own country. In addition to two points for a win and one for a draw, there was a point for each goal scored. At the end of it all, the Italian side with the most points would meet the English side with the most points.

We were with Fiorentina and Lazio and I was fit for our opening match at Molineux, against Fiorentina, the 1969 Italian champions. They had Amarildo, the man who had stepped up so successfully to help Brazil retain the World Cup in 1962 after Pelé had been injured in the group stages. Frank gave Amarildo little chance to shine and we won 2-1 with me, amazingly, hitting our second goal from 30 yards. We then beat Lazio 1-0 thanks to a Mike Bailey cross-shot but the Italians got very angry when they thought Phil Parkes had dropped the ball over the line and the referee waved play on. It all got quite heated and, according to the report in the Express & Star, Hugh Curran was booked once and I was booked twice. I did not get sent off, so the rules must have been different! Giorgio Chinaglia did get his marching orders, though, for persisting to argue about whether Lofty had let the ball cross his line. It flared up again afterwards and the police actually locked the Italians in their dressing room for a while.

Then it was over to Italy and we had a great 3-1 win over Fiorentina, only to lose to Lazio 2-0. There were fears of trouble after the goings-on at Molineux but the game passed off mostly without incident until five minutes from time. For some reason, their keeper Michelangelo Sulfaro raced to the edge of his penalty area and struck Bertie Lutton. The referee had no alternative but to send him off. I suppose it was a case of Michelangelo hitting the roof – or should that be the ceiling? Against Fiorentina, John Richards scored his first senior goal. Little did we know it, but he would go on to add another 193. So we ended up joint second best English team on 12 points with Middlesbrough, just behind Swindon. A couple more goals at Molineux and we would have been in the final, although it sounded like an occasion well worth missing. Swindon won it 3-0 against Napoli in front of a hostile 55,000 crowd in Naples. The home fans were so incensed by the showing of their team that they threw stones and beer bottles, then ripped up seats and threw them as well. With 11 minutes to go the ref abandoned the match, because of the danger to the players, and Swindon were declared the winners.

We all like to play in a cup final but Frank and I agreed we were not too miffed about missing out on that one. After that we settled down to three weeks of watching the 1970 World Cup finals on TV before pre-season training came around again all too quickly.

Chapter Six

Dream Partnership

Before 1970-71 got under way, there was more foreign travel for us, namely a three-match trip to Germany and the Netherlands at the beginning of August. We beat Stuttgart 2-0 but lost 4-1 to Hanover and 1-0 to Groningen. We had a couple of new recruits, signed by McGarry, and both were larger-than-life characters – Bobby Gould and Danny Hegan. Another signing was by the boss himself. He agreed a four-year contract.

In the game in Stuttgart, McGarry used 15 of the 16 players on tour, Dave Woodfield taking over from Frank at half-time. Frank was paired with John Holsgrove for the second game but could not have guessed in his wildest dreams the position he would occupy against Groningen. It all started on the flight from Stuttgart to Hanover when Phil Parkes fell ill and, on arrival, had to be rushed to hospital for an appendix operation. His deputy against Hanover was John Oldfield but he twisted his ankle in the game and he, too, was now out of action. Young Rod Arnold was then flown out to join us but, unbelievably, he also picked up an injury. That completed a hat-trick of crocked keepers. So guess who played in goal in our final game? That's correct – Francis Munro. He did not do badly, either, although our defence did their best to ensure he had as few shots as possible to deal with. He was beaten only by a Martin Koenan penalty, given after Frank had clashed with home centre-forward Bjorne Jenzen.

Frank's display prompted a rare reaction – praise from Bill McGarry. Phoning back to the Express & Star, the boss said: "He was really excellent and, in respect of the six-yard area, he showed better measure and control than many a full-time goalkeeper. He said he was ready to have a go and when it was found Groningen could not lend us a man, as we had hoped they might, Frank was in like a shot." His display between the sticks was no surprise to Les Wilson, who recalled many years later: "Frank loved to play in goal whenever he had the chance. He was a very decent shot stopper and a very capable keeper." Fortunately, when Hanover came to Molineux a few days later, at least two of our keepers were fit again and Frank could revert to his central defensive role. The Germans won 2-1 and our fans, already disgruntled at an increase in admission prices, gave us the slow handclap. It was quite a welcome for Messrs Hegan and Gould. Bobby had given us a bright start by heading a goal but the Germans' skipper Hans Siemansmeyer scored a couple of crackers, one a free-kick which went through our defensive wall and the other a 25-yard shot.

Somewhat surprisingly, McGarry decided to start the League season with Les Wilson, rather than Frank, alongside John Holsgrove. The boss may have felt Frank had a poor game against the Germans but he was by no means the only one. Nevertheless, for the opening game, at Newcastle, he of the 13 who travelled was the only one not to see any action in a 3-2 defeat. When, four days later, we lost 4-2 at home to Derby, Frank was in the reserves for the game with Derby reserves the same night. It was but a brief exile. Having seen us lose two matches, conceding seven goals in the process, McGarry recalled Frank, in preference to Les, and it soon became clear he was back to stay.

We lost four of our first five games, the last 4-1 at Nottingham Forest, where John Holsgrove had to come off after only 27 minutes because of a groin injury. As John Richards was our sub, it put more responsibility on Frank and he accepted it easily. Phil Morgan, in the Express & Star, wrote: "Ironically, having regard to the margin, the most notable contribution came from Frank Munro, who moved into the middle on Holsgrove's departure." Dave Woodfield was out after having a cartilage operation, so, with Holsgrove sidelined for our trip to Ipswich, Frank and John McAlle were paired together in the centre of defence. They were perhaps caught napping when Colin Viljoen strolled through to score after 15 minutes but soon got their act together. Then Hughie Curran turned the match on its head in the space of eight minutes, scoring two goals and making one for Bobby Gould, his first for the club. Ipswich hit back with a late penalty from that man Viljoen but this gritty win marked the start of a special partnership between two very different players who complemented each other perfectly.

Woodfield's and Holsgrove's misfortune created the opportunity for the Munro-McAlle pairing and they made it work. Scouse was still only 20 and Frank 22, so they were young men with bright futures. Not that John Holsgrove was anywhere near being a veteran; he was only a couple of years older than Frank and had done a great job, totting up a couple of hundred appearances for us. Sadly, it turned out that Duggie Woodfield had made his last appearance for Wolves. The 3-2 win at Ipswich saw us embark on an undefeated run of nine games, including six wins in a row. With Bobby Gould and Hugh Curran helping Derek Dougan knock in the goals, we were starting to make an impact. We had another striker waiting in the wings, too. John Richards made a number of impressive appearances as substitute and it was no surprise when he established himself in the team the following season. Frank was in good form and a newspaper report of our 1-1 draw at Crystal Palace at the end of November noted: "Wolves centre-half Frank Munro must have impressed watching Scotland team boss Bobby Brown."

Things were going well on the field for Frank but he was in for a shock off it – a letter from the Inland Revenue that left him speechless. It informed him that, because he was paying Wolves only 25 shillings (£1.25) a week rent, it was considered a benefit in kind and therefore he owed the Revenue some £400. He came into training that morning with a face like thunder, not realising he was far from the only one who had received such a letter. We, too, were smarting like hell. Surely the club must have known this and for us to owe £400 each in back tax was a heavy burden to bear. In 1970, that was a hell of a lot of money. The only way forward for Frank was to buy his own house, so nobody could accuse him of getting a benefit in kind. On New Year's Day, 1971, Frank and Margaret were house-hunting and finished up on a new estate in the Compton area of town, where building had started on new homes. Surprise, surprise, by sheer coincidence, my wife Barbara and I ended up in the same place.

Frank and Margaret had already decided on a Hathaway cottage in Forton Close, as it was going to be called, subject to the club giving him a mortgage. Likewise with Barbara and myself. Next day, we both went into the club office to see secretary Phil Shaw and find out if there was any way we could have a mortgage from the club. "I'll put it to the board," said Phil and we had to leave it at that until the next board meeting. We waited in trepidation, neither of us having had a mortgage before – or ever been able to afford one – and worried that someone else might nip in and buy while we were awaiting a decision. Finally, we got the go-ahead, the good thing being that Frank and I did not have to do a thing because the club solicitors sorted out all the paperwork.

It was an exciting time for Frank with a brand new house to look forward to on top of the likelihood of a long stint in Wolves' first team. We both moved in before the gardens had been finished, before the fences had been put up and even before the numbers had been fixed to the doors, which led to a bit of confusion for Frank on one memorable occasion. We had gone to training in my car because Margaret wanted to go shopping in town, using Frank's car. Arriving back in my car, Frank realised he had not got a key – Margaret had the only one. "No problem," Frank said, "there's an upstairs window open and there are some builders' ladders. I'll just climb up and let myself in." The Hathaway cottages were not very high, so the upstairs window was only 15ft off the ground. The ladder in place, up went Frank, opened the window and was half way in when he suddenly stopped. "What's up?" I asked. "This isn't my bedroom furniture," he said. "In fact, it's not my bloody house." With that, he scurried down the ladder, removed it from the house and put it back where he had borrowed it from. Fortunately, Margaret soon returned with the key to let him in. It was a long time before I let him forget not knowing where he lived. I used to say: "Now remember when you've been out, your house is the one with the red door."

Some time later, he got his own back on me when I was driving us home after a late night out. I was in one of those black and yellow VW Beetles which we hired for a nominal fee. Approaching Forton Close, Frank said "Get some speed up as you enter the cul-de-sac then switch the engine off as we approach our section and coast round the corner, so the wives won't know what time we arrived home." I thought it was a good idea and switched off the engine as I neared our corner but the car did not turn. I had forgotten that switching off the engine would activate the steering lock. So I went straight on and into a neighbour's drive. Restarting the engine not only woke up our wives but half the neighbourhood. Frank was still laughing when he got out of the passenger seat. He said: "That's strange" and I asked: "What is?" Quick as a flash, he answered: "The same thing happened to me the other night." There was rarely a dull moment with Frank. Moving to Compton coincided with the refurbishment of the nearby Mermaid pub on the Bridgnorth Road. It was a very popular place and, being so close, it naturally became our local for years, not only for Frank and me but for the rest of the lads.

The season was by now well under way and Frank had revelled in his new defensive partnership with John McAlle. Scouse had been tried in the team on McGarry's arrival and then dropped for almost the whole of the next season. In 1969-70, he was named in the starting line-up just five times and in three of those he wore the no 8 shirt. He also went on as sub seven times, five of which were to replace a forward. Did the manager not think that he was ready or did he think he was not good enough? We shall never know but I do know that he was more than good enough a season later when he teamed up with Frank to form a formidable pairing. An injury to Frank in the home game with Stoke led to a rare example of misjudgement by our manager, though. We had to travel to Oxford for a League Cup second-round tie and one had to question the decision of Bill McGarry to play The Doog at no 5. Dougan had been a centre-half as a youngster and always fancied himself in that position and no doubt had been bending the ear of the boss to let him show what he could do there. The Doog had gone on as sub for Frank for the whole of the second half against Stoke and not done too badly as an emergency defender. Knowing Derek, he probably thought he had shown that he was like the great John Charles – equally good at centre-half or centre-forward. If so, he was deluding himself. At Oxford, The Doog proved he was a striker, not a defender, as we lost 1-0. Although John Holsgrove was also injured, there were other replacements waiting in the wings, yet McGarry went down a different road. Thankfully, normality was quickly resumed.

Frank felt sorry for John Holsgrove, who for so long had been a stalwart at the back and repeatedly shown he was highly dependable. However, the new kid on the block, John McAlle, had now taken his place and he and Frank were gelling nicely. A fine servant to Wolves, Holsy eventually moved on and Scouse would be a first-choice central defender for nine seasons. His total of 509 appearances puts him sixth in Wolves' all-time list. Frank, by the way, is at no 20 with 371.

A measure of how things had improved for us came when we drew 0-0 at Spurs, who had earlier beaten us 3-0 at Molineux. The Tottenham boss Bill Nicholson, one of the most respected managers around at that time, said we had gone from looking the worst team in the League to now looking a very good side and actually singled out Frank for praise. He said: "Frank Munro played very well at centre-half and gave our front men very little scope." Top words from a top man. Things had by then started well for us in the Texaco Cup, a competition for 16 clubs from England, Scotland, the Irish Republic and Northern Ireland. We got past Dundee and Morton in the first two rounds and eventually triumphed in the final as well but, strangely, won all our away games, then struggled at home.

It all began in familiar surroundings for Frank as we beat his old rivals Dundee 2-1 at Dens Park. Bobby Gould and Jim McCalliog put us in control before Gordon Wallace quickly replied with a goal for Dundee. The locals must have been impressed with the lad who used to play for the club down the road, the marauding midfielder having been transformed into an accomplished central defender. I remember the match had a painful ending for Ken Hibbitt, who sustained a nasty head injury in the last minute and had to be carried off on a stretcher. He needed a fair few stitches and left the ground sporting a huge bandage. While we were in Scotland, Frank, not for the first time, had kept a coach full of players waiting but this time it was not his fault. We were about to leave our hotel in Edinburgh to train at Tynecastle, Hearts' ground, when Frank got stuck in a lift. He was in there for about 20 minutes before his yells for help were heard and an engineer sorted it out. Dundee held us to a goalless draw in the second leg when we had most of the play but could not take our chances. The nearest we went was when Jim McCalliog's shot hit the bar late on.

We won 3-0 in the first leg against Morton at Cappielow in the next round despite the best efforts of Bobby Collins. The gifted former Celtic, Everton and Leeds man, the club's player-coach, was still a useful performer despite being nearly 40 then. Bobby Gould struck after 19 minutes and Derek Dougan made it two six minutes later, from one of my crosses. A centre from Derek Parkin enabled Gouldy to head a third in the final few minutes. They gave us a fright in the second leg. With the diminutive Collins again running the show in midfield, they went two up through Gerry Sweeney in the first half and Campbell on the hour. Fortunately, Hugh Curran, who was back in action after eight games sidelined by a leg injury, went on for The Doog and scored eight minutes after Morton's second goal to calm things down and give us a 4-2 aggregate win. Derry City had us rattled for long spells, too, when we visited Northern Ireland in the semi-final but Gouldy snatched the only goal with eight minutes to go. The second leg was over three months after the first one and we beat them 4-0 to reach the final against Hearts, who had begun their campaign in the competition by putting out Burnley. They lost 3-1 at Turf Moor, where a certain Steve Kindon scored before being carried off on a stretcher, but then won the return leg 4-1. Like us, Hearts seemed to do better away, winning 5-0 at Airdrie, where Donald Ford hit four goals, and 2-1 in the semi-final at Motherwell after a draw at home. They looked certain to go out in front of a 25,000 second-leg gate at Fir Park until a last-minute goal by sub George Fleming took the tie into extra-time, in which Ford hit the winner.

So Frank was into his third cup final and it would prove third time lucky. The trend of away wins continued when we won the first leg 3-1 at Tynecastle, with Hughie scoring twice. There was a neat line in the Glasgow Evening Times from Shearer Borthwick. "Many of the 26,000 crowd came prepared to hail a Bannockburn and remained to see a Flodden," he wrote as one of several compliments about us which confirmed we were becoming a useful side. "They demonstrated that the basic art of passing the ball with economy and the minimum of effort is still one of the most vital aspects of the game," he added. "They could achieve in one quick stab at the ball things that took Hearts two or three passes." Hearts still gave us a scare by going ahead through a Donald Ford header on seven minutes, his eighth goal in the tournament, but I had one of my better games and had a part in each of our goals, first laying on an equaliser for Mike Bailey. I was also in the move that saw Mike O'Grady put Hughie through to give us the lead on 31 minutes and then I managed to lay on his second near the end.

Alas, the Glasgow Times man would not have been so impressed by our display in the second leg, in which our indifferent home form continued. Having had a field day in Edinburgh, I hardly did a thing right at Molineux. We were awful but lost only 1-0, so the cup was ours on a 3-2 aggregate. George Fleming scored after 24 minutes, so the game was on a knife edge for over an hour. All right, it was not a major tournament, they were not dancing in the streets of Lower Gornal and Bilston, nor did we have an open-top bus tour of Wolverhampton town centre. But, after some lean years, it was a welcome piece of silverware for the Molineux cabinet and there were more than 28,000 fans there to see us collect it.

That man Borthwick from the Glasgow Evening Times had a little dig at Frank by commenting: "Eddie Thomson was superb, outshining his opposite number, Anglo-Scot Frank Munro, who has been tipped for a recall to Scottish colours and whose reputation stands so high at Wolverhampton." Yet, in the Glasgow Herald, the report noted: "Hearts' crisp, competent play broke down on the 18-yard line, where they found Munro, the Scottish internationalist, a stumbling block." Funny how two men can watch the same match and come up with differing opinions. Certainly, Thomson had not outshone Frank in the first leg at Tynecastle. Teams in the Molineux leg on Monday, May 3, 1971 were:

Wolves: Parkes, Shaw, Parkin, Bailey, Munro, McAlle, McCalliog, Hibbitt, Gould, Dougan, Wagstaffe (O'Grady). Hearts: Cruickshank, Sneddon, Kay, Thomson, Anderson, Veitch, Townsend, Laing, Ford, Wood, Fleming.

Our Texaco Cup triumph might have received greater acknowledgment nationally had the second leg not been played on the same night as a somewhat important game in North London. Arsenal beat Spurs at White Hart Lane thanks to Ray Kennedy's goal to clinch the League title. The following weekend, they would beat Liverpool in the FA Cup final to complete the Double.

Chapter Seven

Scotland Calling

Things did not go too well for us in the FA Cup in our Texaco Cup-winning 1970-71 season. After beating Norwich 5-1, we lost 2-1 at Derby, where John Richards scored his first goal in the competition. Frank had been doubtful for the Norwich game, having sustained a rib injury in our 2-0 Boxing Day win at home to Everton, and the comments of the Daily Express's Peter Ingall said much about the progress our young centre-half had made: "Wolves cannot afford to be without Munro, one of the key men in their successful run this season. Since being switched from wing-half, he has matured as a fine defender and plugged the gaps in what was a vulnerable defence." When we beat Chelsea 1-0 in mid-February to go third in the table, the same paper noted "No-one showed more class in the Wolves defence than the powerful Frank Munro."

Frank and John McAlle were forming a great partnership at the back and, taking into account the League Cup, FA Cup and Texaco Cup, played almost 50 games each that season. John was the perfect foil with his no-nonsense approach. Frank had the finesse and John the raw exuberance of youth. It was a combination that worked and, as a side, we clicked. We finished fourth in the League – the club's best in the First Division since 1960-61, when Stan Cullis was manager. This meant we qualified for Europe and would play in the UEFA Cup, which had been introduced to replace the Fairs Cup. And do you know what? We did not even get a 'well done' from Bill McGarry.

It had been a more than satisfying season for Frank. He cemented his place at centre-half and won a fourth under-23 cap, although the Scots were unimpressive in losing 1-0 to Wales at Swansea. At least Frank in that game played in what was now recognised as his best position. He was among old friends as Martin Buchan was his partner at the back while, at full-back, was Jim Hermiston, who had made his Aberdeen debut on the same day as Frank made his. The team fell short, though, against a Welsh side who consisted of two First Division reserves and a collection of Second and Third Division players. They had been depleted by the withdrawal of two of their higher-profile players, Liverpool striker John Toshack and Leeds midfielder Terry Yorath, which made the defeat all the more inexcusable in the eyes of the critics. The Welsh, according to reports, were far better organised and the only goal was a 67th-minute header from Peter Price of Peterborough to a corner by Cyril Davies (Charlton). Malcolm Munro did not pull any punches in the Glasgow Evening Times, writing: "There was no power, no command, no authority – no nothing." He added: "It was a fantastically negative entertainment performance that would boost bingo, TV and cinema audiences anywhere."

A recurring theme among managers, pundits and fans in Scotland was that the national side would benefit if most of the players were home-based. If I remember correctly, every now and then there would be a groundswell of opinion saying there should be a limit on 'Anglos' – those who 'defected' to clubs south o' the border. That was the feeling of many, usually when there were poor results. No less a figure than Celtic legend Jock Stein joined in the debate after this under-23 game. He said: "I don't suggest you write off every Scot who crosses the border but I think that too often the fact they have gone to England has helped them win a place. You need only pick up a soccer magazine to read of some English manager insisting that Bobby Brown or the selectors should pick his player for Scotland. What do they think our young footballers play up here . . . shinty?"

Brown was under pressure, not just because of this game but, more important, because of a poor display by the seniors in a 3-0 Nations Cup defeat by Belgium in Liege which left them with only one win and three defeats from four qualifying group matches. Maybe the "let's have fewer Anglos" view received a strong airing at Brown's meeting with the Scottish FA selection committee following these two defeats because, for the under-23 game against England, he announced a squad with only one player not from a Scottish club – Francis Munro of Wolverhampton Wanderers. It was virtually certain Frank would start as he was the most experienced central defender but he took a knock in our 3-0 defeat at Leeds and had to withdraw. Arsenal midfielder Eddie Kelly was called up and became the only Anglo in the side who drew 2-2 with England at Hampden. Versatile George Connelly (Celtic) played at centre-half and the team received a favourable Press.

Soon after the game, Frank had his say on the home-based issue. In Goal magazine, he said: "I think the whole argument about all-tartan teams is nonsense. All the players down here play their hearts out for Scotland, just as any man would. Surely it's of no importance where you play. What does count is ability. That's all that should be considered when teams are being picked." Brown, despite the good showing of his under-23s against their English counterparts, stressed: "Although we had only one Anglo-Scot in our team, I have no intention of switching to an all-tartan policy." Still the misery went on for Scotland when they lost their next European Nations Cup qualifier 2-0 to Portugal in Lisbon, where Jim McCalliog won his fifth cap, although he was replaced by Drew Jarvie after an hour. From never having had a man play for Scotland in their history, Wolves could now claim two as Hughie Curran had played against Austria in a World Cup qualifier in November, 1969. By the end of the season, maybe they could boast three?

Although he had missed out on the chance to impress Brown at Hampden, Frank felt he had done enough in the season to show he was ready to step up as a full international – despite the opinion of that fella from the Glasgow Evening Times. He thought he might make Scotland's squad for the Home International series, the British championship. Wrong! A squad of 16 were named for the first match, against Wales, with an additional six to be added for the other two games. Frank was not in either group, although there was representation from Molineux as Hughie Curran was in the additional half dozen. As for the Anglos question, the 22 players consisted of 13 home-based and nine English-based men. This tournament between England, Scotland, Northern Ireland and Wales had been moved to the end of the season to try to raise its sagging profile. Disappointed he was not wanted by his country, Frank was able to taste some international action when he joined our squad for a trip to play the Israel National XI a week after our Texaco Cup final success. We won 3-1 in Tel Aviv after leading 1-0 at the break, thanks to goals from Derek Parkin, Paul Walker and Bobby Gould. Italian-born midfielder Giorgio "George" Borba replied. Back home, we still could not forget football as we made a trip south to play a testimonial game for two Brighton stalwarts, keeper Brian Powney and defender Norman Gall. We were back, after a 2-0 win, in time for the start of the Home International Championship and Frank thought it would be only of academic interest to him. Wrong again!

Scotland were still at a low ebb and drew 0-0 with Wales on the opening Saturday. Frank may have paid some attention to the game but did not attach much importance to the fact Billy Bremner and Davie Robb, another lad from Broughty Ferry, had been injured at Ninian Park. After all, one was a midfielder and the other a forward, so there would be no emergency call from Mr Brown. Wrong once more! Totally out of the blue, Frank was asked to link up with the squad. The manager explained to the Press: "We will not know the extent of Bremner's and Robb's injuries until they report in the morning. I am taking no chances, however, and Munro is a young man who has been in my plans. He will be useful to have in the party." Frank was taking a break back in Dundee to look up friends and family when told to report to Largs. "This is a terrific chance for me," he said, "and I will have to delay getting a holiday. I travelled to Dundee for a spell with my family. I explained the situation to Mr Brown and he pointed out I have been in good form lately and that was good enough for him." It was a boost to Frank's morale but he hardly expected to get a taste of the action. Wrong yet again! This was the side named to play Northern Ireland on Tuesday, May 18, 1971:

Clark (Aberdeen), Hay (Celtic), Brogan (Celtic), Greig (Rangers), McLintock (Arsenal), Moncur (Newcastle), Lorimer (Leeds), Green (Blackpool), O'Hare (Derby), Curran (Wolves), Gray (Leeds). Subs: MacRae (Motherwell), Dickson (Kilmarnock), Munro (Wolves), McLean (Kilmarnock), Jarvie (Airdrie).

Frank was close to his boyhood dream of playing for Scotland. As for the Anglos factor, it obviously had not come into Brown's consideration as there were only four home-based players in the starting XI, although four more were among the subs. Scottish morale sank even lower at Hampden, though, with a shock 1-0 defeat at the hands of a side whose attack was led by Derek Dougan. It was hardly a match to remember for Scotland but it was memorable for Frank as he went on with 19 minutes left for Arsenal's Frank McLintock, who had taken a knock, to win his first cap. Frank and The Doog were club-mates but this was an international and Derek did not hold back. "I brought the ball down on the edge of the box and waltzed past him," recalled Frank. "He chased after me and hacked me down. I said 'What the bloody hell?' and he just said: 'There are no friends in this game.'" Dougan set up the 14th-minute winner, although unintentionally. He took a long run at a corner and connected poorly with a header that was diverted home by John Greig's knee. Scotland were ineffective up front, particularly John O'Hare, who was replaced by Drew Jarvie at half-time. Hugh Curran, reports agreed, was their best forward but received scant support from O'Hare and little service from wingers Peter Lorimer and Eddie Gray. It may have been a grim result but two Wolves men in a Scotland team was one for the record books.

Next up were England at Wembley and Brown made five changes to the starting XI. Again Frank was among the subs and this time he had 45 minutes of action to collect cap no 2. After Martin Peters had headed England in front, Hugh put Scotland level but two goals by Martin Chivers made it 3-1 before half-time and that was the final score. Frank replaced an injured Hugh and at least ensured the home side did not score again. He recalled: "Martin Chivers was running amok, so the manager moved Frank McLintock into midfield, Billy Bremner into attack and sent me on. I marked Chivers and the score did not change." Although Scotland lost, the display gave Frank satisfaction. The Glasgow Herald report confirmed he 'added useful height and weight to the collapsing defence.' While the second-half changes suited Frank, there were reports that McLintock had been far from happy and he and manager Brown had 'a right go at each other' according to the legendary Desmond Hackett in the Daily Express. He quoted a Scotland player, without naming him, as saying: "McLintock was really riled when Brown told him he was going to be moved into midfield so Munro could come in at the back." The source added that he thought McLintock was going to throw his bag at Brown in anger as the atmosphere turned really nasty. "Frank then wisely decided he must do his best for Scotland regardless of his position." Hackett, in his inimitable style said the Scots, after a promising first 20 minutes, had 'collapsed like a deflated bagpipe and brought soccer shame to their country.'

The defeat meant Scotland finished bottom with one point from three games and a disappointing season continued when they met Denmark at the Idraetspark in Copenhagen in a Nations Cup qualifying game. The Danes had lost their previous five games in Group 5 but won 1-0. Frank started for the first time to collect a third full cap. It was great news but tempered by the fact he played at right-back in a back four. He had previously played midfield, centre-forward and centre-half but full-back was something new. A vital international was hardly the place to start a new career but, as I have said before, he only worried if he was not playing. That Anglos thing reared its head again with him, Hugh Curran and Newcastle centre-half Bobby Moncur the only English-based players in the side. That prompted a comment from Glasgow Herald man Malcolm Munro as he assessed the line-up in his big match preview: "This is an angry, hungry Scottish team which intends to prove we don't need all those big Anglo names." Brave words but the sort that end up being eaten. Scotland flopped again.

Despite his best efforts, Frank had a tough evening in his unfamiliar role and ended with a booking. It seemed strange logic to play him there. Jim Parkinson's report in the Glasgow Herald said: "Munro, the Wolverhampton centre-half, was a disappointment in the right-back position. The Danes pressured him severely." Of course they put pressure on him! They probably worked out very quickly that here was a man playing in a position totally foreign to him. Scotland had hoped their new cap, Tommy Forsyth of Motherwell, might revive their fortunes but Parkinson reckoned he found the pace beyond him. Davie Robb of Aberdeen took over from him at the start of the second half. Finn Laudrup, father of Michael and Brian, scored the only goal just before half-time, curling a low free-kick round the Scotland wall and into the corner of the net. That the Danes did not make the scoreline really embarrassing was down only to keeper Bobby Clark, who made a string of fine saves. As well as a booking, Frank picked up a bruised leg.

Five days later, he had recovered and made it four caps when he played against the USSR in a friendly in Moscow. Again the Scots were beaten by the only goal. Gennadi Evriuzhikan of Dynamo Kiev scored after 25 minutes with only about 20,000 fans there to witness it in the vast Lenin Stadium. At least Frank was played in a more familiar position in midfield and had a much better game. The Scots fielded two newcomers, Hibs full-back John Brownlie and Motherwell defender Bobby Watson, the latter winning his only cap. The Glasgow Herald noted: "In the middle, Munro, Watson and Robb pushed the ball with great abandon to Forrest and Scott on the wings." And the Glasgow Evening Times confirmed: "Most of the midfield play pivoted around Francis Munro." Ron McKinnon of Rangers, playing in his 28th and final international, and skipper Pat Stanton of Hibs were in the central defensive positions. Afterwards, manager Brown said: "Chances were missed, I'll admit, but I believe that on the night we were the better organised team. Certainly, we had the best players in Brownlie, Scott, Munro and McKinnon."

Probably by accident rather than design, ten home-based Scots were in the starting XI in Moscow, three from Frank's old club Aberdeen – Clark, Stanton and Jim Forrest. Somewhat in contradiction to his previous statements, manager Brown told Pressmen on the flight home: "I was particularly pleased against Russia that there was a preponderance of home Scots. Without losing sight of such players as Munro, Eddie Gray and Eddie Kelly, it would be satisfying to have teams containing a large proportion of home players. Perhaps more opportunities would exist for continuity of selection. More preparations could be achieved at Largs with try-out games against Scottish clubs and second division teams."

Maybe this was part of a 'comprehensive blueprint' he was due to submit to the Scottish FA selection committee the following month but, if he did present his plans, they were soon of little relevance. Napoleon famously paid the price for defeat in Russia but this was not so much Bonaparte as 'Brown depart' as the long trip proved to be the last for the Scotland boss. On July 26, 1971, after a two-hour meeting at their Park Gardens headquarters in Glasgow, the Scottish FA sacked him from his £4,000-a-year post. With Brown in charge, Scotland won only nine of 27 games and lost ten. In the Glasgow Evening Times, the border issue was mentioned yet again when Malcolm Munro wrote: "I think where Brown made his big mistake was in going cap-in-hand to English clubs for players. Too often, there were last-minute let-downs from the Anglos." Brown was his country's first full-time manager when appointed in 1967 and started on a high when Scotland famously won 3-2 at Wembley to become the first side to beat the 1966 legends after their World Cup triumph. It was a bit like the film career of Orson Welles, who started by making Citizen Kane and never matched it. Brown's reign ended on a low note by finishing bottom of the British championship, followed by those defeats at the hands of the Danes and Soviets. Scotland had lost six and drawn one of the last seven games with Brown at the helm. At least Frank had cause to be thankful to the manager as he had given him the honour of playing for his country, even if his two starts were not as a centre-half.

Not taking anything away from Frank, his partnership with John McAlle must have helped tremendously in his getting picked for Scotland and I know Frank would have been the first to admit this. Confirmation that they were now established as our no 1 central defensive pairing came with the departure of stalwarts John Holsgrove and David Woodfield, John to Sheffield Wednesday in August, 1971, and Duggie to Watford the following month. John made over a hundred appearances for Wednesday but, sadly, Duggie was hit by injury and had to hang up his boots after just a few games while at Vicarage Road. He moved on to Watford's coaching staff, however, and it did not surprise me that he made a good job of his new role.

Before the new season began, we wondered if we were going to see the exit of our beloved boss. Sir Matt Busby, having briefly taken the Manchester United manager's job again after Wilf McGuinness's 18-month reign, announced he was retiring for good this time. Wilf reverted to trainer-coach of the reserves and speculation was rife about who would get English football's plum job. Bill McGarry was among those mentioned. In the Daily Mirror, the respected Harry Miller said: "McGarry's drive, his qualities as a coach and the ability to get the best out of players appeals to United." The papers do not always get it right, of course, and despite the supposed admiration for our leader, they appointed Frank O'Farrell from Leicester City. He lasted only a season.

Chapter Eight

European Adventures

Pre-season training......everybody hates it but it has to be done. Frank used to dread it because he was not the best of long-distance runners, nor the hill-climbing type – and that was all we did on Cannock Chase; run, run, run, up the hills, down the hills, around the hills. The only respite he got was among the trees, where the manager could not see him. He was not on his own. Lofty Parkes, Hugh Curran and I, plus a few more, usually brought up the rear. Frank and I once tried to steal a march on the others and it backfired on us. After the running had taken us a good way from where our driver Sid Kipping had parked the coach, Bill McGarry told us to make our own way back. Frank and I reckoned on this particular occasion that if we went as the crow flies, through the trees and bracken, we might surprise the others by being first back. It was going quite well as we picked our way carefully through the undergrowth until a wild animal jumped out in front of us. It was a blur but it frightened the life out of us and we ran like hell, much faster than at any time during the morning, until we were far enough away to glance at the 'wild beast.' It turned out to be nothing more than a young deer that was far more scared of us than we were of it. After that, we had to rest to get our breath back – and stop laughing at ourselves for being so daft.

Frank was quite a gambler, like many Scotsmen, and, apart from the horses, he had a weekly go on the pools coupon. But he was not used to the workings of it, especially the perms. He came into the dressing room one Monday morning with quite a smile on his face and a spring in his step. "What's up, Frank?" somebody said, "You look full of beans this morning." "I've got eight draws on the coupon," he replied, pulling out a piece of paper. "This is my copy." He had done a perm of 13 numbers but did not realise that, although he had eight draws, they had to fall in one line. Checking his coupon for him, the lads could not find more than five in any one line. There was no sympathy from us and it was a very grumpy Frank Munro who took part in training that morning. Still, he had a great season to look forward to in 1971-72, as we all did.

We had qualified for the UEFA Cup and nobody in the team, with the exception of one player, had played in a European competition before, so we were not sure what to expect. You remember who that one person was – Frank, of course. He had played for Aberdeen, scored their first goal in Europe and added two more to complete his hat-trick. Now his job was to stop goals, not score them. We were amused to read in the Daily Mirror that we might encounter a less severe Bill McGarry in the new season. He told the paper: "I think I have mellowed a bit this past year. In the past, if we played badly, I'd slate the players publicly. I still slate them but now it's between them and me." Frank and I did not detect much mellowing, I can tell you.

We had a good start to the season, losing only one League game in the first eight. Unfortunately, we also went down 4-3 in the League Cup to my old club Manchester City at Maine Road. What a game! We led 3-1 with 12 minutes to go, then City hit us with three goals in six minutes. Our first games in Europe followed, against Portuguese side Academica Coimbra. McGarry had sold Bobby Gould but he had a special player to take his place – John Richards, who scored on his European debut as we won 3-0. In the return leg at Academica, a game Frank missed through injury, The Doog hit a hat-trick to give us a 4-1 win. Alas, Danny Hegan was sent off for retaliation and was banned for three games. Gerry Taylor deputised ably for Frank and his partner at the back, John McAlle, scored, having also done so in the first leg. John also scored in the League Cup at City and had netted a couple against West Ham in Kansas City in 1969. Little did we know that those three he scored in September, 1971, would prove to be the only goals he would ever manage in League and cup games for the club. Talk about a purple patch! Against West Ham, he completed a strange sort of hat-trick as he also put through his own goal.

Soon after the game in Portugal, there was a morale boost for Frank, courtesy of his old boss Tommy Docherty. With Bobby Brown gone, Scotland turned to The Doc as a caretaker and he would eventually be named full-time manager. His first game in charge was against Portugal in the European Nations Cup and he named Frank in a squad of 16 for the game at Hampden Park. There was every chance Frank would start but he had to pull out as he was nursing a troublesome groin strain and was due to see a specialist. He was not 100 per cent fit, so withdrew from the squad and Sheffield United's Eddie Colquhoun was given his debut as the Scots won 2-1. The Doc did not forget Frank, though, and named him in his squad for the next game, a Nations Cup qualifier against Belgium in early November, 1971. But Frank was still not fully recovered from his groin injury and Bill McGarry again pulled him out, telling the press: "He struggled in our match against Ipswich. I want him to play for Scotland but I agree with Tommy Docherty on having players 100 per cent fit." It was a pity as, with Colquhoun unavailable, Frank was the only recognised centre-half named and looked certain to start. Instead, 18-year-old Willie Young, then of Aberdeen and later of Spurs and Arsenal, was drafted in, although Martin Buchan and Pat Stanton played as central defenders in a game the Scots won 1-0. To make it worse, if he had played, Frank would have been back on very familiar territory. The game was staged at Pittodrie, which was bursting with over 36,000 fans.

For their next international, a friendly against the Netherlands in Amsterdam, Colquhoun was recalled to partner Stanton. Later in the season, Billy McNeill of Celtic and Newcastle's Bobby Moncur were given their chances. Frank was just as good as any of them as a centre-half – better than most in my opinion – but through that untimely injury he had missed the chance to climb ahead of them in the pecking order. For some reason, he was overlooked after that and left in the international wilderness. He would have to wait four years before collecting more caps. Who knows what might have happened if he had not had to cry off from those two games? It could have been the start of something on the international scene for him, especially as Scotland's fortunes rose dramatically under The Doc.

As I said, the Mermaid pub was our local and Frank, myself and a few of the lads would go down early in the week to have a few beers, sometimes in Frank's car, sometimes in mine or sometimes in both. It just depended where we were going after. Many a time, Frank would end up at Solly Wernick's casino, playing roulette until the early hours. Let me make this point – neither Frank nor I would be out drinking the night before a game. Contrary to what people might say, we were professional and never indulged close to an important game. One night, I was driving down to The Mermaid when I saw Frank walking down the road. I pulled up and said: "Jump in, Frank." He replied: "No, I'm having a walk down to the pub. It's a lovely night and I feel like a walk." "OK," I said, "I'll see you down at The Mermaid." I could not understand it. I had never seen him walk anywhere before – not when his car was there, anyway. About three-quarters of an hour later, I saw his car pull up outside the pub window and Frank got out and came in. Puzzled, I asked what had happened. He explained that Bill McGarry had had a go at him that day about his weight and he thought it best he walked to the pub in future. But, about halfway there he encountered a barking dog which he had to pass. No chance! Frank was frightened of dogs, as big as he was, so, having almost got to the pub, he walked all the way back home for his car.

Another thing which petrified him was the needle. For many of the trips we went on, an injection was necessary or you would not get into the country. We had to make sure he was in the sitting position when he had the jab just in case he fainted. You can imagine everyone lined up and Frank was the only one sitting down. John Dee, who covered Wolves for the Express & Star after Phil Morgan retired, swears that Frank once asked the doctor: "Can I have an injection for the injection?" An unnecessary bit of pain came our way before we made the trip to play Academica in our UEFA Cup campaign. The Wolverhampton medical officer made us have inoculations against cholera, thinking Coimbra was in Spain, where there had been traces of the disease. The outbreak was, in fact, a thousand miles away, so Frank had a sore arm for no reason.

He and John McAlle had developed a really good understanding in our defence and, with the support of Derek Parkin and Bernard Shaw, the back four looked more than adequate. Frank, however, was still struggling with the injury that forced him to drop out of the Scotland squad and finally he had to take a rest, missing three League games and our next European trip. We were nonetheless in confident mood for the second step on the UEFA trail – against ADO Den Haag. He travelled with the squad for the first leg in The Hague and saw Gerry Taylor continue in the side without letting us down. We were under pressure all game but managed to break away and score three goals for a win which put us in the pound seats for the return leg. By the way, on the same day, there was a small item of news – Nottingham Forest had signed a 19-year-old from Distillery called Martin O'Neill. Frank was back for the Molineux game against ADO, which we won 4-0 for a second successive 7-1 aggregate victory. The unusual thing about the home game against Den Haag was that we had three own goals. The one we scored without help from our visitors was from The Doog. The big wins added up to a tremendous start to our campaign in a major European tournament and the manager must have been well satisfied with what we had done. If he was, he did not let on.

Frank really hated McGarry because, no matter how well the team did or how well he personally played, there was no praise from him whatsoever. No 'well done' or a pat on the back. The other thing was that you could not put forward your point of view. Frank always said that if we had been given the freedom to use our own skills and take chances, we could have been even better. But you were not allowed to use your initiative with Bill McGarry. Frank always referred to the Leeds team when making this point. Anybody in that side, he would stress, could play anywhere if the need arose and then return to their normal positions when the time was right whereas McGarry was too regimented in what he wanted you to do. Frank laughed when, many years later, he saw Bobby Gould talking on a Wolves video. Bobby had long since left and, in the video, was heard to say "The boss wasn't very pleased after the game." Realising what he had said, he added "See, I still call him 'boss' now even though it was years ago. You can tell that I was frightened to death of him." If somebody with Bobby's experience was scared to death, the younger lads must have been petrified.

Frank, however, was not frightened as he proved in a game against Leicester. As the players came into the dressing room at half-time, McGarry went absolutely berserk at our goalkeeper Phil Parkes, calling him all the names under the sun over a defensive error. Frank intervened. "It was my fault, not Phil's," he said. "No it fucking wasn't," said McGarry. "I should know," replied Frank, "I gave the ball away." "No you didn't," bawled McGarry. "I should know, I was on the pitch," said Frank calmly. With that, McGarry stormed out of the dressing room, knowing he was wrong but stubbornly refusing to admit it. The mere fact that Frank stood his ground left McGarry in an embarrassing situation – that was why he marched out.

Carl Zeiss Jena were our next UEFA opponents; a team who were rarely heard of in football circles because they came from behind the Iron Curtain. They were relatively small as far as other European clubs were concerned but it is the dark horses that one does not know about that can be a surprise package. Not having a scout to check them out beforehand, we did not have much to go on, so we were really in the dark as to how good they were. Realistically, they could not have been that good because they were all semi-professionals who worked at the Zeiss factory making lenses and microscopes but, there again, they had already got through two rounds, so we were going to have to be on our toes. They had beaten Lokomotiv Plovdiv 4-3 on aggregate in the first round after winning the home leg 3-0, then they put out OFK Beograd 5-1, drawing 1-1 at home before winning the away leg 4-0. The town of Jena was enough to put us off. It was dark, dismal, cold and, to top it all, there was snow on the ground. However, that did not put Frank off. He relished the thought of playing on a white carpet. He felt a little sorry for the folk of Jena, living so restricted a kind of life, very regimented, not being able to go out into the world. Still, that was not his problem and there was a game of football to be played.

It was a dour game on a pitch that was hard to play on but Frank loved it. We won 1-0 through a John Richards goal after only 12 minutes. The Doog brought a couple of good saves from their keeper late on but most of the time it was a case of hanging on against a Carl Zeiss side who had provided six players to the East Germany team against England at Wembley a year earlier. It was in keeping the home side quiet, marshalling those around him, that Frank came into his own as Alan Williams confirmed in the Daily Express: "The quick and firm covering by Frank Munro and his defensive aides gave them no chance to level that early Richards goal." That view was endorsed in the Daily Mirror by their man Peter Ingall: "With centre-half Frank Munro never putting a foot wrong, Wolves played it tight at the back with the result the East Germans' sudden attacks rarely carried a real threat," he wrote. There was still the return to come but this proved easy on a normal pitch at Molineux with goals from Ken Hibbitt and two from The Doog seeing us home. The opposition thought Wolverhampton was a wonderful place when they were allowed a day's Christmas shopping prior to flying home.

So we were through to the quarter-finals. By then, we were in mid-season with a pretty good record, losing only six League games out of 26. However, we were out of the League Cup and went out of the FA Cup 2-0 in a replay at Leicester after being held 1-1 at home. This was just after we had beaten Manchester United 3-1 before nearly 47,000 at Old Trafford. Despite playing in the centre of defence, Frank had by then still managed two League goals during the season – one in the 1-1 home draw with Coventry and the other in a 2-1 win at Leicester three weeks before we lost there in the Cup.

We still had plenty to go at for the rest of the campaign, with the UEFA Cup and the First Division. We were going well in the League if not as well as in the previous season and were climbing the table. To use the old saying, we just took each game as it came and treated one no differently from any other. In Europe, our next opponents were the mighty Juventus. The Italian giants had put out Aberdeen in the second round and then beat Rapid Vienna home and away to join us in the last eight. We were really looking forward to this challenge. None of this meant anything to Frank, of course. His attitude was that it was just another game to look forward to. As long as he was playing football, he was perfectly happy. He did not know anything else; he was not fazed; football was his whole life. We were away in the first leg and our interpreter-cum-ambassador was another giant of a man, a former Juventus player and an idol of the Turin crowd, the great John Charles. The former Wales star, who in his prime proved equally outstanding at centre-half or centre-forward, travelled on the same charter flight and was eagerly anticipating meeting some old friends when we got there. Did I say 'some'? There were thousands of them when we arrived in Turin. Big John's reputation was second to none and it was as if the whole city had turned out to greet him. It was the same at the training ground, which, incidentally, Juventus shared with Torino – the same arrangement as the stadium. Each day at training, there were at least

3,000 watching us go through our routines. John was mobbed and lost among a sea of supporters.

The game itself was thrilling, end to end, and finished 1-1, which was a great result for us. Jim McCalliog equalised after Pietro Anastasi had put Juventus into the lead in the first half. In the Daily Express, there was praise from Alan Williams for the dynamic duo in the centre of our back four: "Wolves refused to be overawed. Their defence, with John McAlle and Frank Munro outstanding, constantly frustrated the Juventus attack." Bill McGarry was still not in the best of moods, though. Maybe it was because of what had happened during the game. He appeared to show dissent at one of the referee's decisions and the official stopped play, then ordered him away from the bench. He had to watch the rest of the game from behind the running track, sitting alongside six policemen. Although it was a good result, there were no words of encouragement or congratulation from the manager as we gathered for an after-match meal in a hotel, miles from Turin, up in the hills. "Nobody is to have a beer," he announced, "and just one glass of wine with the meal." He did not say how big a glass, though.

One person who did not take any notice of McGarry was John Charles, who drank as if it was going out of fashion and had to be helped to his room by Frank and Lofty Parkes. They put Big John to bed but had not reached the end of the corridor when they heard him coughing and spluttering vigorously. Thinking he was choking, they rushed back to his room, only to find that he had lit himself a cigarette. They had no option but to confiscate the packet and waited by the bed until he had dropped off to sleep. It was a job well done and, because McGarry had gone to bed by the time they got back to the hotel bar, they treated themselves to a bottle of wine – each!

The tie was by no means over as the Italians were hard to beat home or away. According to 'Big John' on the plane home, though, it was all over. "They will send a depleted team and half of them will just go through the motions," he proclaimed. Frank replied: "I don't know about that. Any Italian side is a problem, depleted or not." Sure enough, Juventus did not roll over but they could not stop us in the second leg in front of 40,421, our biggest home gate of the UEFA campaign. Danny Hegan scored a scintillating 35-yarder to send us on our way and when The Doog scored, it was virtually all over. Frank nearly spoiled an immaculate performance when he handled to give Juventus a late penalty. Helmut Haller, one of the German World Cup runners-up against England at Wembley in 1966, scored to give us a fright but we got there in the end. Danny was a very capable deputy for our injured skipper Mike Bailey and made us all laugh after the game. Every time he went into his pocket, he would say: "All right in there, Helmut?" To be fair, he did have Haller 'in his pocket' for most of the game and proved to us all that he was a very good footballer, in fact a brilliant one on his day.

Who would have thought it? We were in the semi-final of the UEFA Cup but it made little difference to Frank. It just meant there were at least two more games against a top European team. Do not get me wrong, he was a highly competitive player but, basically, he just loved playing so much that it was a case of the more the merrier. In the summer, I do not think he would have had a close season, given the choice. He relished the semi-final because we were paired with Ferencvaros of Hungary and knew we had just two games to overcome to get to the final. Budapest is a beautiful place, full of history and wonderful statues, plus the River Danube, but we were not there to admire the views. We had a game to play and what an exacting one it was in the Nep Stadium. John Richards gave us the lead in the 20th minute but Ferencvaros equalised with a penalty from Istvan Szoke. The Hungarians then took the lead with a goal from their star international forward Florian Albert and it stayed that way until very late in the game when Frank popped up to head a well-deserved equaliser from my corner. Phil Parkes had kept us in the game by saving a second Szoke penalty – with his feet. It was a pleasing result, with two away goals and a draw into the bargain. No wonder half our team finished up at The Mermaid that evening, our flight home following the afternoon kick-off conveniently getting us back in time for a drink or two.

One hurdle to surmount and we were in the final but there was a disappointing crowd for the second leg, considering the importance of the game. There were 28,262 at Molineux as opposed to 48,000 at the Nep Stadium. Mind you, we had nine competitive games in April and I suppose our fans could not be expected to go to every match. At least the gate was 41 more than our average home League attendance for the season. The Ferencvaros game was the third at Molineux in the space of eight days and what our fans lacked in numbers they more than made up for in noise and enthusiasm, which always gave us an extra lift. They must have lit a fire under Steve Daley, who took my place as I was suspended. Steve scored after just 20 seconds. Bernard Shaw also missed the game as, like me, he had been booked in the first leg. It was a great start and then Frank headed no 2 before the interval. Kenny Hibbitt took a corner from the left and, when it went right across goal, Jim McCalliog returned it for Frank to head home from just to the left of goal in the six-yard area. It looked as though we would go comfortably into the final but Lajos Ku scored for Ferencvaros and we were under pressure for quite some time, culminating in Lofty saving another Szoke penalty. Again he did so with his feet. We held on gamely and that was it.....we were in the final of the UEFA Cup.

While we had been doing wonders in Europe, our form in the League had plummeted. At one stage in mid-season, we had gone ten games unbeaten, the ninth being that win at Old Trafford against a United side who were top of the table at the time. That had us talked of as possible title contenders but we were brought down to earth on our next visit to Manchester, when we lost 5-2 to City. Around our two games with Ferencvaros, we lost four League games in a row and eventually finished ninth, but only 11 points behind champions Derby. Yet, after that win at United, we had 31 points compared with Derby's 33. It was a 2-1 home win over Derby that had started us on that unbeaten run and if only we could have kept up our form in the League, who knows what we might have achieved? It has been said before but I will say it again – 'if' is the biggest word in football.

What disappointed us most, Frank included, about our UEFA Cup final was the fact we were to play Tottenham. After what we had gone through to get there, we would sooner have been playing anybody from any other country in the final. We had faced a Portuguese team, a Dutch team, an Italian team, a Hungarian team and an East German team and to now meet a side we regularly faced was a big anti-climax. Anyway, Spurs it was and Frank would be the first to admit that it was always a treat to play them because of their attacking flair and open style of play. His disappointment was not with the Tottenham team but the fact we were to play an English team. How he wished it could have been a club from Siberia or Outer Mongolia – wherever that is!

We usually played well against Spurs and this was no exception. Yet we fell behind to a Martin Chivers goal 12 minutes into the second half of the first leg at Molineux. Chivers climbed above Frank to head home a Mike England free-kick. A quickly taken free-kick by Danny Hegan enabled Jim McCalliog to level but then, two minutes from the end, Chivers scored again, this time with a shot from nearly 30 yards. It was no good blaming Phil Parkes as the ball swerved two yards on its way to the goal. The modern ball swerves all the time and keepers are used to it but, in our day, it was very unusual for it to deviate from the original flight path. We were 2-1 down, but we were not out of it yet.

Before the second leg, there was a very important League game – one which had little significance to Wolves but meant everything to Leeds, who could complete the Double by just drawing. They had won the FA Cup by beating Arsenal at Wembley and two days later were due to face us at Molineux. There was contact in the build-up, informing us there would be a certain amount of money for us if we just went through the motions and let Leeds win. In particular, Frank and the other defenders were targeted. Bill McGarry got wind of the approach and, on the morning of the match, called us all into a meeting in the centre circle at a deserted Molineux. He was so paranoid about people listening in to what was being said that he called us out of earshot of anyone but us. His statement was straight to the point. "If any of you don't perform tonight, I will personally lead an inquiry as to why you didn't and, furthermore, should any of you be found guilty of not performing to the best of your ability, I will make sure you never again kick a ball for this or any other club."

Frank thought this statement was harsh, to say the least. As a defender, many things can happen. You can give away a penalty, play somebody onside, handle the ball unintentionally – all sorts of scenarios which were totally innocent. What it did do was put extra pressure on all our players. Frank knew McGarry was right in what he said but thought the manager could have handled it a little differently. McGarry certainly knew how to put us all under pressure. We were all frightened to try anything in case it went wrong but the more the game went on, the more natural we became and it turned out to be a humdinger of a match. It was significant that we won – if only to prove that nobody took a bribe – but it just goes to show what goes on behind the scenes.

I helped set up the first goal for Frank with a short corner on the right. Bernard Shaw's cross was deflected by Johnny Giles to Frank, who sidefooted home from the corner of the six-yard box. Frank used to recall: "When I scored, Billy Bremner called me a 'Scottish bastard' – and he was more Scottish than I'll ever be." We hammered another nail in Leeds' Double hopes mid-way through the second half. Danny Hegan sent the ball through to John Richards, who put it into the path of Derek Dougan and he fired it home low from just inside the penalty area. Frank used to talk about how Leeds then 'threw everything but the kitchen sink at us.' He added: "All of a sudden, Norman Hunter and Jack Charlton were playing up front as well." All they got for their efforts was a consolation goal from Bremner. Liverpool were playing at Arsenal that night and could have sneaked the title with a win but they drew and so Brian Clough's Derby were champions. They finished on 58 points with no fewer than three clubs bracketed behind them on 57 – Leeds, who had by far the best goal average, Liverpool and Manchester City.

Having helped decide the destiny of the title, we looked forward to the second leg of the UEFA Cup final nine days later. Again, we did not get the goals our performance deserved. Everybody agreed we had probably been the better team over two legs but Spurs held us 1-1 and took the trophy. There were more than 54,000 at White Hart Lane that May night and we really did play well. Alan Mullery headed them into a 3-1 aggregate lead and I, of all people, pulled one back with a long-range shot with my left foot from out on the right. We went near once or twice to taking the final into extra-time, Frank going close with a header. He was still disappointed that it had been Tottenham and said: "Nothing against them but it would have been that much better if we could have played somebody from abroad." Teams in the second leg:

Tottenham: Jennings, Kinnear, Knowles, Mullery, England, Beal, Gilzean, Perryman, Chivers, Peters, Coates. Subs not used: Daines, Evans, Naylor, Pratt, Pearce. Wolves: Parkes, Shaw, Taylor, Hegan, Munro, McAlle, McCalliog, Hibbitt (Bailey 55), Richards, Dougan (Curran 84), Wagstaffe. Subs not used: Arnold, Parkin, Daley.

Mullery, the skipper, was saying farewell to Spurs. He had been out with a pelvic joint injury for much of the season, then went on loan to his old club Fulham. It was our misfortune that he returned to Spurs in time to score that vital goal in the second leg. It's interesting to note from those line-ups that the only non-British player on the pitch was Joe Kinnear – and he was from the Republic of Ireland. How times have changed!

Chapter Nine

Around The World In Thirty Days

What a season 1971-72 had been – and it still wasn't over. We had finished in a respectable position in the League, played a tremendous part against Leeds in deciding the destination of the title and reached the final of the UEFA Cup at the first attempt. In all, we had played 57 League and cup games, Frank being involved in all but six of them. However, that was not all. Bill McGarry had informed us we were touring Canada, America, New Zealand and Australia at the end of the domestic campaign, starting with a game against Aberdeen in San Francisco four days after the second leg at Tottenham. It was a case of dashing from North London to North America with hardly time to gather our thoughts, never mind take a rest.

The first four tour games were nostalgic for Frank because we were to play his old club in San Francisco, Seattle, Vancouver and, lastly, in the stadium in which we played that famous game in 1967 in Los Angeles. Everybody was shattered as we travelled. It was a long trip in the wake of our exhausting game at White Hart Lane and it showed in our first fixture. We even had jet-lag on top of the tiredness, so you would have thought McGarry would have some sympathy as we opened with a defeat. Not likely! He lost his temper and flew into a rage and Frank was on the end of one of his lambastings, having already been smarting at the fact it was Aberdeen who handed out the 3-1 beating. Jimmy McCalliog was our scorer.

It was the same in the next game against Aberdeen in Seattle three days later. We lost 3-0 and McGarry again blew his top. But good news filtered through afterwards that our manager was to leave the tour. Frank could not have been more pleased but the boss's departure was not to be until after our next match. That came two days later in Vancouver, where this time we were 3-0 winners thanks to goals from John Richards, Kenny Hibbitt and Hugh Curran. We were pleased when we heard McGarry was leaving after the game and were determined to make it a good send-off, if only for our own peace of mind so the boss would depart quietly and leave everyone in a good mood. Alas, another rumpus was looming on the horizon. A wealthy acquaintance of ours named Brad, who had had a good win on the horses, had organised a party for us after the game. An added attraction was that he had paid for half a dozen 'ladies of the night' to attend just to brighten up the occasion. Half-way through the evening, McGarry realised who they were and admonished Brad about the women. Brad stood his ground and told McGarry it was his party and if he did not like it he should leave – which he quickly did with his tail between his legs. He was not seen again until the next morning.

However, we had been misinformed. McGarry was not due to leave until after the final Aberdeen game, in Los Angeles. How would his mood be following the previous night's telling-off from Brad? In actual fact, his mood was pretty good, considering. It must have had something to do with the fact he was off the next day. We were also in a good mood – win today's match, get rid of McGarry and everything would be fine for the rest of the tour. We won 4-0 and Frank helped himself to a goal while a John Richards hat-trick accounted for the others. We had played four games in eight days and, out of a party of 15 players, 13 had played some part in all four games. Only two to sit out a game completely were Kenny Hibbitt and Jimmy McCalliog. Then it was like Euston Station at Los Angeles air terminal. We were going to New Zealand and The Doog and Danny Hegan were arriving from London to join us, having played in the Home Internationals. They were in high spirits after helping Northern Ireland to a surprise win over England at Wembley. John Richards was off to join England under-23s for a three-match tour of Eastern Europe, where he played in all three games and scored in the 3-0 win over Poland in Warsaw. With McGarry on his way to some rendezvous, there were so many comings and goings. Frank said to me: "I thought football was a simple game."

Arriving in New Zealand without our manager was like being let off the lead. The restrictions had gone and we felt as though a weight had been lifted. Now it was time to enjoy ourselves. On our first night Down Under, the phone rang at 12.30am in the room I was sharing with Mike Bailey. It was Frank laughing and saying: "Listen to the radio. I've requested a record. It's on next." Mike and I listened intently and heard the DJ announce: "This one is for Frank from England." His choice was Sylvia's Mother, by Dr Hook, and, do you know, we never did find out why he requested that record, why he phoned to tell us it was coming on or the significance of it. It was a complete mystery.

Sammy Chung and physio Toby Andersen were now in charge of the tour and it was a far more relaxed atmosphere. The thing that annoyed Frank was that if McGarry had any suspicions that players might be cheating on their wives, he threatened to expose them. Now, we had reason to wonder whether he was playing away, as it were, and that seemed to be OK. Since joining Wolves, McGarry had always been a sergeant major type, football-orientated and full of good morals. A bastard to deal with, he was always right – or thought he was. One of his favourite sayings was "Think the right things and you will do the right things." It all sounds fine until women become involved and that is precisely what we suspect might have happened to McGarry. Rumour was that he got involved with another lady, a member of the squash club he used. Squash was a game he excelled at.

Back to the tour . . . it really was a whistle-stop trip – play a game, then move on. We began with a tough one against South Island which we won 3-2 before a capacity crowd of 14,000 at Newmarket Park, Auckland. Derek Dougan and Hugh Curran put us two up after 20 minutes and, when Warren Fleet scored soon after the break, The Doog quickly restored our two-goal advantage before a penalty from Earle Thomas gave us a late fright. The second game against an Invitation XI at Basin Reserve in Wellington was much easier. The Doog scored twice in the first five minutes and Jim McCalliog and Peter Eastoe got two each in the second half to give us a 6-0 win. Finally, we beat South Island 2-0 at English Park in Christchurch. We looked a weary outfit in this one and the home side held us at bay until the final 18 minutes when Frank and Peter Eastoe were the scorers. We were not helped by being strictly limited to only two subs and, after the Auckland game, The Doog had a go at New Zealand FA chairman Jack Cowan for insisting on this, saying: "If both coaches want more than two substitutes, there's nothing simpler than the two parties getting together and deciding just that. Stick to your rules in international or other important competitions, but this was no more than a friendly." The New Zealanders obviously thought otherwise. The matches were a serious business, more than mere friendlies to them.

A fixture that was classed as friendly but turned out to be far from it was played in Montreal on the same day as our Christchurch game and it certainly attracted Frank's interest when we heard about it. While we had set off for New Zealand, his old club Aberdeen had stayed in North America to play five more games. In the fourth of these, against Montreal Olympics, Aberdeen opened the scoring just past the hour with a Joe Harper penalty. Booing fans let off fire-crackers in the stands, then started hurling cans, shoes and rubbish at the visitors, and finally many of them stormed the pitch to try to attack the players. Referee Stan Tait quickly called a halt to the proceedings and, after half an hour of officials and police trying in vain to restore order, the game was abandoned.

Nothing remotely like that happened to us in our opening game in Australia but it was certainly no friendly as far as the home side, the Australian National

XI, were concerned. They were really up for it and we were beaten 1-0 at the Olympic Park in Melbourne before a 10,000 gate. Gerry Taylor replaced Frank for the second half and the goal did not come until eight minutes from time, through delightfully-named winger Attila Abonyi. The Sydney Morning Herald reported: "It was a red-letter day for Australian soccer – the first ever win over an English professional team." Jim Rooney, a lad from Frank's old home town of Dundee, paved the way for the goal, forcing John McAlle into a hurried back pass when Phil Parkes had left his line. The ball struck Lofty and fell just right for Abonyi. The Herald was probably closer to the truth than it imagined when it added: "Wolves frankly seemed to have done too well on Melbourne hospitality. Either that or they are weary of football." The second statement summed things up, apart from for Frank, of course. He never wearied of playing.

Afterwards, Sammy Chung said: "I can assure you there will be more effort in the second match. I am bitterly disappointed at the way the boys played. Nevertheless, Australia should not have scored that goal. Our keeper touched the ball no more than five times during the second half." Recalling the game in an interview with the Wolves Heroes website many years later, Frank said: "Our opponents were very committed, as Aussies always are, and Hugh Curran received a lot of stick from his markers." Abonyi the goal hero was not Attila the Hun, but Attila the Hungarian, having been born in Budapest and emigrated to Australia aged ten at the time of the revolution in his home country. He played 89 times for his adopted country and was a member of the Aussie side who reached the 1974 World Cup finals. His standing in Oz football was such that Abonyi Place in the Sydney suburb of Glenwood was named after him. Teams on Sunday, June 11, 1972:

Australia: Reilly, Harris, Wilson, Schaefer, Hogg (Nyskohus 55), Richards, Mackay, Rooney, Baartz, Alston (Vojtek 55), Abonyi. Wolves: Parkes, Shaw, Parkin, Hegan, Munro (Taylor HT), McAlle, McCalliog, Sunderland, Curran, Dougan, Daley (Wagstaffe 73).

It was a similar story when we met the same side at the Sydney Sports Ground the very next day before a crowd of 18,803. Hugh Curran, who grabbed our equaliser 17 minutes from time, was sent off in the closing minutes of a 2-2 draw when he finally cracked and hit Ray Richards, who had scythed him down. Frank remembered: "We were still tired following the game 24 hours earlier and after a long flight from New Zealand but we were fired up because of the treatment Hughie received." Australia had got off to a flying start with a goal timed at 20 seconds after kick-off. Winger Billy Rogers raced down the left and centred for

Ray Baartz to slot home. Frank put us level in the seventh minute and this is how the Sydney Morning Herald reported it: "Australia's defenders stood and admired Hegan's corner kick and centre-half Frank Munro trundled in to head home from close range." Baartz restored the lead with a solo effort after 35 minutes, evading four tackles in a 60-yard run. Then came Hughie's goal followed by his final flourish. He nearly got away with it as referee Tony Boskovic was following play but linesman Frank Jones drew his attention to the prone Richards, and Hughie was told to leave, which he did to a pelting of rubbish from some fans. Boskovic did not show the diplomacy you would expect from a referee. Referring to us, he told reporters: "They were poor sports who could not take it." Cheers, ref!

Chairman John Ireland, who had assumed charge of the squad in McGarry's absence, came in afterwards and, straight-faced, gave Hughie a right telling-off – for not hitting the Aussie harder. That sort of thing was what made the players hold the chairman in such great affection. Fortunately for Hughie, who had received a lot of provocation, the Australian Soccer Federation took a lenient view and announced that no action would be taken. The FA here could also have carpeted him but nothing more was heard of the incident. The Aussies were gearing up for their World Cup qualifying campaign the following year and, on the evidence of their displays against us, it was no surprise they made it to the finals in West Germany. Aussie newspaper The Age summed up the mood of our hosts: "For the first time, Sydney fans witnessed the spectacle of English soccer playing second fiddle to a select band of brilliant Australians." It added that several fans had been involved in a brawl after the game and police made several arrests. I suppose that was Hughie's fault, too. Teams in this game were:

Australia: Corry, Harris, Wilson, Schaefer, Nyskohus, Richards, Rooney, Baartz, Rogers, Alston, Butler. Wolves: Parkes, Taylor, Parkin, Hegan, Munro, McAlle, McCalliog, Sunderland (Hibbitt HT), Curran, Dougan (Eastoe 73), Wagstaffe.

A month before we took on the Australia XI, Dundee, the team down the road from Frank's old club, beat them 2-1 in Adelaide. So I suppose we were expected to beat them, too. The Scots also defeated a Northern Rivers XI during their tour by the emphatic score of 16-1. While our games against the Aussie national side attracted a fair bit of attention, what really excited the locals was the imminent arrival of the Brazilian side Santos, complete with their star attraction Pelé. With the great man in the side, their friendlies were sold out. After our game in Sydney, there was a less demanding 6-2 victory for us over a Queensland XI in Brisbane, with 18-year-old Peter Eastoe helping himself to a hat-trick. It looked as though it might be quite close when we led only 3-2 at half-time but the home side then faded. The Doog, Kenny Hibbitt and Jim McCalliog were our other scorers. A see-saw encounter with South Australia followed in Adelaide and we won 3-2 after the home side went one up after only four minutes. A minute later, I hit the post and Danny Hegan slotted in the rebound. Kenny gave us the lead on 20 minutes but they soon equalised and looked like holding out for draw. But, with three minutes left, Jimmy Mac's through pass somehow got through the South Australia defence and Alan Sunderland nipped in to hit the winner.

Before the Adelaide game, we had a couple of days' break which we all relished. But there was no relaxing after it as we had to play our final game the next day in Perth. We beat Western Australia 3-0 in front of about 15,000, which was pretty sizeable for a game in Oz in those days. I scored one of my rare goals and the others came from Jim McCalliog and Peter Eastoe. So, a very tired squad flew home the next day, having played 12 games in 29 days, each one in a different city, starting in San Francisco and ending in Perth. We won eight, drew one and lost three. Young Eastoe was top scorer with seven goals while Frank took great pleasure in pointing out that he had scored three times as many as I did.

It was a tiring tour; not so much the games we played but the travelling in between. We covered many thousands of miles getting from one venue to another. By the time we won in the beautiful city of Perth, we had circumnavigated the world, or so it seemed. A season that began on August 14 ended on June 18 and saw us play 69 matches – only seven short of the equivalent of two Premier League seasons. Or, as Frank said: "That's a game more than two Scottish League seasons put together." He was spot on as the top flight in Scotland consisted of 18 clubs playing 34 games a season. He was impressed by Australia and really enjoyed it there, which explains why he settled down so well there many years later. Over again to Frank's recollections with Wolves Heroes – "Most of us enjoyed the travelling even if hanging around in airports became boring. We were able to sample the Aussie beer, Sydney was a great place and Perth was incredibly clean. I loved the country so much that I went back there to live for quite a while."

When we finally got home after that epic trip, there was barely four weeks' breathing space before we had to report back for training. And, would you believe, we were soon on our travels again for a pre-season warm-up in Sweden! Most of us felt the new season had come around all too quickly – but not Frank, of course.

Chapter Ten

Semi-Final Sadness

So let me sum up Frank's career at Wolves up to the end of 1971-72 and the good things that had happened to him. In the previous two full seasons, he had gone from bit-part player to a first-class centre-half and Scotland international. He had played 44 senior games in his first full season, helping us finish fourth in the League and win the Texaco Cup. The season after, he played 51 games, seeing Wolves to ninth in the First Division and runners-up in the UEFA Cup. It had been two years of considerable progress, evidence of which could be found in that famous old publication, Football Monthly, which did a two-page article on him in their November, 1972, edition. The piece, by Ray Bradley, included a quote or two from me and said: "On their good days, Wolves are one of the most inspiring teams in the land, a team brimming with talent and tireless energy. On other days, they are liable to lapses in concentration when their defence is frequently exposed to the quick counter-attack that rebounds after all-out commitment to attack. On such days, it is often the courage of defenders like their Scottish international centre-half Francis Munro that stands out above other talented team-mates. For nearly four seasons now, Munro has been a tower of strength in a Wolves defence that has wobbled under pressure. His performances are generally more noted for their quiet efficiency than the spectacular achievements of the glamour men up front like sharp-shooter John Richards, the wily Dougan or the wizard wing play of Dave Wagstaffe. Yet the high level of performance and the consistency of Munro in Wolves' rapid rise to the fringe of top honours in the last few seasons is fully recognised and respected by his team-mates."

That was where the article turned to yours truly and my comment was: "Frank has been a pillar of strength in the defence for three seasons now. For my money, he's the best centre-half in Britain." I can assure you I really meant those words, for Frank really had reached the top when it came to being an accomplished central defender. The article included a few quotes from Frank as well – "I quite enjoyed my spell at wing-half but I much prefer playing at centre-half because I'm facing the play all the time. At wing-half, you can get caught out by a swift counter attack if you're backing up and this can leave you struggling. At centre-half, you've got time to read the situations and have the advantage of facing the play. Now I wouldn't want to play anywhere else." Any suggestion he was one of the game's hard men was refuted by Frank, who told Bradley: "I think I'm quite the opposite. There are times when you have to go in hard to win tackles but I do it fairly and to win the ball. Manager Bill McGarry has told me to be harder but I prefer to try to win my battles by getting there first and using the ball constructively. I see no point in being destructive."

I think the feature gives some indication of how Frank liked to play his football as a centre-half. There is no doubt he could be tough when necessary but he was like all good defenders – he could read the game and be in the right place at the right time. He was class in that respect. By the time 1972-73 arrived, he was an established member of the side. I would go further and say he was one of the mainstays. He was by no means scared of McGarry – in fact, he really hated him – but he felt that, having been in the team only two or three seasons, he did not want to rock the boat. So he would usually bite his tongue. However, he was still firmly of the opinion that should McGarry release his stranglehold on team tactics, then the better the team would be. He also knew that there was very little chance of this happening because McGarry liked to be in total control.

We used to sit and talk tactics in hotels, when McGarry was not around, of course, and Frank was the first to advocate that we ought to play the Leeds way, which meant you played the game the way you saw fit at the time. This would not have been difficult as we had great strength in depth in our squad and players could adapt to other positions for short periods. Put this to McGarry and the balloon would have gone up as he was not the sort of person to listen, full stop. He was a total one-off, unapproachable, self-opinionated and thought he was above everyone else. The reason he had that opinion was that you were not allowed to answer him back or give your side of a story because he was the boss and, in football, whatever the boss says goes. Well, it did in our day. Not that Frank always toed the line. On occasions he would risk the boss's anger, like at a match at St Andrew's in the early 1970s when Frank reckoned Trevor Francis was the Birmingham danger man and told John McAlle to man-mark him even though McGarry had not given any such instructions. The boss realised what Frank had done but, to his great surprise, Frank did not get a rollicking.

When talking about his previous managers, Frank could not recall any of them being as self-centred or contrary as Bill McGarry. It was perhaps a good thing that he decided to bite his tongue. If he had aired his views, there would have been a confrontation and only one winner. Bearing in mind our views about the boss, we had to laugh about what our skipper said just before the start of the new season. McGarry had been strongly linked with taking over at Coventry City in succession to Noel Cantwell. Wolves did not want him to go and eventually it was announced he had signed a new contract and was staying. The Daily Express report said the news would please the players and quoted Mike Bailey: "We all think the world of the boss." I can tell you those sentiments expressed by our skipper were certainly news to Frank and me.

After the dizzy heights of 1971-72, we could not help wondering if the new season would be an anti-climax. We did win a bit of silverware before it even began when we retained the Rous Cup in Gothenburg. We defeated local side Gais 4-3 on penalties, after the game ended 1-1, then beat Everton 2-1 in the final before just over 3,000 fans in the massive Ullevi Stadium. Believe it or not, D Wagstaffe was one of our successful penalty takers against Gais. Kenny Hibbitt got the winner in the final. He went on as sub for Danny Hegan immediately after John Connolly had wiped out the lead given us by John Richards. Within five minutes of appearing, Kenny slotted home a Steve Kindon cross to give us victory. Frank was in great form and was named man of the tournament, even if it was a tournament of just two games per side. By coincidence, we had beaten Gais 3-2 on penalties after a 3-3 draw to win the cup a year earlier.

We then came down to earth when, back on English soil, we made a quick exit from the Watney Cup by losing 2-0 to Bristol Rovers at Eastville. It was, though, our third game in five days and Frank, our hero in Sweden, became our villain in Bristol. He brought down former Albion winger Ken Stephens and that enabled Bruce Bannister to open the scoring from the penalty spot for the Third Division side. By the time Stephens hit the second goal three minutes from time, Frank had limped off. He was fit for the start of the League season but I was sidelined, so it was a good job we had signed 'The Tank' – Stevie Kindon – from Burnley and also had Steve Daley to call upon. Frank and the lads made a losing start to the First Division campaign, going down 2-1 at Newcastle and 5-2 at Arsenal. The home striking duo of John Radford and Ray Kennedy were really on song at Highbury, one of the very few occasions when Frank and John McAlle were given the run-around. We then won four and drew one of our next five League games but it would have been five out of five if Frank had not presented Southampton with an equaliser in a 1-1 draw at The Dell. Jim McCalliog had put us one up and we were in control until Frank tried to lob the ball back to Phil Parkes and saw it sail over Lofty for an own goal. Bill McGarry did not pull his punches afterwards:

"Frank tried to be too clever. He had time to put the ball away – a silly goal and it cost us the match." Frank could not argue with the boss. He knew he had made a silly error and I am pretty sure he learned a lesson from it.

We got back on track and lost only once in the next 15 games. A spell which included two League Cup games and two in the Texaco Cup saw John Richards score 13 times. Our only defeat was in the League at Anfield, where Liverpool won 4-2 by scoring three times in the last 15 minutes. Jim McCalliog was sent off there. He remonstrated with a linesman after Liverpool had been awarded a penalty but went too far and actually pushed the official backwards. JR's two goals in the Texaco Cup helped us beat Kilmarnock 5-1 at Molineux in the first leg of the first-round tie. Frank missed the game through injury but was able to travel back to his native land for the second leg and a goalless draw at Rugby Park saw us through. Some Wolves record books have Brian Owen down as playing in this match but they have it wrong. Frank definitely wore the no 5 shirt but his total appearances for the club remains at 371, as the same record books wrongly have him playing in the away UEFA Cup game with Academica Coimbra.

In the second round of the Texaco Cup, we were knocked out by Ipswich. We lost 2-1 away and then 1-0 at home. This proved a blessing in disguise really because it meant we could concentrate on the FA Cup, League Cup and League. Soon after the start of the season, McGarry signed Derek Jefferson from Ipswich to provide some cover for our central defenders and Frank soon discovered that things could go wrong for our new colleague. It happened when Derek came into the side in early November at West Ham as John McAlle was having to play at left-back. The Hammers had just scored and Frank noticed that, on the muddy pitch, Derek was still on his knees as we all lined up to kick off. Frank yelled: "Derek we're kicking off, what are you doing?" "You've got to help me," said Derek. Frank did not know what to do – whether to call over the ref or shout for the doctor. "What's wrong?" asked Frank. The reply was surprising: "I've lost one of my contact lenses. You've got to help me find it!" "Derek, they'll be attacking again in a minute," pointed out Frank and attack the Hammers did, with Derek still on his knees in the Upton Park mud. Fortunately, Frank was able to clear the ball into the crowd. The referee appeared and asked Derek what his problem was as he was still on all fours. The ref gave a wry smile when told and said that he could hardly hold up the game while we looked for a 'needle in a haystack.' So Frank was partnered for the rest of the match by a player with virtually one good eye. Amazingly, we still managed to draw 2-2.

In the League Cup, we were lucky enough to be drawn at home in the first four rounds. We beat Orient in the second round, followed by Sheffield Wednesday and Bristol Rovers. Frank managed to score at both ends in the 3-1 win over Wednesday. When John McAlle, again playing left-back that night, put over a cross, Derek Dougan headed the ball goalwards and Frank nodded it into the net. That was after 17 minutes, two minutes after Kenny Hibbitt had fired us in front from the penalty spot. The Doog headed our third on the hour, then Frank managed to turn a John Sissons cross into his own net. Our old pal John Holsgrove was in the Wednesday line-up while Derek Jefferson made his debut for us and very quickly made it clear his approach was of the no-nonsense variety, in stark contrast to the more subtle style of Frank. After conceding five free-kicks, Derek was booked soon after half-time for a late tackle. Scouse was again at full-back with Derek alongside Frank when we brushed aside Rovers 4-0 but was back partnering Frank when we met Blackpool in the fifth round, the quarter-final. We did well to get away with a 1-1 draw at Molineux with a goal from Jim McCalliog saving the day. Keith Dyson scored for Blackpool. Surprisingly, in the replay at Bloomfield Road a week later, the crowd of 19,812 exceeded the one at Molineux by over 2,500, which was a superb turn-out for a Second Division club. We were the ones who played like a Second Division team and were very lucky to win by the only goal, scored by The Doog.

McGarry did not say a word after the match. Although we were now in the semi-final, we knew it had been a poor performance. However, for him not to make any comment was very unusual. We were staying at the Norbreck Hotel on the sea front and our faithful driver Sid Kipping drove us back there afterwards. As the bus pulled on to the car park, McGarry stood up from his usual seat at the front, turned round to face us, then let rip with a torrent of abuse about the way we had played. This went on for fully 15 minutes and, just when we thought he had finished, he came out with: "By the way, nobody leaves this hotel tonight. If I find out any of you have attempted to go out for a drink, you will be back home to Wolverhampton with a hefty fine waiting for you when you get there."

With those words, he left the bus. This was typical McGarry – no right of reply for us and no night out in Blackpool. Yet, as a result of that game, poorly though we played, we were in the semi-final. Tottenham were our opponents and we were hoping the two-legged affair would produce a different result from that of the previous season in the UEFA Cup final. Sadly for us, the home leg produced exactly the same result – a 2-1 defeat. The second leg at White Hart Lane brought a 2-2 draw after extra-time that saw Spurs through to the Wembley final, in which they would beat Norwich. Frank missed the return, although he had just finished a two-match suspension. He was still nursing an ankle injury from the first leg at Molineux.

That replay with Blackpool had consequences for John McAlle, the other man now firmly established in the centre of our defence. His progress had been noted by Sir Alf Ramsey, who named him, along with John Richards, in the England under-23 squad to face Wales at Swansea. But it was scheduled for the day after our Blackpool trip, so the club withdrew them from the international. Tommy Taylor of West Ham and Kevin Beattie were the central defensive pairing and Scouse never did get the cap he deserved at that level. He was 23 the following January.

Out of the Texaco Cup, out of the League Cup and realistically in with no chance of winning the First Division, we were left with the FA Cup as our only route to glory. By the time the third round arrived, we had more than held our own in the League, with ten wins, six draws and nine defeats. The draw for our first hurdle could hardly have been tougher – Manchester United. One thing in our favour was that it was at home and we had already beaten them 2-0 in the League there. We had 40,000 at the Cup game and the only goal came from skipper Mike Bailey. We were on our way. Amazingly, in the week before the tie, there was a report speculating that Bill McGarry would be prepared to let Frank go in a deal that would bring United striker Ted MacDougall to Molineux. The Daily Express claimed: "Wolves are still hoping to clinch a deal for Ted MacDougall, Manchester United's unsettled striker. They have offered cash and a player – possibly defender Frank Munro. Total value of the deal would be about £200,000."

United's boss at the time was Tommy Docherty – funny how he keeps cropping up in Frank's story – and he denied there had been a bid by Wolves. Docherty, who had barely begun his reign at Old Trafford, had just signed big Jim Holton from Shrewsbury but the newspaper's Midland reporter Alan Williams, who usually had reliable sources, reckoned Holton was seen as a long-term investment and The Doc was likely to be interested in a defender of Frank's First Division experience. While the Express named Frank as the likely defender involved, the Express & Star did not. Their report said McGarry had confirmed he had spoken to Tommy Docherty and had offered for MacDougall a cash sum and 'an as yet unnamed defender.' A day later, the paper reported that The Doc was now saying MacDougall was not for sale, United having rejected bids from Wolves and the striker's old club, Bournemouth. Alan Williams was usually spot on with his inside information but it is still difficult to understand why McGarry would have let Frank go. Having said that, nothing McGarry did would have surprised us.

Thankfully, no more was heard of it. No disrespect to MacDougall but, if such a deal had gone through, I reckon our loss would have been United's gain. A few weeks later, MacDougall was indeed sold – to West Ham for £150,000. He played only 24 League games for the Hammers before moving on to Norwich.

In the FA Cup, another 1-0 win at Molineux, this time against Bristol City with John Richards on target, saw us through to the fifth round, where we were drawn against Millwall. Another JR goal and another 1-0 home win was the outcome. Our luck held for the sixth round when we were paired with Coventry on March 17 – St Patrick's Day. It's a day that has gone down in Wolves folklore but not for anything that happened during the 90 minutes. McGarry blew his top even before the match, never mind at half-time or full-time. It was all because of a freak accident during the pre-match kick-about. Our substitute Steve Kindon was firing in shots and one caught Derek Dougan unawares and hit him so hard that he collapsed and needed treatment. Our beloved boss raced on to the pitch to see if The Doog was hurt and also to give Kindo a right ear-bashing. Thank goodness, McGarry did not see me and Frank laughing our socks off. We were not alone! Despite Kindo's best efforts, The Doog was able to play and helped get us off to a flying start.

Frank had a significant part in the opening goal after only six minutes. His towering header out of defence was nodded on by The Doog on the half-way line and John Richards galloped through to score. When two Coventry defenders sandwiched Richards in the second half, Kenny Hibbitt fired home the penalty. The Sky Blues had a couple of decent strikers but, as the Daily Express reported: "Colin Stein and Brian Alderson were snuffed out by Frank Munro and John McAlle." This put us into the semi-final against Leeds, the Cup holders and the team we had denied the Double at the end of the previous season. It was a match we all wanted to play in but one Frank might have missed. A week after we beat Coventry, we were at Elland Road in the League. We played well and deserved our 0-0 draw but Frank pulled a hamstring after about half an hour. Typically, he stayed on until the final few minutes, which may not have been in his or our best interests. He had been skipper as Mike was out. In fact, such was the pile-up of injuries that we had to play youth-team coach Brian Owen in defence against Sheffield United in our next game. So Frank and Mike were both doubtful for the semi-final with hamstring problems. After breakfast at the team hotel, the pair talked with McGarry and Frank pointed out it was a big risk to play both when they were only about 80 per cent fit. These were the days of only one substitute and Frank told the boss: "If you lose both of us, you'll be a man down against the best team in the country." For once, McGarry must have listened as he told them he was playing Frank, as skipper, and Mike would be on the bench.

Leeds were the most feared team around with every player an international and very experienced in every department, although they had Norman Hunter and Eddie Gray sidelined. The game was at Maine Road, where every one of our team felt comfortable playing. We were all up for it when we arrived in Manchester but it proved an anti-climax even though they lost Jack Charlton, by then nearly 38, with a pulled muscle in the first half. Barry Powell missed a chance when clean through and John Richards seemed to be denied by what looked like hand-ball on the line. It was clearly not our day and Billy Bremner scored the only goal on 69 minutes. A left-wing corner by Johnny Giles was headed clear but Peter Lorimer, from outside the area, hooked a high ball back in over his head. It might have gone out but Kenny tried to clear and succeeded only in slicing across goal to the lurking Bremner. The goal was the only one we conceded in the Cup that season. After that, John Richards hit a left-foot shot which looked a certain goal, only for it to rebound off the inside of the post, then The Doog almost equalised. By then, Mike had been thrown into the action and his long free-kick fell perfectly for The Doog but his header went agonisingly wide. Teams at Maine Road on Saturday, April 7:

Leeds: Harvey; Reaney, Cherry, Bremner, Charlton (Jordan), Yorath, Lorimer, Clarke, Jones, Giles, Madeley. Wolves: Parkes; Taylor, Parkin, Shaw, Munro, McAlle, Powell, Hibbitt (Bailey), Richards, Dougan, Wagstaffe. Attendance: 52,505. Referee: P Partridge (Durham).

After the game, McGarry said he blamed himself, explaining: "I chickened out. I picked the wrong team. I should have played Mike Bailey. Bailey, the player who could have won it for us, was sitting on the substitutes' bench. It was a problem I lived with all through Friday: Whether I could risk both Bailey and Frank Munro in the same team when they were not 100 per cent fit. My instinct told me that I ought to play Bailey because there is a time and place when certain players ought to be there. For Bailey, Saturday and Maine Road was the time and place. For what must be the first time in my managerial career, I went against instinct. Yet, as so often happens in this sort of situation, Munro had no trouble and had a fine game. Because of that, playing Bailey would not have been a risk."

Many years later, Frank recalled: "He played Barry Powell and Mick came on for the last 20 minutes or so. He got through the game and I got through but McGarry blamed me. He said: 'If I'd have played the two of you, we'd have beaten them.' I can remember the goal as if it was yesterday. I could have walked the ball out of the box. It was coming down and I shouted to Ken (Hibbitt) 'Leave it' but he kicked it and the ball spun away in the air and it went to Bremner." Frank added: "That was the greatest disappointment ever for me – that game. We'd never have a better chance than that of going to the final. We'd have beaten Sunderland as well, don't worry about that." Of course, Sunderland, then in the Second Division, caused a huge Wembley upset by beating hot favourites Leeds 1-0 in one of the great finals.

Frank was furious after the defeat. We had been without our inspirational skipper but Frank maintained that The Doog, John Richards and I did not perform on the day. He did not tell Derek and John as much but he certainly told me on the way home. Looking back, he was right. If ever a team were there for the taking, it was Leeds but we did not take advantage. For a man so calm before a game, Frank could sometimes have a short fuse on the field and, a couple of weeks after our defeat, he managed to get himself sent off after a bout of fisticuffs with Ipswich's Colin Viljoen at Portman Road. They swapped several punches before referee Gordon Kew gave them their marching orders. That created a Football League record at the time as Kew was the first referee to send off seven players in a season. Viljoen told the Daily Express afterwards: "I was blatantly obstructed and we should have had a penalty. Then I was struck and I hit back in self defence. Was I supposed to stand there and just take it?" Wisely, Frank and manager Bill McGarry chose not to comment to the press but the boss had plenty to say to our hero in the dressing room. It was not Frank's finest hour. The three-match ban incurred for his impression of Joe Frazier, coupled with a hamstring injury, meant he did not play in the final five League games of the season.

We finished a commendable fifth in the League and had lost in the semi-final of two cups. It might sound like a successful season but it is not if you are a professional because the hardest place to lose is in a semi. So near yet so far. Nobody remembers the losing FA Cup semi-finalists, although, at the beginning of the next season, we met the other losers Arsenal in a game at Highbury to decide who officially was third in the competition. We won 3-1 but it was meaningless. I don't think it even rates a mention in the list of honours contained in the Wolves programme. Frank managed to play in only one of our last eight games but still ended 1972-73 with 32 League appearances to his name. By the end of the campaign, he was not fully fit, so there was no chance of him playing for Scotland in the Home Internationals. Yet many must have wondered why he did not get a call-up earlier in a season when the Scots played home and away World Cup qualifying games against Denmark. Instead, they went for Eddie Colquhoun of

Sheffield United and Martin Buchan of Manchester United. Frank was surely a better all-round player than either of these two.

England certainly showed up the pairing in February, 1973, when they met Scotland at Hampden in a special game to mark the Scottish FA's centenary. England won 5-0. What a first game as Scotland manager that was for Willie Ormond! He had been appointed after Tommy Docherty left for Manchester United. Ormond named no fewer than five United players in his starting line-up that night – Alex Forsyth, Buchan, Lou Macari, George Graham and Willie Morgan. The only non-Anglos were keeper Bobby Clark and Kenny Dalglish, then still with Celtic. For the Home Internationals, Ormond turned to two previously uncapped players – Jim Holton, a rugged no-nonsense centre-half, and Derek Johnstone of Rangers. They made their debuts in a 2-0 win over Wales in Cardiff but the Scots then lost four in a row as the season came to an end.

Another season over for Wolves but what was happening off the pitch? Mr McGarry was dyeing his hair all of a sudden. Yes, it was a nice deep auburn and we all had a good idea why. On more than one occasion, when we played in London, Sid, our coach driver, was instructed to drop him off at the Holiday Inn, then continue into Kensington, where the rest of the party would disembark at our normal overnight base, the Royal Garden Hotel. We thought it was perfectly obvious what McGarry was up to and he seemed to make no attempt to hide it – but he would no doubt have fined any player for doing this and no doubt exposed him in the newspapers.

Chapter Eleven

Wembley Wonders

Was 1973-74 going to be the season we at last won something or were we to miss out yet again? We had been so near in the past few seasons but it just had not happened for us. We were now back in the UEFA Cup as well as the usual FA and League Cups and maybe we could win one of these? We got off to a rousing start (pun intended) when we again won the Rous Cup in Sweden, overcoming Oergryte 3-1 and then Leicester 1-0. Alan Sunderland got the goal in the final when he headed John Richards's cross past Peter Shilton after 20 minutes. Confirmation of Frank's standing was the fact he was named skipper, with Mike Bailey still sidelined. He was able to collect the trophy from Sir Stanley Rous himself, the man who started out as a referee, became secretary of the Football Association and then president of FIFA. This was the third season running we had collected the trophy.

We made a good start in the League with two home wins – against Norwich (3-1) and Sheffield United (2-0). Then things went badly wrong. Starting with five successive defeats, we went 14 League games with only one win. We were successful in the first round of the UEFA Cup, though. The away first leg against Portuguese side Belenenses attracted fewer than 9,000 and we won it 2-0 with John Richards and Derek Dougan on target. It was 2-1 to us at Molineux but unfortunately we did not progress past Lokomotiv Leipzig in the next round even though the second leg produced one of our most exciting displays and reinforced Frank's feelings that we should be allowed more freedom in our playing style. Having lost the away leg 3-0, no-one gave us a chance but we had nothing to lose and just went for it, all-out attack. It worked and we all but pulled it round. The final score was 4-1 and it was one of the most exciting games Frank had played in. He even scored. It was a game that really proved his view about what we might achieve if we did not have to stick to McGarry's rigid approach. All the goals came in the second half. Steve Kindon started it off, then made a goal for Frank. Lowe got Leipzig's vital away goal on the break, only for The Doog immediately to put us back in it. Kenny Hibbitt made it 4-4 on aggregate with eight minutes still to go but we just could not get the extra goal to see us through and they went through via the away goals rule. .

So that was one competition we were not destined to win but things were going quite well in the League Cup. We comfortably got past Halifax away, 3-0, then a 1-1 draw at Tranmere brought them to Molineux, where goals from Barry Powell and The Doog saw us edge home 2-1. Next came Exeter at Molineux and another goal from The Doog and two each from John Richards and Kenny Hibbitt put us through to the fifth round with a 5-1 win. Now it was Wolves v Liverpool for a place in the semi-final. Sounds exciting, doesn't it? Well, it was played on a damp, cold December afternoon, the crowd a measly 16,000. Nothing to get excited about. The reason for the small turn-out was the power-saving at the time due to the cuts during industrial disputes that winter. Floodlights could not be used but, if it had it been an evening game, there would have been at least 35,000 there, probably many more. Fans could not afford to have the afternoon off work as well as having to pay to go to the match – it was just too expensive for the man or woman in the street. Exciting or not, we won, John Richards wrapping it up for us with a brilliant solo effort. We were through to the semi-final.

Frank fondly recalled the goal in that excellent book, Those Were The Days, telling author Clive Corbett: "John was fantastic. I think he put four years on Derek Dougan's professional life. He was so quick and brave. I think the best goal he scored, and I've told him so, was the one against Liverpool. Larry Lloyd had three yards start on him but John's power and bravery got him there and he smashed it with his left foot, a fantastic goal that showed what he was all about." The next game after the Liverpool win was at home to Chelsea in the League and we beat them 2-0 with John getting both goals. Alas, trouble and Frank sometimes went hand in hand, as this game proved. Something incensed him and he went chasing after Peter Osgood following a scramble in the Chelsea area and the scuffle that followed earned them both a booking. Frank was sent reeling and the Chelsea centre-forward raced away to the centre circle. Rather than let it be, Frank sprinted upfield, charged into Ossie and it was handbags at two paces. McGarry hit the roof and told Frank he had acted like an idiot. He could hardly argue and was banned for two games, the first a 2-1 home win over Southampton on New Year's Day in which I scored my first League goal for over two years.

Derek Jefferson stood in for Frank against the Saints and again four days later when we met our old friends Leeds in the FA Cup third round. It looked as though we might gain revenge for the semi-final defeat the previous year when John Richards deflected home an Alan Sunderland shot soon after half-time. But, with time running out, referee Roger Kirkpatrick adjudged that Barry Powell had fouled Billy Bremner – and Peter Lorimer fired in the penalty. Frank was back for the replay, which had to kick off at 1.30 on the Wednesday but still pulled in nearly 43,000. We did well until six minutes from the end when Mick Jones headed the only goal.

That was at the start of January and, at the end of the month, two games would decide whether we made it to Wembley for the League Cup final. Surely we would do it this time – just defeat Norwich, who were struggling to stay in the First Division. After beating the mighty Liverpool, we would never have a better chance of getting there. No disrespect to Norwich but we preferred to play them, rather than Manchester City. The other team in the last four were Plymouth, so City must have been even happier than us with the draw. Norwich were having a dreadful season and had managed only two League wins from 24 games, which was why they were firmly entrenched at the bottom. We had a rehearsal because we had to play them in the First Division on January 19, with the away and home legs against them in the League Cup to follow on January 23 and 26. The League game proved to be a non-event as both teams kept their cards close to their chest, not wanting to show their hand. The result was a 1-1 draw with nothing much learned.

The first leg of the semi-final was at Carrow Road and Norwich proved tougher opponents than we thought. But a goal from John Richards gave us a 1-1 draw and we were happy with that, with the home leg to come. Ian Mellor scored for the Canaries. There were 20,000 at Norwich and 10,000 more at Plymouth to see them take a first-half lead through Steve Davey. City salvaged a draw, thanks to defender Tommy Booth. You would have thought our draw would have satisfied Bill McGarry – but no. We got back to our hotel in Bury St Edmunds and he laid down the law. "You get one drink and one drink only," he stressed, although, for a change, he was paying – or, rather, Wolves were. He settled the bill and then disappeared to bed. "Why does he have to be like this?" asked Frank. "We've got a good result away, you would think he would be happy with the second leg to come at Molineux."

By contrast, soon after McGarry 'retired,' who should appear but John Bond, the Norwich manager, to have a pint and socialise with our lads? "Comes to something," said Frank, "when the opposition manager spends more time with us than our own manager." Bond had already socialised with his own players after the game so, consequently, it was late when he arrived at our hotel. McGarry would never have dreamt of doing something like that. Bond was good company and all the lads enjoyed his views on different aspects of the game. He failed to stop the Canaries getting relegated that season but it did not surprise us when he took them back at the first attempt. The second leg of the semi was tight, as you could imagine with so much at stake. It was played on an FA Cup Saturday as both of us had been knocked out. Once again it was John who got the all-important goal, the only one of the game, and that took us through. It was a great feeling after the disappointments of the previous season.

Four days later, Manchester City beat Plymouth 2-0 at Maine Road, so we knew our opponents. It meant I would be facing the club where it all started for me while Frank would be playing against a fellow countryman he had admired for many years – the great Denis Law, who was enjoying an Indian summer with City after so many years of success with their great rivals United. It had taken us seven games to reach the final, in contrast to City, who needed ten. They required three to get past Walsall in the second round, starting with a goalless draw at Fellows Park. It was goalless again in the replay at Maine Road before the second replay saw City win 4-1 at Old Trafford, Franny Lee grabbing a hat-trick. Lee also got the only goal in the third-round victory away to Second Division Carlisle, then York held them 0-0 before losing 4-1 away, with Rodney Marsh scoring three. It was in the quarter-final that City finally met another side from the top flight for the first time. They held Coventry 2-2 at Highfield Road and won the replay 4-2. When City beat Plymouth in the second leg of their semi, it meant Franny had scored in each round that season and his total was eight goals.

We were at Wembley at last and due to face one of the best sides in the country. In a golden period a few years earlier, City had won all the domestic trophies under the Joe Mercer and Malcolm Allison regime but those two were gone now. In charge was Ron Saunders, who had led Norwich to the final in 1973, only to lose to Tottenham at Wembley. Saunders would make it a hat-trick of finals in 1975 when he took Aston Villa there. Frank was as enthusiastic about going to the twin towers as any of us, yet he only went and put his chances of playing in jeopardy thanks to an incident in our very next game after beating Norwich. We drew 1-1 at Molineux with Stoke, who were parading their new signing from Chelsea, Alan Hudson. Frank clashed with their former Spurs and Scotland winger Jimmy Robertson and was promptly sent off after 63 minutes. Not everybody in a crowd of over 30,000 saw what happened but one man who mattered did – the referee, Harold Hackney. Frank was staring at a three-match ban and the games would be Birmingham at home, Manchester United away and . . . the League Cup final.

Just when things were going well and he was at the height of his powers, he faced missing a dream game. That occasional hot-headedness had surfaced once more and it could cost him dearly. However, there was a way out – an appeal. Six days after the Stoke game, the club exercised their right to lodge one after reading the referee's report and the hearing would be after the final. It was a way out but Frank had aimed a blow at Robertson and knew that morally he had no grounds to object to his sending-off. Many years later, he recalled: "I should have been banned for Wembley." So he did not face the music until 12 days after the final and Robertson kindly went to give evidence on his behalf to the FA disciplinary committee in Sheffield. It had no effect and Frank was inevitably banned for three games. He missed the chance to face three top sides and Derek Jefferson stood in for League games against Liverpool, Manchester City and Tottenham. What did matter was that Frank could play at Wembley on a memorable day for Wolves players and fans. On the day of the hearing, Frank became our lone first-team Scot as Jimmy McCalliog was transferred to Manchester United for £60,000.

While Frank was lucky, Phil Parkes could do nothing about missing the final. He suffered a hairline fracture of his ankle in training on the Monday after the semi-final second leg. It was a cruel blow to him but he was the sort of bloke to wish all the best to his deputy, Gary Pierce. Defeats at Sheffield United and Everton meant we slipped dangerously close to the relegation area but we got a welcome home win over bottom-of-the-table Birmingham. Able to play because of his appeal, Frank scored a rare goal, the only one of the game, when he headed home my corner after 14 minutes. Blues keeper Gray Sprake claimed someone had fouled him but the ref was not interested. Frank spent the rest of the match ensuring Kenny Burns had no chance to shine. Burns was leading the visitors' attack as Bob Latchford had been transferred to Everton in the midweek. In the next game, there was an unusual sight at Old Trafford as Manchester United keeper Alex Stepney stepped up to take a penalty against us. He had already scored twice that season from the spot but Gary Pierce saved this kick. A 0-0 draw brought us another welcome point but it was no help to United, who were then bottom but one in the table and destined for the unthinkable – relegation. Remember the Denis Law back-heeled goal for City that sent them down?

All thoughts of the League were put on hold as we turned our attention to the League Cup final. One man who did not think our central defensive duo would be a match for City's all-star attack was Malcolm Allison, who by then was manager of Crystal Palace. He gave his pre-match prediction in the Daily Express and reckoned Mike Summerbee would be the big danger: "I can see him pulling Wolves' central defenders out to the left. And if Summerbee is checked, if Wolves push up on him hard, he has the technique to play the ball across to Marsh, who will be playing slightly behind the forward strikers. Law and Lee. Now there is no more subtle passer of the ball than Rodney Marsh. I expect the finesse of his passing to undermine McAlle and Munro and supply the alternative line of attack to Summerbee." Well, Allison was a good coach and knew his football but he was well wide of the mark with this view of how things would go at Wembley. No way were John and Frank undermined.

All looked set for a great game and it certainly lived up to its billing. It was a cracking match, end to end, with not too many chances to start with but, as the game continued and opened up, a goal was bound to come. Frank and John McAlle were magnificent against a forward line of household names – Summerbee, Colin Bell, Lee, Law and Marsh. All five were experienced Wembley performers. In contrast, we only had one player, The Doog, who had played at the famous old stadium. The game was not very old when Frank made his presence felt. Marsh went galloping through and met a human brick wall in the shape of Frank. That set the pattern for the match, with our no 5 coming up with clearing headers, vital tackles and cool interceptions. He hardly put a foot wrong.

City's defenders were also under threat from him and, twice in the space of a few minutes, he nearly set up a goal. First he found himself in acres of space to meet my right-wing corner and direct a sharp header goalwards. Unfortunately, their keeper Keith MacRae was perfectly positioned to collect. Then Kenny Hibbitt took a corner from the left and this time Frank headed back across goal for Alan Sunderland to produce a shot that was goal-bound. John Richards accidentally deflected it and saw the ball hit the post. Kenny finally broke the deadlock. It was a mis-hit shot but the goal was not against the run of play. We had definitely taken the game to City and deserved to be ahead. Probably the only time Frank and John McAlle were caught napping was when City equalised early in the second half. Rodney Marsh centred from the left and Colin Bell was unmarked and had all the time in the world to score. Soon after that, Frank got himself booked when he tackled Franny Lee from behind.

John Richards hit the winner with just a few minutes left. I played my part in that goal – because I was off the field! McGarry was about to take John off as he was struggling but then I pulled up and I was the one who left. While Barry Powell was waiting to go on as sub, City gave us a scare with a Colin Bell shot that grazed the bar. So JR stayed on and was there to hit the winner. Fate must have been on our side that day. We were pleased it did not go to a replay as that would have been at Stoke. No disrespect to the Potters but their old Victoria Ground was a far cry from playing at Wembley.

Taking nothing away from the goalscorers Ken and John, it was our back four who paved the way for victory. To look after a forward line that Manchester City put out that day – I think they had something like 120 caps between them – was an achievement in itself and they fully deserved the plaudits. So take a bow Geoff Palmer, Derek Parkin, John McAlle and Frank Munro. This has to rank as one of Frank's best ever games. He was superb – and, just think, he might have missed it all through that nonsense with Jimmy Robertson. Gary Pierce, on his 23rd birthday, also played a blinder in goal. The majority of the team were young in football terms. The Doog, Mike Bailey and I were past 30 while Frank and Derek Parkin were 26. The other five were all 24 or under.

Frank swapped shirts with Denis Law immediately the final whistle sounded and it was lucky for us he did. We asked McGarry if we could keep the Wembley gear – the strip we had played in and the tracksuits we wore to walk out in. "No" was the emphatic answer, "you can only keep the shirts." He had obviously seen Frank was wearing Denis's shirt and did not want to rock the boat at such a joyous time. It was such a petty thing. The tracksuits were no good to anybody else with Wembley '74 emblazoned on them. Presumably, they were just left in a cupboard to rot and be thrown away when Molineux was rebuilt. There is a picture in Denis's 2012 book, Denis Law, My Life In Football, of him wearing Frank's shirt as he congratulates Derek Dougan during the celebrations. The caption says Denis cannot remember with whom he changed shirts. That is such a pity as swapping with a Scottish legend he had long admired meant such a lot to Frank. I am told Denis no longer has the Wolves shirt and cannot remember what happened to it. He may have donated it for auction but it would be great to know where that shirt is. Teams at Wembley on Saturday, March 2, 1974:

Manchester City: MacRae; Pardoe, Donachie, Doyle, Booth, Towers, Summerbee, Bell Lee, Law, Marsh. Sub: Carrodus. Wolves: Pierce; Palmer, Parkin, Bailey, Munro, McAlle, Sunderland, Hibbitt, Richards, Dougan, Wagstaffe (Powell). Attendance 97,886 (Receipts £165,000). Referee: D Wallace (Crewe).

In the evening after the victory, the team and wives or girlfriends were treated to a banquet at the Hilton Hotel in Park Lane and Frank had extra reason to recall it. "That was the night I started smoking," he told Those Were The Days author Clive Corbett. "I asked a waitress to bring me a packet of Benson & Hedges. McGarry went mad at me." Back home, Wolverhampton Council decided to honour the team with a civic banquet and, during the evening, McGarry's wife, Connie, came over to our table with a menu for the lads to sign. Frank and I were sat at the end of the table and she asked us to add our signatures and pass it on to the others. As she was stood there, I asked her if she was enjoying herself. "Not really," was her reply. Amazingly, she then came out with a remark that made it clear she knew who the 'other woman' was in McGarry's life. I will not repeat her exact words but, take it from me, there was no misunderstanding her meaning. This was the first time Mrs McGarry had let slip that she was aware of what was going on. Frank and I looked at each other absolutely gob-smacked.

Chapter Twelve

After The Glory

After all the celebrations, it was business as usual with the League. There were still 11 games left and plenty of points to be had. We picked up 13 from those final games – it was only two for a win then – which meant we finished 12th. With a cup for the cabinet, it was a successful season. Frank had appeared in 49 games, quite a few more than usual because of our League Cup campaign. Manchester City struggled, though, and, after winning only one of their next nine games following the final, they sacked Ron Saunders. Former skipper Tony Book took over but Saunders soon gained employment again, being named boss of Aston Villa, where he built a side who would become League champions and then European Cup winners, helped by the goalscoring of a centre-forward by the name of Peter Withe.

It was noticeable that, after the final, The Doog was given a back seat and was substitute in seven of the last eight matches of 1973-74. Several players were handed a chance to take his position, including Alan Sunderland, Steve Kindon and that man Withe. Something that baffled both me and Frank was why McGarry could not see the potential of Peter. He was a natural successor to The Doog, yet McGarry sold him for a relatively small fee, the worst Wolves sale of the century. Everybody knows that Peter went on to gain more honours than any one of us Wolves players, including the League Cup twice, and League title with Forest, and the European Cup, European Super Cup and League title with Aston Villa. His record speaks for itself and Frank was always very impressed with him as a footballer and as a colleague – but there was no arguing with Bill McGarry.

In the summer, Scotland, unlike England, were off to the World Cup in West Germany and many pundits thought Frank would be in their party, although he had been in the international wilderness for a few years. He was certainly at the height of his powers and in probably the best form of his life. After his display at Wembley, Express & Star man John Dee had written: "Munro must have made sure of a place in Scotland's World Cup squad with his ice-cool judgement and efficiency glowing throughout." A month and a half after Wembley, we drew 0-0 at West Ham and there was an endorsement from their England international midfielder Trevor Brooking, who said: "We just didn't get going but give credit to Wolves' back four. They were brilliant and Frank Munro must be good enough for Scotland's World Cup squad." McGarry, to be fair, also backed Frank's credentials for a place in the squad. He did not pull any punches: "Frank is the best centre-half in Britain. I have been saying all season he is different class from Jim Holton. To compare the two is to compare a cab horse to a Rolls Royce. Surely Willie Ormond must think about him for Germany." Frank had his say, too: "All I ask is that Willie Ormond takes a look. I desperately want a place. All I want is a chance. To me, the greatest honour is to play for my country. It is great to win a cup final in front of 100,000 at Wembley but that is nothing to the thrill I got when I pulled on a Scotland jersey and heard the roar of the Scots fans."

Frank was named in the preliminary squad but did not build up his hopes as there was no place for him in the party for the Home Internationals announced the same day. And, as expected, he was omitted from the final World Cup 22. Ormond and the selectors obviously did not rate him highly enough and preferred the rugged Holton of Manchester United to play alongside Martin Buchan. Gordon McQueen of Leeds and John Blackley of Hibernian were the other central defenders in the squad. In fairness to Buchan, he had become a very accomplished defender. On the day of the announcement, Frank said: "Well, that's life. Naturally I am disappointed. Now I must look forward to next season." Briefly, there was a chance of Frank still going to Germany when Holton pulled out of a pre-World Cup friendly against Belgium which enabled McQueen to win his first cap. There were fears Holton had sustained a ligament injury which would rule him out of the finals and the general opinion in the Scottish press was that Frank would get the vote ahead of Rangers' Derek Johnstone as replacement. It proved to be purely academic as Holton recovered and played in all three of Scotland's games, which saw them win one, draw two and fail to qualify from their group.

Since Frank's debut in 1968, Wolves had come a long way – as, indeed, had he. Even if the Scotland team manager did not see it as such, Frank had clearly established himself as one of the best centre-halves in the Football League. And he was part of a side who had had a hectic but enjoyable few years, highlighted by the winning of the League Cup, and with many more highs on the way. It had really started in 1971, when we finished fourth in the League and won the Texaco Cup. Just winning something gave the whole side a sense of well-being and belief. This fillip led to better things. Reaching the final of the UEFA Cup the following season was a magnificent achievement when you consider we were travelling into the unknown, with only Frank having tasted European competition previously. Then came two semi-finals in one season and finally winning the major trophy I believe we deserved – the League Cup. It had been a great four or five years for the players and the fans and Frank had played a major role in our success. With a little bit of luck, we might have had more to show for our efforts but I think most fans I speak to rate that team as the best at Molineux since the great Stan Cullis era. After all, it was full of some legends like Derek Parkin, Mike Bailey, Derek Dougan, John Richards, Kenny Hibbitt and Frank. Modesty prevents me from putting myself in that company, although I was inducted into the club's Hall of Fame in 2013, so somebody must have rated me!

After the glory of Wembley '74, things were to take a turn for the worse. You could call it a case of after the Lord Mayor's Show. The next season proved an anti-climax and, even before it began, Frank made headlines. He said he wanted to go on the transfer list, feeling the new deal offered him was not good enough. How serious he was, I do not know but he put his request in writing, only to get short shrift from McGarry. The manager told the Express & Star: "It will be put before the board at their next meeting. My recommendation will be to turn it down." I am sure that if the directors had agreed to Frank's request, there would have been no shortage of top clubs after his signature. All was finally settled the day before the new season, the Express & Star reporting: "The former Scottish international has settled his differences with Wolves and signed a new contract. At the same time, the board has turned down his written transfer request. Munro asked for a move during the close season and, with his contract concluded, was in dispute over terms. McGarry said the dispute between player and club had been resolved amicably." In other words, Frank got himself an improved deal.

When the season got under way, we got knocked out at the first hurdle in all the cups – Fulham in the Football League Cup, Ipswich in the FA Cup and Porto in the UEFA Cup. We were beaten 4-1 in Portugal and did our best to turn it round but a 3-1 win at Molineux was not enough. Willie Carr was signed from Coventry and made a memorable debut as we beat Chelsea 7-1 but, despite a 12th-place finish, the cracks were beginning to show. We no longer had the dependable Jim McCalliog, who had for some reason fallen out with McGarry – well, that was not difficult, was it? Jim briefly joined Manchester United before moving to Southampton, with whom he would gain an FA Cup winner's medal against United in 1976. Yes, the old guard were moving on as The Doog played in only six League games (three as sub) and I played just 13. The defence were still the same established one that Wolves fans could reel off like a mantra: Parkes, Palmer,

Parkin, Bailey, Munro, McAlle. Gary Pierce did share the goalkeeping duties with Lofty, however. A feature of the season was that Kenny Hibbitt, rather than John Richards, was our top League scorer. Ken hit 17, helped by no fewer than nine from the penalty spot. John collected 13.

It was clear McGarry was desperate to find a successful partner for John and the solution was there all the time. Unfortunately, he could not see it. Had he persevered with Peter Withe, what a partnership that would have been! McGarry gave Peter only nine starts that season and only four of them were with JR. For the rest of the time, it was usually Steve Kindon up front and occasionally Alan Sunderland. At the end of the season, Peter went to Portland Timbers and McGarry sold him to Birmingham before the start of 1975-76. Some may have thought his chance of making a real impact in English football had gone. Little did they know.

As I said, we finished a respectable 12th despite all the upheavals and Frank had another excellent campaign with 35 League appearances. He was still at the height of his powers and it was no more than he deserved when he at last got a recall to the Scotland side. I still cannot believe he was ignored so often. Jim Holton was still first choice in the centre of their defence, playing alongside his United team-mate Buchan, but broke his leg against Sheffield Wednesday in December, 1974. That eventually paved the way for a recall for Frank to international duty, although Gordon McQueen and former Aberdeen man Buchan were at first the favoured central defenders along with Kenny Burns of Birmingham. However, the fifth cap of Frank's career came when Willie Ormond decided to draft him in as a late replacement for a friendly against Sweden at the Ullevi Stadium in Gothenburg in April, 1975, after Buchan withdrew because of a thigh injury. With Colin Jackson of Rangers making his debut alongside Frank, a goal four minutes from time from Ted MacDougall, another debutant, earned the Scots a 1-1 draw. Malmo's Thomas Sjoberg had put the Swedes ahead just before half-time and an error from Frank, whose intended header back to his keeper Stewart Kennedy lacked power, might have brought another goal had Mattson not dragged his shot wide. In a team including Kenny Dalglish, Graeme Souness and Lou Macari, Frank soon put that behind him and acquitted himself well. Respected Glasgow Herald correspondent Ian Archer reported: "Jackson and Munro were firm and capable defenders."

Not that the Scotland match got much attention south of the border. The same night, England beat Cyprus 5-0 in a European Championship qualifying match at Wembley, with Malcolm Macdonald scoring all five goals. That set the anoraks searching the record books for the last time an England player had scored that many in a full international – a search that unearthed the name of Tottenham's Willie Hall, who had done it against Ireland at Old Trafford in 1938. Buchan and McQueen were the central defensive pairing a month later for another friendly when Portugal were beaten 1-0 at Hampden, where Derby's Bruce Rioch won his first cap. But Frank was in the squad for the British championship, which began four days later. He was still not first choice, though, with Colin Jackson playing alongside McQueen. First up was a trip down to Ninian Park, where Wales took a two-goal lead after 36 minutes thanks to John Toshack and Brian Flynn. Jackson and Rioch then scored in the space of seven minutes in the second half but Jackson had to go off 13 minutes from time and Frank went on to collect his sixth cap. The Scots held out for a 2-2 draw.

Three days later, Frank was in the starting line-up as Jackson's deputy and he and McQueen ensured the Northern Ireland strikers got little scope on a warm night at Hampden as Scotland won 3-0 with goals by MacDougall, Dalglish and Derek Parlane. It was an encouraging display and had a crowd of 64,696 chanting "Bring on the English!" Glasgow Herald man Ian Archer said: "McQueen was blond and steady, Munro swarthy and uncompromising." That win set things up perfectly for what was, in Scottish eyes anyway, THE game of the season – the annual clash with England. It was no surprise when Frank kept his place in the team for Wembley. Under Don Revie, England had not had a sparkling season and had drawn their Championship games with Wales and the Irish. So Scotland needed only a draw to become champions. The Scottish fans headed south full of optimism and Frank was in a side who fancied their chances. Bookmakers William Hill reported they had taken a bet of £2,000 at odds of 3/1 on a Scotland victory. The optimism lasted barely seven minutes, though, by which time Gerry Francis and Kevin Beattie had put England two up. Those who reckoned at that time that Scottish keepers were not up to much got more evidence as Stewart Kennedy of Rangers, impressive against Northern Ireland, was at fault with both goals. A third from Colin Bell was answered by a Rioch penalty but Francis and David Johnson struck in the second half, so it was 5-1 to England and a day to forget for Frank. For the record, the teams on Saturday, May 24, 1975, both lining up 4-4-2, were:

England: Clemence; Whitworth, Watson, Todd, Beattie; Bell, Ball, Francis, Keegan (Thomas 85); Channon, Johnson. Scotland: Kennedy; Jardine, Munro, McQueen, McGrain; Rioch, Dalglish, Conn, Duncan (Hutchison 61); Parlane, MacDougall (Macari 71).

Surprisingly, Kennedy was set to keep his place for Scotland's last game of the season, in Romania in a European Championship qualifier. But he injured an ankle in training, missed the game and was never chosen for his country again. Sheffield United's Jim Brown was given his first cap while, in front of a 52,000 crowd at the Stadionul National, Frank kept his place to win his ninth and final cap. Leeds had lost to Bayern Munich in the European Cup final in midweek and Billy Bremner and Joe Jordan were supposed to link up with the Scotland squad for the vital qualifier. To the anger of Willie Ormond and the Scottish officials, the pair did not get in touch to tell them they were injured and would not be arriving. Said Ormond: "I was looking for Billy to organise the game in midfield and for the mobility of Joe up front. Their absence is a big blow."

Scotland trailed from the 22nd minute to a Dudu Georgescu goal but Frank's central defensive partner McQueen popped up to grab an equaliser in the last minute. The Scots felt they should have been awarded a goal ten minutes before the break when a Parlane shot went in via Macari's knee. However, the referee's verdict was that the ball had gone into the net via Macari's hand. Ormond was adamant that it was a perfectly legitimate goal. After the debacle of Wembley, the Scots, with Aberdeen's 20-year-old Willie Miller making his debut, had bounced back in style in a game played on one of the hottest days of the year. Brown, despite his competent debut, was never chosen again. Speculation was rife that Ormond would lose his job but he stayed in charge for another two years.

So ended the international career of Francis Munro. Many players never win one cap, so he was rightly proud to have amassed nine, yet I am not alone in believing his country should have made better use of his talents. In his prime, I believe he was in the Bobby Moore class. He was definitely in the same mould with great command, great skill and great ability to read the game. In the first Scotland international of the following season, there was a certain irony in the fact that Frank's place went to Buchan, the player who had to make way for him when he joined Aberdeen. Buchan won his 19th cap, on the way to a final total of 34, when he played in the 1-0 win over Denmark in Copenhagen.

Chapter Thirteen

Promotion Skipper

With three defeats and three draws in the opening six League games, the writing was on the wall for us from the very start of 1975-76. Of the first 15 matches, we won just two in collecting a mere eight points from 30. One of those wins was 5-1 at home to Sheffield United and they managed only four points from their opening 15 fixtures. No wonder they were bottom, with Wolves immediately above them. The first League win of our season came against Birmingham at Molineux just after we had come from two down in the League Cup second-round tie at Swindon to earn a replay. Yet Frank did his best to miss the Blues game as only he could. Apparently, he had just finished shaving when he rushed downstairs, still in the process of getting dressed, to watch the football preview programme, On The Ball, on TV. "I fell downstairs," recalled Frank. "My knee swelled up badly and when I got in (to Molineux), I told McGarry I could hardly walk. My knee was killing me but he said 'If you can walk, you can play.' They found some tape and strapped it up and I had an even bigger bandage put on at half-time." Peter Withe was leading the Blues attack by then but Frank kept him quiet, although it was a painful 90 minutes.

It was a real bottom-of the table clash, which is probably why McGarry insisted on Frank playing. Even worse than us, Blues had lost four and drawn two of their first six games. We won 2-0 thanks to two rare goals from Willie Carr after Kenny Hibbitt had blasted a first-half penalty high into the South Bank. Frank, not surprisingly, was unable to play when we beat Swindon in the League Cup replay three days later. We did manage to win successive games to take ourselves briefly out of the relegation zone and the second of those, 5-1 at Burnley, saw Frank play a part in a bit of club history. Steve Daley and John Richards kicked off and the ball was played back to Frank. He passed to Steve Kindon, who sent John Farley away on the left. When the winger's cross came in, Burnley keeper Alan Stephenson could not hold it and Richards was there to put home the rebound. The goal came 15 seconds after kick-off and is believed to be the fastest goal in Wolves history.

After a goalless home draw with Derby, we were soon back in trouble as we lost five in a row, one of which saw Frank taking issue with Tommy Docherty, who had been a such an understanding boss when their paths crossed at Chelsea. Now The Doc was in charge of Manchester United and we lost 1-0 to them at Old Trafford just before Christmas. Booked in the first half, John McAlle was sent off in the second but there were allegations afterwards that Docherty had influenced the dismissal. John claimed that as they left the field at half-time, the United boss told him he was going to tell their striker Stuart Pearson to provoke him to get him sent off. John said The Doc also told him he would see the referee Kevin McNally about him. When John tackled Pearson in the second half, he claimed the United man made it look worse than it was and he duly got his marching orders. A report in a national newspaper quoted Frank as saying: "Docherty said he was going to get Pearson to provoke John and get him ordered off. Then he went after the referee. It's a terrible state of affairs. I have always thought Doc was great but I lost a lot of respect for him yesterday."

It could have got out of hand and The Doc, who denied saying anything to John or talking to the ref, at one stage threatened to report McAlle to the Football League for a possible charge of bringing the game into disrepute because of his allegations. However, within a couple of days, both clubs announced they would be taking the matter no further. McGarry did have a parting shot at Pearson, saying: "He went down like a dying swan and should get an Oscar for it."

I was not involved for most of the season and eventually went on loan to Blackburn, who I later joined permanently. That run of five defeats was what probably defined the Wolves season. We scored only one goal in that run – and that was a Kenny Hibbitt penalty in the 2-1 home defeat by Middlesbrough. Scoring goals was our big problem. Of 51 we managed that season, 19 came in four games, so we managed just 32 from the other 38. A rare highlight of the campaign was an FA Cup run which had Frank and the rest briefly dreaming of a Wembley return. I got a recall from my Blackburn loan spell to face Charlton in the fifth round and it was my injury which enabled John Richards to create FA Cup history. He went on and scored all the goals in our 3-0 win, which made him the first sub to hit an FA Cup hat-trick. Visions of Wembley became stronger when, without me, the team drew 1-1 at Manchester United in the quarter-final and raced into a 2-0 lead in the replay. Alas, United turned it round to win 3-2 in extra-time.

From what I could gather from Frank about the Molineux time I missed, it seemed McGarry was panicking when it came to who should partner John Richards. He tried Steve Kindon, Alan Sunderland, Norman Bell and finally brought Bobby Gould back. None of the pairings was the success he had hoped for. Indeed, the team as a whole were not a success. When they managed to beat Newcastle 5-0 at home, thanks to John's hat-trick, they lifted themselves out of the relegation zone with four games to play. Crucially, they then lost at Arsenal three days later. Frank and the rest of our defence were caught out 20 minutes from time when veteran centre-half Terry Mancini chose that night to score his first and only League goal for the Gunners to give them a 2-1 win. It was hardly a happy League debut for Martin Patching. A 3-1 defeat at Coventry followed before a home win over Norwich gave a glimmer of hope. It all came down to winning the last game of the season and hoping Birmingham would lose at Sheffield United. Only trouble was the visitors to Molineux were Bill Shankly's Liverpool, for whom a victory would see them pip QPR for the title.

With John Toshack and Kevin Keegan forming a legendary strike partnership, Wolves needed their top-class centre-half pairing to curb them. Sadly, both John McAlle and Frank missed the vital game. A sore knee had kept Frank out against Norwich and John damaged knee ligaments in that game. He did some training on the Monday but did not make it and Frank was also doubtful – more than that, he was an almost certain non-starter. He said: "I was having a cartilage out the next morning. My knee was three times the size it should have been. I could hardly walk. McGarry asked me to play and I fell out with him. I actually grabbed him." Frank was bitterly disappointed. A niggling injury was getting worse and now he was to miss the decider. He was idling away his time on match-day morning, watching the lads loosen up and doing a few sprints, when Sammy Chung surprised him by telling him the boss wanted a word. Limping along the corridor, he wondered what McGarry wanted. As soon as he got in, he realised and was furious. "Couldn't you just play tonight, before you have the op?" asked the manager. It was obvious McGarry was thinking of himself and not Frank's career. Frank was amazed and angry McGarry had the audacity to ask him. In a rush of blood, he grabbed him by the lapels of his jacket and forced him back against a filing cabinet. "Don't you ever ask me to risk my career for your own ends," he said and, with that, he pushed McGarry away and stormed out.

Once he had calmed down, Frank could not believe what he had just done and what the consequences might be but he need not have worried on that score. Wolves lost 3-1 to Liverpool, despite Steve Kindon giving them a half-time lead. As it turned out, even a victory would not have saved us as Birmingham, a goal down at Sheffield United at the break, managed a 1-1 draw. The Blues equaliser was scored, ironically, by Kenny Hibbitt's brother, Terry. Although worried about losing his temper and man-handling the manager, Frank nevertheless felt it was worth it, whatever the consequences. It was something he had wanted to do for years. He was not a violent man by any means, although he had his moments, and all that pent-up frustration had to give one day. What would be the outcome?

McGarry felt he was the manager to get us back into the top flight and must have told the board that. Steve Gordos, who helped with a large part of this book, was a sub-editor on the Express & Star sports desk at the time and remembered the paper carrying a story about McGarry wanting to stay. Steve actually wrote the headline, which ran something like: "McGarry plea: Give me Second chance." When McGarry saw it, he blew his top and rang the sports editor to complain. He was angry because he said the headline made it sound as though he was down on his knees, pleading. Even if he was not begging, he was certainly hoping to carry on. So there were a few days of worry for Frank. He wondered what action McGarry might take against him if he remained. Frank need not have fretted, though, as McGarry would soon be master of Molineux no more. However, it was 11 days after the Liverpool game before the board decided the boss had to go.

Frank was relieved that his altercation in the manager's office had been followed by McGarry's departure. If he had stayed, the manager would no doubt have come down like a ton of bricks on him. As it turned out, those words Frank spoke angrily in the office under the stand in Waterloo Road were the last he ever uttered to McGarry. A lot of teams claim they were too good to go down but, in our case, we all felt it was true. We should not have been relegated and getting us back at the first attempt would be a fairly easy task.

There was another casualty of the club's relegation but one that did not go down well with the players. Chairman John Ireland had brought McGarry to the club and did not want him to be fired. He was a lone voice on the board and the outcome was that, after 22 years as a director, 12 of them in the chair, he quit the board. Harry Marshall, the club's 45-year-old chief shareholder, took his place and John agreed to become president. His comment to the press was: "In the right way, presidency of the club would be a great honour. In the circumstances, I fear it is a means of getting rid of me. Everything has been done with unseemly haste. The present team, with two new players, is capable of a quick return to the First Division. It's a good side." Marshall countered: "It was obvious changes had to be made and we've made them." Well, John Ireland was just about spot on with his view – except they did not need even a couple of signings in order to get straight back. The squad were more than capable of achieving that task.

What of the future for Frank and for managerless Wolverhampton Wanderers?

His operation and convalescence would sideline him at least to July. But would the new manager want him? It worried him slightly but everyone who knew him was sure that a place in the team would be found for him. He was too good a player for Second Division football. One thing was certain, whoever the new man might be.......Frank was free from the shackles of Bill McGarry.

There was briefly talk that our old pal The Doog might come back as boss. He was by then chief executive at Kettering Town. He would have been up for it but the board must have thought better of it, as he was still finding his feet on the administrative side. Former Albion boss Don Howe was said to be a front-runner before a decision was finally announced on June 19, 1976. After several interviews and much to-ing and fro-ing, the new manager was none other than Sammy Chung, who for so many years had been McGarry's assistant. Chairman Marshall said they had received 70 applications and added: "We were overwhelmed but the man we wanted was right here on our doorstep. Sammy is a players' man – he has their confidence. We have always been impressed with his ability and believe he will make a great manager." Sammy, whose contract was said to be worth £16,000 a year, had been in Sweden when he received a call to get back to attend a board meeting to be told he was the chosen one. He likened his appointment to that of Bob Paisley following in the footsteps of Bill Shankly at Liverpool: "I have to live down the name of a well-known manager. Bob couldn't be a Shankly and I can't be a McGarry. Like Bob, I shall try to do it quietly and efficiently."

During the close season, Frank had the operation on a knee he had suffered with for many years. He knew Sammy well, having been with him roughly seven years and was used to his training sessions. By the same token, Sammy was used to the ways and whims of all the lads in his charge. Unlike Bill McGarry, you were able to put your side of the story to Sammy and he would listen. He might not agree but he would hear you out and discuss the problems. Frank's recovery was slow – he missed the pre-season tour to Sweden – and Sammy was not happy. On the eve of the opening Second Division game, against Burnley, he explained to the press that Frank's cartilage operation was taking a lot longer to mend than at first thought, so he played him in the reserves at Manchester City. Mike Bailey, who had been tried at centre-half on the tour, was played there alongside John McAlle and the side made a steady start. They lost only one of their first eight League games and conceded a mere six goals.

Recovery was a painful process for Frank and he had to work particularly hard to make sure he got back to full fitness. By the time he reached that point, the Bailey-McAlle partnership could not be disrupted as far as Chung was concerned and relations between Frank and the new boss were not the best. Frank felt he was in danger of becoming sidelined and he wanted first-team football. A couple of days after a 6-1 victory at Hereford, the manager told the Express & Star that Frank was not for sale but was available on loan. "He has not asked for a transfer and I have not put him on the list," he said. "I have never wanted him to leave us. The trouble all boils down to the fact that he hates playing in the reserves." Chung confirmed he had received many letters from supporters who were unhappy at the thought of Frank leaving Molineux and added: "He came to see me last week to ask if he could get away for a month to play. I agreed because I want to help him at a difficult time. I can't put him in our team because of our great start to the season."

That's when it was reported that Hereford, managed by ex-Chelsea defender John Sillett, were going to sign Frank. A headline in the Daily Mirror of Tuesday October 5, 1976, announced "Hereford sign Munro on loan" and the attached report said: "Hereford have agreed to pay Wolves £40,000 for Frank Munro, their Scottish international centre-half. Munro joins Hereford today on a month's loan and the deal – double their previous record buy – will go through at the end of it." That, so it seemed, was that. Frank's Molineux career was virtually over. It may well have been, too, had it not been for what happened later that evening when Southampton came to town. It's amazing how words can come back to haunt you and the great start Sammy had spoken of came to an abrupt end only three days after the slaughter at Edgar Street as Southampton triumphed 6-2, with our old pal Jim McCalliog among their scorers. The following day's Express & Star carried the headline: "Frank Munro to stay with Wolves". The paper revealed that Sillett had been unsuccessful in trying to get him, although it confirmed Frank had talked to him in the hope that, if he proved his fitness, he would sign for the Bulls permanently.

That Southampton drubbing changed everything and Chung realised he needed the big man at the heart of his defence. To make matters worse, if Wolves had won, they would have gone top of the table as leaders Chelsea lost 2-1 at Bristol Rovers the same night. Frank definitely did not want to leave Wolves and told Daily Mirror man Dave Horridge: "I was due to have final talks with Hereford after the Southampton game. Then the boss told me I was wanted here. That was the best news I have had in months." You may like to know Southampton had recorded their first League win of the season only three days before visiting Molineux. They beat Fulham 4-1 at The Dell and the Londoners had George Best sent off after 67 minutes for 'foul and abusive language.' It was the first day refs

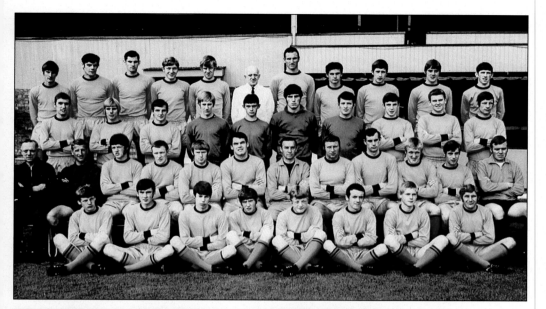

Top: One of the earliest Wolves team pictures Frank Munro was seen on. He is one in from the left on the back row at a time in the late 1960s when the club still wore all gold. The same attire was sported when he demonstrated his ball skills for the camera but black shorts made a popular return (left) in 1969.

Frank, help! There's unease in Wolves' defence as keeper John Oldfield and Spurs' Alan Mullery go tumbling at Molineux. Derek Parkin, a half-hidden John Holsgrove and Les Wilson are the members of the back four closest to hand in this sticky situation, with Munro out of view.

Another Wolves team group, this time with Frank standing between keepers John Oldfield and Phil Parkes. The side were about to click in a big way by reaching the final of the UEFA Cup as well as the last four of the main two domestic cups, all in the space of 12 months. Frank would no doubt have approved of this picture......Bill McGarry isn't on it!

Munro looks on approvingly as Phil Parkes demonstrates the safest of hands to frustrate Newcastle striker Malcolm Macdonald during an early-season meeting at St James' Park. The two Wolves men had a good understanding, although Frank was known to pull the occasional stunt by ducking under the ball. They also remained close friends right to the end.

Above: Frank and Billy Bremner see to the pre-match formalities at the Leeds v Wolves meeting in August, 1971, in the unusual setting of Leeds Road, Huddersfield. The game, which produced a 0-0 draw, was switched as a result of crowd trouble at Elland Road a few months earlier. The two clubs contested an epic Molineux battle at the end of 1971-72, with the Leeds captain as the central figure. Right: Mike Bailey is hoisted aloft by youngsters Barry Powell and Alan Sunderland after the 1974 League Cup triumph at Wembley. Frank is the odd man out in a photo also featuring Geoff Palmer and Gary Pierce - the centre-half's decision to wear Denis Law's Manchester City shirt ensures that.

Three contrasting images from different stages of a tremendous career.......above: Frank hurtles into a challenge in the last of his 371 League and cup appearances for Wolverhampton Wanderers. We didn't know it was his farewell at the time but it was a happy occasion, with a Wolves side already crowned champions winning 1-0 at Burnden Park against a Bolton team who consequently missed out on promotion to Brian Clough's Nottingham Forest. Left: Frank (background) walks out for the 1967 Scottish Cup final as an Aberdeen player. A decade or so later, he was in the colours of Celtic and facing the men from Pittodrie more than once. The skippers in this photo are Harry Melrose and Billy McNeill. Below: The spotlight has switched to Australia, with Frank fourth along from the left on the back row on this South Melbourne team photograph. Immediately to the left of him is Alun Evans while another former Wolves man, Bertie Lutton, is standing on the right-hand end of the back row.

An afternoon out at Molineux.......a major highlight for Frank following his return from Down Under. Left: With his partner from later years, Naomi Hackner, as they arrive at the funeral of Derek Dougan in 2007. Below: With old Molineux favourite Peter Knowles at the game at Willenhall Town's Noose Lane ground that was held in 1994 as an important money-raiser for Frank at his time of great need.

The saddest of days..... Dave Wagstaffe, John Richards and Mike Bailey, watched by Phil Parkes, gather in August, 2009, for Frank's funeral. Such was his great popularity that even little-seen former Wolves favourites like Jim McCalliog and Danny Hegan made the effort to be among the large congregation. Waggy was a coffin bearer and found a smile as he met up afterwards with Margaret to reflect on the many happier times. All guests at the wake received a token inviting them to raise a glass to the much-loved subject of this book.

HAVE A DRINK
ON
FRANK

A last pictorial reminder of the man he was........a well-tanned Frank in Melbourne in 1979 with Sammy Wright, who he described as one of the best young prospects he had ever seen at Wolves. Below: Grant (left) and Stuart with their mother Margaret after the ashes interment at Molineux in August, 2013, with the family album open at an appropriate page.

had used cards in the Football League but George did not have the honour – if that's the word – of getting the first red one. That bit of history fell to yours truly. It took only 36 minutes for me to see red playing for Blackburn against Leyton Orient at Brisbane Road. I got my historic card for arguing but we had the last laugh. Bobby Svarc scored the only goal of the game 13 minutes from the end. Maybe my dismissal would have attracted more attention had George not also gone. He was always huge news, so all the attention was focused on him. I would like to think I will be remembered for what football skills I may have possessed but no doubt the only place in football history for David Wagstaffe will be as the first man to receive a red card in English football!

After the Southampton defeat, there was an 11-day gap until the next League game and Frank was back in the team during the blank weekend for a friendly at Bristol City, where he looked good in a goalless draw. He was then given his first League outing of the season at Hull, Mike Bailey being sidelined by a hamstring injury. A former antiques dealer by the name of John Hawley, who had signed professional forms only in August, stole the headlines at Boothferry Park, scoring the goals that gave Hull a 2-0 win. Despite this, Frank had a satisfactory game and subsequent displays meant he was clearly back to stay. After that, Wolves lost only two of 25 League games as he not only took over Mike's position in defence but also the captaincy. Sammy obviously had to forget any opinions he might have about Frank the man because his team needed Frank the player. Mike, then nearing 35, made one more appearance as sub and one more start before ending an illustrious Wolves career. He was recognised as the club's best skipper since Billy Wright and, in my opinion, is somebody they have never been able to replace to this day.

In his third game back in the team, Frank scored what would prove to be his last goal for Wolves. It came at Blackpool on October 30, 1976, in a 2-2 draw that was marred by the actions of a few mindless Wolves fans. Kenny Hibbitt had given us (I'll use that term, although I was no longer involved) a third-minute lead, only for Derek Spence to prod home a free-kick within two minutes, the ball going in via Steve Kindon's head. Paul Hart headed in from another free-kick to make it 2-1 to Blackpool just after the half hour, then it started. Early in the second half, home keeper George Wood was pelted with stones and coins from behind his goal. The referee took the players off for nearly ten minutes and an announcement was made that the game would be abandoned if the trouble continued. Fortunately, there were was no further bother and Frank grabbed the equaliser on 68 minutes. He was unmarked at the far post to head Kenny's corner powerfully home. It was a vital point as it kept us hot on the heels of Blackpool, who were second at the time. The crowd trouble resulted in 20 arrests and ten fans had to go to hospital for treatment.

Maybe Frank's display made Sammy realise he was vital to the team despite any differences which had developed between them. Certainly, Express & Star reporter John Dee had no doubts about the effect the big man had had on the side. He wrote: "Munro had an outstanding game alongside John McAlle. Lack of concentration did bring a couple of bad passes from him but the rest of his performance was full of the poise and polish he has shown over the years. The return of the Scot to the back four has made such a difference." The successful run with Frank at the heart of the defence set down a firm base for a return to the First Division, which Wolves duly achieved as champions ahead of Chelsea. Having been omitted for the first nine games of the season, Frank started all the remaining 33 as he skippered the team back to the big time. Despite the success, only one Wolves player, John Richards, was named in the PFA Second Division team of the year. Mind you, the voting was done with a third of the season still to go. Chelsea had three men in it.

Although Wolves were doing well and looking a decent bet for promotion, it did not really change things – Frank and Sammy still did not see eye to eye. It was different when Sammy was the coach under Bill McGarry; he was approachable and only too happy to try to help sort out any problem. However, it seems that, when coaches become managers, their attitudes alter over time. Sammy was a likeable chap but it was perhaps inevitable he would change once he became manager and set about stamping his personality on to the job.

The year of 1977 was a momentous one for Wolves – it was their centenary. Frank, the other players and a host of former favourites were at the celebration banquet at the Park Hall Hotel in Wolverhampton at the end of January for a special night that was a chance to forget on-pitch matters briefly. It was around then that Mike Bailey, for so long Wolves' inspirational skipper, said farewell to Molineux, former Blues boss Freddie Goodwin having signed him for Minnesota Kicks. Next day, Frank was formally appointed first-team skipper while John Richards was named club captain. Mike would have liked a painless exit but it was not to be. During his final training session, someone accidentally stepped back on his foot and broke a bone in it. I had better not say who the culprit was but, suffice it to say, he was the heaviest man on our books and was often known as 'The Tank.' He was also the same player who KO'd The Doog before that FA Cup-tie with Coventry.

PROMOTION SKIPPER

Wolves had beaten Rotherham in the third round of the FA Cup and the first game after the centenary dinner was in round four – a 2-2 draw at Ipswich, where many thought Wolves had been denied a goal as a John Richards shot seemed to drop over line. It was a view backed up by television replays, so even then there was a case for goal-line technology. Frank was hurt at Portman Road and failed to appear for the second half because of a stomach injury. He had to miss the replay, in which Colin Brazier deputised in a 1-0 win. It was the promotion push, not the Cup, that really mattered and Frank was fit to lead the side to three wins and a draw in four February games as the momentum increased. A 1-0 fifth-round Cup win over Chester meant a quarter-final against Leeds who, almost inevitably, won by the game's only goal before nearly 50,000 at Molineux. That defeat came in a run of four successive League wins which helped ease Frank's disappointment at missing out on yet another semi-final in a cup competition.

Being skipper made Frank a proud man, the team clinching promotion with a 0-0 draw against Plymouth in front of 16,000-plus fans at Home Park. Frank led the players into the directors' box afterwards to salute the 4,000 Wolves supporters who had made the long trip. They did not know it but they had just witnessed the last act in a famous partnership – Frank's fellow central defender John McAlle had limped off to be replaced by Kenny Todd and would miss the last three games of the season. Munro and McAlle, it would turn out, had played their final match together. When people recall that very useful Wolves side of the 1970s, the pairing that is usually mentioned first is the Dougan-Richards strike partnership, yet it can be argued the Munro-McAlle duo in the middle of our defence was just as much a factor. What is often overlooked is that Frank and Scouse were together for seven seasons while Doog and JR's partnership lasted only three.

The last home game of 1976-77 brought a 1-1 draw with Chelsea that suited both sides. It clinched the title for Wolves and ensured promotion for Chelsea, who had Tommy Langley to thank for giving them a half-time lead. Frank played his part in the equaliser. He thought he had scored when he fired in a shot after John Richards had flicked on a Kenny Hibbitt cross but Peter Bonetti managed to save with his foot. Richards was first to react, as he was so often, and fired home the loose ball. There were over 34,000 present, the best gate of the season, as proof that the fans had been gradually wooed back after the disappointment of relegation. Nine of the first ten home fixtures had seen crowds of under 20,000 but eight of the remaining 11 were above that milestone. The attendance for the Chelsea game could have been bigger but the club had decided to make it all-ticket in a bid to combat the hooligan element.

The final fixture of the season was also a huge occasion, with a massive crowd crammed into Burnden Park, where Bolton needed a win to keep alive their promotion hopes. They were fourth in the table, two points behind Nottingham Forest, with a significantly worse goal difference, no play-offs and the top three to go up. A season would not be allowed to end this way now but Forest had finished their programme and Bolton, who were managed by Ian Greaves, needed three points from their final two games to pip them. With two points for a win, they could not afford a defeat against Wolves or that was the end of the story. Wolves scored early through Kenny Hibbitt and then held out as the home side threw everything at them. A strapping defender named Sam Allardyce, then only 22, several times went close to scoring but even the efforts of Peter Reid in midfield and the old Manchester United winger Willie Morgan could not turn things round. Greaves reckoned the goal by Hibby was offside, adding colourfully: "If not, I'm a Japanese coalminer." The defeat meant Bolton could still equal Forest's points total if they won their last game, at Bristol Rovers, but the goal difference – this was the season it replaced goal average – was far too big to make up. In the event, they managed only a draw at Eastville, so this was the top of the table at the end of the season:

	P	W	D	L	F	A	GD	Pt
Wolves	42	22	13	7	84	45	39	57
Chelsea	42	21	13	8	73	53	20	55
Nottm Forest	42	21	10	11	77	43	34	52
Bolton	42	20	11	11	75	54	21	51

Recalling the match some years later, Frank said: "Bolton should have gone up and I felt sorry for Ian Greaves. We were already champions and went out for a stroll but then started to play a little bit. They had about six six-footers in the team but we kept them out. To be honest, they should have beaten us twice that season." So Wolves had, in effect, got Forest promoted and possibly changed the course of football history. The following season, Brian Clough's team took the First Division by storm to become champions and then won the European Cup two years running. Maybe they would still have reached those heights had they missed out on promotion in 1977 but who knows? What no-one could have known is that Frank had played his last competitive Wolves game. He had not even finished it as an injury at Bolton saw him replaced by Bobby Gould, who then, for the final few minutes, had to don the keeper's jersey when Gary Pierce was hurt. The match was a farewell trip for one of our best-loved behind-the-scenes characters – Sid Kipping, our coach driver. A lovely man, always immaculately dressed, he had driven the team all over the country for 20 years. Another feature of a successful season was that Wolves had four ever-presents. Gary, Geoff Palmer, Derek Parkin and Steve Daley each played in all 42 League games while Alan Sunderland missed only one, Kenny Hibbitt two and John McAlle three.

Chapter Fourteen

Back Home

I don't think Frank dreamed for one minute that he would never again kick a ball in English competitive football, but that proved to be the case. The knee ligament injury sustained at Bolton meant he could not go on Wolves' three-match end-of-season Norwegian tour and he was still not available for the final game of 1976-77 – the one at Molineux against Manchester City to mark the club's centenary. But he still made an appearance before kick-off to receive the Second Division championship trophy from Birmingham City director Jack Wiseman, a member of the Football League management committee. Few among the 15,000 who then watched Wolves lose 2-1 would have guessed Frank was taking a farewell bow as a Wolves player. Also saying goodbye that night – but knowingly – was Wolverhampton's Jack Taylor, the man who refereed the 1974 World Cup final between West Germany and the Netherlands. Jack, the third Englishman to take charge of a World Cup final, refereed the centenary game and fittingly had as linesmen two fellow Wolverhampton referee stalwarts in Alex Hamil and Terry Bosi.

There were few thoughts in Frank's head about quitting Wolves, as far as I was aware, and evidence of that came in an interview with him by Maltese sports journalist Alfred Camilleri, for many years the president of the Malta Wolves Supporters Club. He makes regular trips to see our games but was still a sports sub-editor on the Maltese newspaper I-orizzont in the summer of 1977 and spoke to Frank, who was holidaying on the island with his family. It is clear from what Frank said that he was looking forward to a season back in the top flight. He talks of relishing the challenge and having a testimonial match during 1977-78. Little did he know how things would suddenly and dramatically change. Significantly, Frank mentioned to Alfred that Sammy Chung had tried to sign centre-half David Needham from Notts County to play alongside him, yet I wonder whether the boss was in fact after Needham to replace Frank? Here is what Alfred wrote:

"Right now, on a two-week holiday in Malta is one of the two captains of Wolverhampton Wanderers, Scotsman Frank Munro. He came over with Exchange

Travel and is staying at Golden Sands Hotel in Ghajn Tuffieha. I say one of the two captains because Munro is the team captain while John Richards is the club captain after Mike Bailey was transferred to the American team, Minnesota Kicks. Frank is here with his wife Margaret and his two sons, ten-year-old Grant and Stuart, who is two years younger. The first thing I asked him was what he thinks of Wolves' chances in the new season after promotion to the First. Munro said that the coming season would be a challenging one to Wolves as they want to prove that they did not deserve to be relegated, which was the opinion of the critics and managers of the other teams. He said: 'We kept the same players, other new ones were drafted in, we moved forward and we hope that, if Lady Luck smiles on us, we will be able to finish among the top five next season. During the close season, the manager tried to buy David Needham but instead he signed for QPR. On the other hand, we have promising young players at Molineux like Colin Brazier and George Berry and they have already played in the first team.'

"The past season saw the centenary of the club while towards the end of the 1977-78 season Munro will be having a testimonial match for his ten years' service to the club. He thinks the past two years were the highlight of his career and it was his good fortune to be present for the big celebrations organised by the club to mark the centenary. I asked Munro about the change of manager and if this affected the players, who went on to win the Second Divison championship. Munro said that Bill McGarry was a disciplined person who did not forgive a mistake that quickly. His successor, Sammy Chung, is a tolerant person and this makes the players play with their minds more at rest, knowing that the mistakes they commit will be put right next time. Chung won the title of Manager of the Year for the Second Division – with a prize of £500 and a gallon of Bell's Scotch Whisky that goes with it – in his first year in the job.

"Regarding some Wolves supporters who criticise frequently, Munro said that they had lived in the successful era of Stan Cullis and Billy Wright, and when things were going bad, some would turn against us instead of encouraging us. On the other hand, he singled out the supporters who followed the team away from home as they stayed loyal in the good and bad times. Finally, I asked Munro if he felt that the ten years he spent with Wolves were happy ones for him. He said that without doubt he was happy in Wolverhampton. He recalled that the 6-2 defeat to Southampton had helped him and meant he was not loaned to Hereford United. He said that after he had an operation on his knee in the summer, it did not respond to treatment and he was going to be loaned to Hereford. However, Chung cancelled the loan that would have become permanent later on. Thus the

Southampton defeat was a blessing in disguise for him as, instead of the Third Division with Hereford, he won promotion to the First with Wolves."

These hardly appear to be the views of a player who saw his future away from Molineux. Alfred paints a picture of an optimistic man, looking forward to returning to the top flight of English football. If he had kept himself fully fit, Frank could surely have served Wolves for a few more seasons but the key word is 'if'. There was another factor, of course – he and Sammy did not get on. Despite this, you would assume that, after his performances in the promotion season, Frank would still be first choice for the no 5 shirt, even if the boss might have welcomed a reason not to pick him. As it turned out, Chung did not have to bite the bullet as Frank was not available for selection at the start of 1977-78, which happily saw Wolves back in the top flight. He played in a pre-season friendly at Brighton, then went down with a chest infection. It ruled him out of the opening League game and Derek Parkin was in central defence as the return to the First Division was marked with a 3-2 win at Bristol City. That was on August 20 and it was not until early September that Frank was fit enough for a few outings in the reserves, although his progress was hampered by a knee injury which sidelined him again.

When he had another reserve game towards the end of September, in a 1-1 draw with Coventry, the Express & Star reported that he had proved his fitness with an impressive display. This might have signalled a return to first-team action yet it proved quite the opposite. On Monday, October 3, the paper reported that Frank was up for sale. Alan Sunderland, Bobby Gould, Phil Parkes, Gary Pierce and John McAlle were also said to be available and Chung explained: "Parkes, Munro and Gould have not asked for transfers but I'm prepared to receive offers for them." It was perhaps no surprise that Parkes and Pierce were surplus to requirements as Chung had just splashed out £150,000 on Blackburn keeper Paul Bradshaw. Yet others were restless, too, as Steve Kindon put in a written request and winger John Farley was also added to the list. Kindon would soon return to his old club Burnley while Farley would move to Hull in the summer.

Inexperienced youngster Colin Brazier was now being selected in the centre of defence, so it was clear Frank, for whatever reason, was not wanted by Chung. On October 14 came news that he was going to Celtic on loan. About half-way through the season, Bob Hazell went into the Wolves team and he would prove a more than useful defender. However, Sammy was still taking a gamble by being prepared to let Frank go. How did manager and player fall out? I am not sure what went on but there was clearly no future at Wolves for Frank as long as Sammy was the manager. Many years later, Frank recalled: "We had a team meeting once and Willie (Carr) said we were playing off the cuff. I agreed with Willie and I probably went a bit too far. I told Sammy that he had been a yes man all his life. He had been a yes man to McGarry and now he was being a yes man to Marshall (Wolves' chairman) – and that was the end."

After agreeing the loan deal, Celtic boss Jock Stein said: "Frank's experience will be a tremendous help." Frank also made sure he said the right things. He told the Glasgow Herald reporter: "I have now achieved an ambition. I have always had leanings towards Celtic and, ever since coming into the professional game, this is the club I have wanted to play for." What a surprise awaited him! Regular skipper Danny McGrain was injured, so Stein made his loan signing captain for his first game, although Frank knew only a couple of players in the team. Celtic needed an experienced man as centre-half Pat Stanton had been injured in the opening League match of the season. It was an injury that was to prove the end of Stanton's career. By the time Frank arrived on loan, Celtic had won only two of their opening eight games and were lying eighth in what was then a Scottish Premier Division of only ten clubs.

Frank's Celtic debut was not one to remember. He scored an own goal as they lost 2-1 at Parkhead to St Mirren, then managed by an up-and-coming Alex Ferguson. There seemed little danger as Lex Richardson sent a through ball into the home penalty area but Frank, harried by Frank McGarvey, tried an overhead kick to clear and put the ball past his own keeper to give St Mirren the lead on 59 minutes. Tom McAdam equalised five minutes later when keeper Donald Hunter could not hang on to a Ronnie Glavin free-kick. Another five minutes on and Billy Stark restored the visitors' lead. He showed great close control as he danced past Frank and Johannes Edvaldsson before firing home from a couple of yards inside the penalty area. Celtic were under strength with both regular full-backs, McGrain and Andy Lynch, sidelined. That put extra weight on Frank's shoulders. The defeat meant the defending champions were bottom but one. 'What a start for Frank' was the headline on the Scottish Daily Express report, in which Gerald McNee noted that his errors had twice put his team in trouble before the opening goal. McNee revealed how Frank had been told he was skipper just before kick-off, adding: "The fairytale turned to nightmare for the 29-year-old Scottish internationalist." The reporter did say: "It would be quite wrong, however, to blame him for this defeat, Celtic's sixth in nine Premier League games. He at least had the excuse of playing in strange surroundings whereas most of the rest had no excuse at all."

The Glasgow Herald man Jim Reynolds reported that there was something of a gala occasion about the game, with European Cup legend Jimmy Johnstone there to acknowledge the fans, Alfie Conn fit after injury and new boy Frank making his debut. The report went on: "The stage was set for a fairytale but, for the Celtic fans, the show was on a par with a Shakespearean tragedy. Munro, undoubtedly a fine player, made a complete hash of his lines and set St Mirren on the winning trail." Looking back many years later, Frank remembered: "Jock Stein threw me the ball at five to three and said I was captain. He didn't introduce me to all the players. The only one I knew was the goalkeeper, Peter Latchford. I just called everybody else 'Jimmy'." With the passing of the years, he obviously regretted leaving Molineux and added: "I should have played two more years at Wolves." Here is how they lined up at Parkhead on Saturday, October 15, 1977:

Celtic: Latchford, Kay, Burns, Edvaldsson, MacDonald, Munro, Wilson, McAdam, Glavin, Aitken, Conn. Subs: Lennox, Casey. St Mirren: Hunter, Young, Beckett, Fitzpatrick, Reid, Copland, Abercrombie. Stark, McGarvey, Richardson, Docherty (Sharp 65). Sub: Dunlop.

The Glasgow Evening Times's football paper, Sports Times, that night proclaimed on its back page "Shocks galore for Munro, Celts" while, on the front, to make matters worse for Celtic fans, the banner headline was "Rangers go on a spree". The other half of the Old Firm had won 4-1 at Motherwell to close to a point the gap on leaders Aberdeen, who had been beaten 2-1 at home by Hibernian. After that unfortunate debut, when he was given quite a runaround by young McGarvey, there was a happier occasion for Frank a week later as he helped Celtic beat his old club Dundee United 2-1 at Tannadice despite going a goal behind after only two minutes. A Ronnie Glavin penalty put them level and Paul Wilson hit the winner 12 minutes from time. Frank, Andy Lynch and Tommy Burns were described in one match report as Celtic's top men. That win came three days after Celtic had beaten SWW Innsbruck 2-1 at home in the first leg of the European Cup second-round tie. Frank was not eligible for that game nor the return, which saw the Austrian club go through with a 3-0 victory. Jim Casey, a 20-year-old Glasgow lad, deputised for Frank as sweeper.

Four days after the Tannadice win came the second leg of the third-round Scottish League Cup clash with Stirling Albion. Frank was in a side held 1-1 at home but they went through 3-2 on aggregate, having won the first leg 2-1. It was a poor display and Celtic were grateful to be gifted an early lead through an own goal by John Kennedy. Trying to freshen things up, Jock Stein took Frank off at half-time, moved Roy Aitken into defence and sent on young Peter Mackie for his debut. However, Celtic failed to convert a succession of chances and were left hanging on for the final 12 minutes after Matt McPhee had grabbed an equaliser.

The next League game provided evidence that Frank might do all right at Parkhead. Celtic came from 2-1 down to win 3-2 at home to Ayr with the winner coming from a Roddie MacDonald header five minutes from time. Joe Filippi was in the Ayr side that day but signed for Celtic a few days later and made his debut in their next game as they staged another recovery, this time at Motherwell. Following a goalless first half, Celtic took the lead but were again trailing before fighting back to win 3-2, centre-half MacDonald again securing victory, this time with 12 minutes to spare. In the Glasgow Herald, Ian Paul reported: "For Celtic, no-one was better than Frank Munro." It was an optimistic note but a false one and, as the season wore on, Frank's form would deteriorate.

It was back to League Cup action and a chance for Frank to make amends against St Mirren, the team who had made his Parkhead debut so embarrassing. Celtic virtually sewed up the quarter-final clash by winning the first leg 3-1 at a rain-swept Love Street but the result flattered them somewhat as Peter Latchford made several fine saves. Joe Craig, who had scored twice at Motherwell, struck twice in the first half and Johannes Edvaldsson just after the break before Bobby Reid's goal gave St Mirren some hope. Although happy with the win, Frank was disappointed that an injury which led to him going off meant he would miss the next League game three days later – the big one, against table-topping Rangers at Parkhead. He had really been looking forward to it as it would have been quite a way to mark the end of his month-long loan. He had to watch, along with a 56,000 all-ticket crowd, as Celtic trailed to a goal by Derek Johnstone but levelled through Tom McAdam five minutes after the interval. Frank was not alone in thinking Celtic were denied a cast-iron penalty when Tom Forsyth sent Joe Craig sprawling. Jock Stein was not too happy, either, but then had to turn his attention to Frank. Three days after the Old Firm game, he secured another month's loan and, as Frank had recovered from his knock, he was able to play in the second leg of the League Cup quarter-final.

After a goalless first half, Celtic beat St Mirren 2-0 at a misty, rainy Parkhead thanks to Paul Wilson scoring one goal and then making another for Johnny Doyle. Alex Ferguson's young side, without their injured top scorer Frank McGarvey, posed few threats as Celtic coasted through 5-1 on aggregate. Suddenly, Frank was eyeing a Hampden Park cup final over a decade after playing at the famous venue for Aberdeen against Celtic in the last stage of the Scottish Cup. It all hinged on whether he made his loan move a permanent deal.

A home League win followed, Aberdeen being beaten 3-2 as Celtic continued a pattern in their recent League games of giving the opposition a goal start. The visitors led through Drew Jarvie on 16 minutes, Celtic equalised with an Andy Lynch penalty, went ahead with a 20-yard drive from Roy Aitken, then allowed Joe Harper to level before Tom McAdam won the match with 15 minutes to go. Watching Celtic had suddenly become a roller-coaster ride and Jim Reynolds in the Glasgow Daily Herald noted: "With Filippi, McAdam and Frank Munro all fitting in well, Stein's men are again playing with all the old familiar confidence."

On the eve of the Aberdeen game, Frank may have noted a snippet of news from south o' the border – Bill McGarry was back in Britain. After a stint as Saudi Arabia's director of coaching, he was appointed boss of bottom-of-the-table Newcastle. Not that far further north, Celtic were in good form and in just the right mood for their League Cup semi-final date with Hearts at Hampden but then the Scottish winter took a hand and temperatures plummeted. The last League game before the scheduled big night in Glasgow was against Clydebank at Kilbowie but the referee halted proceedings with the score 1-1 at half-time after the players had done their best to cope with a pitch like a skating rink. There was no let-up in the weather and both semi-finals were postponed, first Rangers v Forfar and then Celtic's game. They were put back to the New Year, so the only way Frank could again savour the atmosphere of a Hampden cup final was if he joined Celtic permanently – and that was still in the balance.

To end his loan stint, Frank helped Celtic beat Partick Thistle 3-0, new terrace hero Tom McAdam opening the scoring with a low 35-yard drive past Scotland keeper Alan Rough early on to set them on their way to ending an eight-match unbeaten League run which had taken the visitors into second place. It was an impressive way for Frank to sign off as Celtic cemented a spot in the top half of the table. But would he be coming back to continue to help the Hoops' revival? He had made quite an impact and Stein told pressmen he wanted him back on a permanent basis. Said the manager: "Frank was very impressive during his spell with us and I would certainly like to see him come back as a fully signed player." However, he said Frank was unable to make a decision because of domestic reasons. Stein did not go into details but the problem, I know, had a lot to do with Frank's desire to have a testimonial. I also believe he would have liked to continue playing for Wolves, as he had put down roots in Wolverhampton. Alas, it would not happen so long as Sammy Chung was in charge. In the edition of December 14, the Glasgow Evening Times quoted Stein's assistant Dave McParland: "We are just waiting to hear from Frank Munro and what his position is." A day later, the paper's back-page headline declared: "Munro – Celts' hopes nosedive." Jock Stein told the paper: "While he would like to join us, there are problems. However, we are still hopeful." The report added that Frank had proved a more than adequate replacement at sweeper for the injured Pat Stanton. Despite his optimism, Stein did not get Frank at that stage. It had the makings of a saga. One press report confirmed that the clubs had agreed a £20,000 fee and said that Frank, despite deciding against the move, remained on the transfer list.

So, rather than play for Celtic against St Mirren at Love Street, he appeared for Wolves reserves against West Brom on December 17. By coincidence, on the same day, Sammy gave 18-year-old Bob Hazell his debut at centre-half against Newcastle at St James' Park, where our old 'friend' McGarry had begun trying to revive Newcastle's fortunes. Chung came off second best against his old colleague as the Geordies won 4-0. Surely that was a game that called for a man like Frank, not a teenager? Incidentally, while McGarry had the bragging rights after the game, it was Chung who had the last laugh. After the win over Wolves, Newcastle won only one of their remaining 23 League games and our old boss tasted the drop from the top flight once again. Wolves also flirted with danger but won their final three games to move clear.

Less than a week after the Newcastle defeat, it was reported in the Express & Star that Wolves had made a record bid of £175,000 for Paul Hart, Blackpool's central defender. That clearly showed that Sammy knew he needed experience in his central defence. There was no possibility Frank would provide it as he was by then sidelined with a groin strain. Two days after Christmas, it became clear the move to Celtic was back on, Jock Stein telling the Evening Times he had spoken to Chung over the weekend and adding: "We have put a proposition to Wolves and we're expecting developments later this week." It was Friday, December 30, 1977, when Stein finally signed Frank. On the same day, Newcastle took a player in the opposite direction, a Morton striker by the name of Mark McGhee, for £150,000. A report in the Glasgow Herald reckoned that, for £20,000, Celtic thought they were getting a bargain in Frank. Wrote sports reporter Jim Reynolds: "The signing of Munro will come as a welcome relief to Parkhead fans, who have come to regard the big defender as something of a lucky mascot. In his two-month trial, he played nine matches and was on the losing side only once – his very first match, against St Mirren. Stein said yesterday: 'We are naturally delighted that Frank has joined us on a permanent basis. He has lots of experience and that is something we need at the back. The signing means we do not have to rush on a youngster.' Stein confirmed Munro will be in the side this afternoon." That match was against struggling Ayr and Celtic were beaten 2-1, which started a five-game losing sequence in the League. So much for Frank being the lucky mascot!

So what was behind the delay in completing the move? When Sammy called Frank in and told him Jock Stein wanted to sign him permanently, Frank had one or two things to weigh up before he made a decision. At first glance, it seemed like a dream move for him – back to his native Scotland and to a world-famous club. But Frank had to consider that he had spent more than nine years and 11 months at Molineux, as technically he was still a Wolves player while out on loan. He was just a week from qualifying for a testimonial awarded for ten years' service. Armed with this information, he went to see Sammy to confront him about his testimonial money if he went to Celtic. Sammy put Frank's mind at rest, telling him he need not worry. He would apparently get the testimonial game, although he had not quite completed ten years' service. That was good enough for Frank and he took Sammy's word for it that he would receive his special game. After 371 appearances for Wolves, six of them as a sub, surely Francis Michael Munro deserved that.

Anyway, he had played his last game for Wolverhampton Wanderers and, in the Express & Star, Sammy paid him a glowing tribute as well as trying to explain the decision to sell. "He has been a tremendous servant to us and I can't speak too highly of what he has done for Wolves in the ten years he has been here. My problem is I have three young defenders – Colin Brazier, Bob Hazell and George Berry – and I have to find ways to get them into the side. The parting of the ways has to come eventually and, now Frank is leaving us, he goes with the good wishes of everyone concerned." While these were fine words, Sammy's remark about his three young central defenders hardly rang true. If he really felt he had to blood the young players, why just a few days earlier had he tried to bring in some experience by signing Paul Hart? No doubt the fans could read between the lines.

So Frank became the legendary Stein's last signing for Celtic as a happy new chapter in the Munro career seemed to lie ahead. His future was settled, Stein offered to pay off his mortgage on the house he had in Compton and also give him a couple of thousand to sort out his removal fees and other costs. Sammy Chung had sanctioned his testimonial match. The icing on the cake, so it would seem, was that he was back home in Scotland, although he had settled in Wolverhampton and had much more of an affinity with the town than he did with Glasgow.

The middle game of those five successive League defeats after Frank's permanent signing for Celtic was an incident-packed affair against Rangers at Ibrox. Frank may have thought Scottish top-flight football far less intense than its English counterpart but he soon came to realise that any Old Firm clash was very,

very different. For passion, there are few fixtures like it anywhere in the world and there was no shortage of that commodity when the sides met on January 7, 1978. Celtic had begun well, only to go a goal down on 35 minutes when Gordon Smith fired past Peter Latchford. Two minutes later, Celtic were convinced they should have had a penalty as Colin Jackson appeared clearly to push Joe Craig in the back. Referee John Gordon said no and was immediately surrounded by nine Celtic players. As the protests continued, he allowed play to re-start and Rangers took a goal-kick which suddenly led to five blue shirts breaking clear with only two Celtic men to stop them. One was Latchford and the other, in glorious isolation, was Frank. John Greig ran almost 70 yards unopposed. The ball was switched to Davie Cooper and then Tommy McLean, who drew Latchford off his line before squaring to Bobby Russell. Frank desperately tried to block Russell's shot but it hit his heel and fell for Greig to score. Alan Herron in the Sunday Mail described it as 'one of the most astounding goals ever seen at Ibrox.'

From the Celtic end of the pitch came a shower of cans and bottles and their favourites declined to re-start the match, only doing so after Stein and trainer Neil Mochan had persuaded them they must carry on. Mochan had to go to the centre circle to remonstrate with his players. Celtic had another good penalty shout denied when a Roy Aitken shot seemed to be scooped away on the line by Alex MacDonald with his arm. They finally pulled a goal back through Johannes Edvaldsson and looked briefly as if they might salvage a point. However, three minutes from time, Latchford could not hold a Sandy Jardine shot and Derek Parlane made the final score 3-1. The Sunday Mail headline screamed "2 Minutes of Mayhem" but, despite the intensity of the match, only two players were booked – John Greig of Rangers and guess who of Celtic? To add insult to injury, referee Gordon was from Newport-on-Tay, near Frank's old stamping ground, Dundee.

In the Glasgow Herald, an article by Jim Reynolds carried the headline "Five Questions for Old Firm referee" and the reporter laid into the official in posing his quintet of queries. Reynolds asked: WHY was what looked like a legitimate penalty claim turned down in the first place? WHY did the referee give everyone the impression he was running towards the touchline to consult his linesman then change his mind when he saw Rangers breaking towards the Celtic goal? WHY did he allow the goal-kick to be taken with Celtic players still inside the penalty area? Rule 16 states: 'Players of the team opposing that of the player taking the goal-kick shall remain outside the penalty area whilst the kick is being taken.' WHY, if he was convinced he had made the right decisions, did the referee then not send off or even book the Celtic players who pushed and jostled him in the centre circle and refused to restart the game? WHY did he not caution Neil Mochan, who had no right to be on the field without permission?"

More League woe followed. At Pittodrie, against a second-placed Aberdeen side managed by Celtic legend Billy McNeill, Frank's old club edged home 2-1 thanks to two goals from former Clyde winger Dom Sullivan. It could have ended all square but Andy Lynch's penalty shaved a post 11 minutes from time. Celtic needed a win but had to wait three weeks for it as snow disrupted the season. To get some action, a friendly was arranged at Ayr and Frank figured in a 5-0 win which saw George McCluskey grab a hat-trick. Welcome relief to the losing run came courtesy of a Scottish Cup win over Dundee. There was no stopping the Celts in their third-round tie at Parkhead as they brushed aside the First Division outfit 7-1. It turned out to be a Monday night spree, although the score was a mere 2-1 at half-time. Then young McCluskey grabbed a hat-trick. It was almost three weeks before the severe weather relented and Celtic got more action, then it was a case of déjà vu as St Mirren went to Parkhead again to win 2-1, just as they had on Frank's debut day.

With harsh weather causing successive postponements, I can imagine Frank's frustration. He would have hated not being able to play. He knew how to enjoy himself when not playing but lived for football. Having no games would do him no favours. Putting aside the League slump, Celtic turned their attentions to winning a place in the Scottish League Cup final when they at last met Hearts in the game that should have taken place before Christmas. Hearts were beaten 2-0 at Hampden before a meagre crowd of 18,804 thanks to first-half goals from Joe Craig and George McCluskey. So Frank was indeed once more set for a Hampden showpiece. Celtic's opponents would be arch rivals Rangers, who had been given a mighty scare by minnows Forfar in their semi-final. The Division Two side led 2-1 with seven minutes to go but Rangers equalised to force extra-time and eventually won 5-2. On the same night, there was more frustration for Celtic and Frank. Holders of the Scottish Cup, they were held 1-1 at home in the fourth round of the competition by First Division Kilmarnock. It took a Roddie MacDonald goal six minutes from time to spare the Celtic blushes – all the more frustrating as the prize was a quarter-final at Rangers.

Three days after their semi-final success, Celtic got their first League win of 1978 – against Frank's old club Dundee United. The only goal came when home defender Davie Narey sent an intended back pass over his keeper's head. That was mid-way through the second half and, by then, Frank was off the field, having been injured just before half-time. Celtic were quickly brought down to earth again when Kilmarnock beat them 1-0 in the Scottish Cup replay at Rugby Park. Frank was ruled out through injury but returned in a 3-0 home win over Ayr a week before the League Cup showdown at Hampden. At least the gate for the final was over 60,000. Alas, there was no fairytale ending as Rangers, then managed by one-time West Brom keeper Jock Wallace, won 2-1 after extra-time. A cloud hung over the final as Rangers winger Bobby McKean had died thee days before it.

Celtic had the better of the first half but there was a costly slip near half-time when Ronnie Glavin tried to let the ball run out for a goal-kick, only for Gordon Smith to hook it back for Davie Cooper to fire home. Rangers looked like holding on but, late on, Johannes Edvaldsson, playing up front, headed in an Alan Sneddon cross. It then took a Latchford save to stop a McLean free-kick winning it for Rangers before the winner came controversially two minutes from the end of extra-time. Latchford could not hold Alex Miller's cross but seemed to have been impeded by Alex MacDonald. Smith put home the loose ball and the goal stood despite Celtic protests. Reaching the Scottish League Cup final was nothing unusual for them. Amazingly, this was their 14th successive final, although eight had ended in defeat. Teams in the final on Saturday, March 18, 1978:

Celtic: Latchford, Sneddon, Lynch (Wilson), Munro, MacDonald, Dowie, Glavin (Doyle), Edvaldsson, McCluskey, Aitken, Burns. Rangers: Kennedy, Jardine, Greig, Forsyth, Jackson, MacDonald, McLean, Hamilton (Miller), Johnstone, Smith, Cooper (Parlane).

Four days after the final, Frank played in a 2-1 defeat at Motherwell and that proved to be his last League start for Celtic. On a rainy night at Fir Park, Celtic led at the break but were then rocked by two goals from Peter Marinello, the winger who a few years earlier had failed to hit the heights with Arsenal after being transferred amid much publicity from Hibernian. A free-kick conceded by Frank for a foul on the winger was fired against the defensive wall by Marinello but the referee ordered a re-take. This time, Marinello blasted home and he beat three Celtic men on a solo run to strike again five minutes later. It had not been a good night for Celtic in general and Frank in particular. Clearly, he had not had the stabilising influence on the team Jock Stein had expected. To make matters worse, Rangers went on to win the League title and then beat Aberdeen in the Scottish Cup final to complete the Treble. After the Motherwell game, Frank was sidelined, suffering from a sore throat, and the team produced one of their best performances of the season in his absence. Fit or not, any chance of a speedy return for him looked remote as Celtic's next game saw them beat Rangers at Parkhead in the League to gain consolation for the League Cup final defeat and the controversial loss at Ibrox. There was no way Stein could make changes and, four days later, Celtic collected their biggest League win of the season when hitting four goals without reply at Partick, who had two men sent off to Celtic's one.

Suddenly, Frank was no longer a key figure and I can imagine him quickly becoming disillusioned. The more that happened, the more his commitment would weaken. It was Catch 22. He made his final Celtic appearance at Clydebank as a second-half substitute for the injured Roddie MacDonald and it was hardly an auspicious farewell as they lost 3-2 to the already-relegated home side. Frank was at fault for the winning goal four minutes from time. He was caught in two minds when the Clydebank keeper sent a long clearance downfield and Gerry Colgan nipped in to score. It was a bad defeat against a team who had won only once in 16 League games. It was also the only occasion Clydebank managed to score more than two in a League game that season. So it was goodbye to British football for Frank – before 9,000 fans on the narrow Kilbowie Park pitch; there could have been better send-offs.

On April 22, 1978, two weeks after the Clydebank game, Celtic beat Partick 5-2 at home and the Glasgow Herald match report made a brief passing reference to the possibility of Jock Stein giving Frank a free transfer. A week later, the paper's back page headline announced "Celtic give frees to five" and a lone paragraph confirmed that Frank could go, along with Roy Kay, Johnny Gibson, John Clifford and Willie Temperley. It was a far cry from the headlines that had accompanied Frank's arrival. In stark contrast, it was front page news a month later that Stein was stepping down as boss. As well as his five League Cup appearances, Frank also played twice for Celtic in the Scottish Cup. In all, he made 21 appearances for them but there it ended. He had secured a footnote in that great club's history by being the last signing made by the great Stein but the dream move had not worked out. Maybe if Frank had had a more dedicated approach, he could have made a go of it and could have found success. The very next season, with 1967 European Cup hero Billy McNeill as manager, Celtic became champions but Frank could only reflect on what might have been. Incidentally, McNeill's move to Parkhead paved the way for a step up the managerial ladder by Alex Ferguson, whose St Mirren team had ensured Frank had such an unhappy Celtic debut. Ferguson went from Love Street to Aberdeen and the rest, as they say, is history.

Frank's 15-year professional career on this side of the world was over. It had for the most part been a brilliant one, befitting a brilliant player. Those fans lucky enough to be at the 1974 League Cup final will have witnessed one of the finest centre-half displays ever to grace the Wembley turf. To keep Messrs Summerbee, Lee, Bell, Law and Marsh at bay was a feat in itself. Even some of the best strikers in Europe scored only ten goals in 12 games against Wolves in our fabulous UEFA Cup campaign of 1971-72. Frank always admitted that the two strikers who gave him most trouble were John Radford and Ray Kennedy, the Arsenal pair of the famous 1971 Double-winning side, for whom he had the greatest admiration. Frank was not in the team, however, when Arsenal won 3-0 at Molineux in that epic Gunners season. John Holsgrove deputised and that proved to be a last Wolves first-team appearance for 'Long John.' Frank could only watch from the stand as Radford and Kennedy scored that night. It was the first of nine wins in a row for the Gunners and the key to them ending as League champions.

When we played Arsenal early in 1972-73, Frank was in the team and he and John McAlle were for once left chasing shadows as Radford scored twice and Kennedy once in a 5-2 home win for the Gunners. It was rare for Frank and John to play second fiddle. As for the rest of the top strikers at that time, none of them ever really bothered Frank – not even "Supermac" Malcolm Macdonald had much of a kick when playing against him. It is some tribute to Frank that, with his four British clubs, he played first-team football in 14 consecutive seasons, amassing well over 500 appearances and over 50 goals. Yet he was still only 30 when he played his final game for Celtic. Looking back in 1998, he reflected: "I had many good years at Wolves. I loved Wolves. I went to Celtic and I tell you Celtic's not a patch on Wolves – and I'm Scottish."

As Jimmy Greaves used to say, it's a funny old game. One minute, you are on top of the world, the next in the depths of despair. So it was with Frank. One day, he was playing in the Scottish League Premier Division. A few weeks later, he was given a free transfer. Playing in the Scottish Premier was a wee bit easier than the English First Division and Frank admitted to me that he did not put 100 per cent into training when he should have done. Consequently, he lost that yard of pace. Standing off players instead of tackling them was just not him. But he still had something to offer, even if finding where to pursue his career was a problem. America was a possibility because, having played there with Aberdeen and Wolves, he knew the standard that was expected. Being played at a much slower pace, it would have fitted in perfectly well with his ability to read the game.

Yet Frank decided on Australia and went out in July, 1978. However, back on a home visit towards the end of the year, he had one last fling to prolong his career on home soil. With perfect symmetry, his last outing in England, on November 27, 1978, was where it all began for him – Stamford Bridge. The Daily Express reported: "Frank Munro was given a 45-minute trial by Chelsea in a 2-2 testimonial game against QPR for former Chelsea striker Ian Hutchinson. Munro has signed a two-year deal for Australian club Hellas but struggling Chelsea could tempt him back into the First Division." With Frank on the field in front of a crowd of under 4,000, Chelsea led 2-0 at the break and, without him, they conceded two goals. But it was only a friendly, of course. Chelsea were bottom of the table at the time and destined to be relegated. Maybe Frank did not fancy joining them or maybe their boss, Ken Shellito, having taken a look at him in action, thought he could no longer hack it at the highest level. Whatever the reasons, the matter went no further and Frank prepared once more for life Down Under.

I think he opted for Australia instead of the bright lights of the USA as he saw football there as suiting his moderate pace even more than the American game would have done. Surprise, surprise....who was to be his new manager at South Melbourne Hellas? None other than ex-Wolves keeper Dave MacLaren. Although they never played together, they certainly knew of each other. Once a decision was made, Frank had not wasted much time getting to Australia. He discovered that football there was on the up. The Aussies had qualified for the 1974 World Cup finals, which heightened interest, and the National Soccer League, which later became the Philips Soccer League, was founded in 1977. I don't know too much about Frank's career Down Under but I do know he got himself sent off. It happened in April, 1979, when South Melbourne Hellas were beaten 6-0 by league leaders Marconi. Soon after Marconi's highly-rated striker Mark Jankovics had scored his second goal to make it 4-0, Frank tried to stop him going through again and was promptly given his marching orders. The Sydney Morning Herald did not go into too much detail, merely stating: "Munro was ordered off for a tough tackle on Jankovics." The same player scored a couple of minutes after Frank's departure to complete a genuine hat-trick – three goals in a row. He must have been good as he hit another treble near the end of the season in a 4-3 win over Brisbane City that clinched the Philips League title. He ended the season as the league's top scorer and one newspaper described him as a '6ft 1in workhorse who will run all day.' That sounds like the sort of player Frank, in his prime, would have had no problem with. Alas, his dodgy knees were taking their toll.

After his spell with South Melbourne Hellas, Frank devoted more time to coaching than playing and Albion Rovers and Hamlyn Rangers, the latter now known as Geelong Rangers, were among the clubs to benefit from his undoubted knowledge. Rangers won successive Victoria Metropolitan League titles, the fourth division in 1983 and third in 1984. I believe Frank also played for Keilor

Park before finally calling it a day as the knee injury kept nagging at him. Someone who can shed a little more light on his life Down Under is Gary Cutler, who was on Wolves' books for a while. The surname may well be familiar to older Wolves fans as Gary's dad, Reg, scored when Bournemouth sensationally won 1-0 in the FA Cup at Molineux in 1957. For good measure, Reg was responsible for a post snapping when he collided with the side netting and delayed the game for several minutes.

After four years at Molineux in which he progressed no further than the reserves, Gary was encouraged by Frank to move Down Under and said that what Frank had visualised for himself as a couple of seasons in Oz turned out to be a stay of ten years. Gary pointed out that Hellas were backed by the Greek community and boasted several players with Wolves connections. As well as Alun Evans and Bertie Lutton, there were midfielder Sammy Wright, whom Frank described as one of the most influential players he had ever seen as a 17-year-old, and Kenny Drakeford, who was to follow Frank to future clubs and remain close to him when he finally returned to Wolverhampton.

Gary recalled that Frank experienced moderate fortunes with South Melbourne Hellas because of injuries, his troublesome left knee restricting his appearances. He believed Frank then moved to Juventus, a team backed by Italian Aussies who were as passionate in Melbourne as they are in Turin. Dave MacLaren eventually became chairman of Albion Rovers, who were predominantly run by Scottish immigrants. By the time Frank became Rovers' coach, he also had a job outside football. "Until then, football had been Frank's only form of employment and was a life he made no secret of being privileged to have lived," recalled Gary, who reckoned Frank's new means of income was not exactly demanding. "Working shifts as a security officer at Melbourne's second airport, Essendon, could hardly be described as hard labour. Once, when asked what the biggest challenge was about having a proper job, he was heard to reply: 'What? Apart from staying awake?' Frank enjoyed the job and the banter with work-mates, especially the boss, an Aussie rules fanatic. They would spend many evenings enjoying arguing about whose game was the better. As was his way, Frank, with his quick wit, rarely came off second best. He took great pride in his home, where a full-size bar became the centre of many an evening. In turn, that was home to one of his Scotland caps, which to all who saw it seemed to mean so much more than it did to him, although there was a sense of achievement underneath. He had been there and done it, after all.

"We both loved a wind-up. Frank played in the 5-1 defeat at Wembley against

England in the mid-1970s and I managed to get a tape of the game. I arranged for a few of the English lads to come round and told Frank the tape was the League Cup final of 1974. Beers were flowing and stories told when the request came to put the game on. When he saw what it was, there was not a name he didn't call me and, thank God, he had bad knees and couldn't catch me as I made a swift exit. He did not let me back into his house for half an hour." Cutler has fond memories of Frank: "He became a second father to me as I was only 20 when I arrived in Melbourne and stayed with Frank, Margaret, Stuart and Grant for the first six months. They were exceptional people and a good family. To play alongside such a complete player, even at that late stage of his career, was an experience for us all and having him around off the field was probably an even better experience. Frank loved his racing and got me to collect him one day as he had a 'red-hot' tip going in the second race at Ballarat, about an hour and a half west of Melbourne. All the way, he convinced himself – and me – that the horse was a certainty, only for it to run stone mother last. We returned to Melbourne with me pointing out his misconception of his punting ability. Although down, he was not beaten and we called in for a beer at the local, where he picked the last two winners. The big man's smile was back. He loved it.

"Post games at Albion Rovers, Frank and his assistant John Innis would often be the organisers of a few beers. There was a selection of good honest Scottish amateur league players in tricky winger Bennie Ferry, centre-halves Andy McMillan and John Creanie, midfielder Kenny Smart, Wolverhampton-born striker Kevin Lloyd and me. We were a willing crew. At a friendly against South Melbourne, Frank was reunited with Tommy Docherty with almost all the players from both teams sitting up until the early hours in the bar listening to the two of them exchanging stories. Dean Hennessey, son of the former Derby and Wales great, Terry Hennessey, had also arrived at Albion and his father was to arrive in Melbourne soon afterwards. Listening to Hennessey and the big man holding court and talking about the game was an experience on its own.

"Lack of available funds to move the club forward, and an average season, meant Frank had only one year at Albion before moving to Hamlyn Rangers and it was a sign of the esteem he was held in that many of the Albion squad travelled the hour's drive to be part of his set-up. Time stops for no-one and, with his knees becoming too painful to play, Frank's retirement and reduced training requirements combined with a few beers and his appetite for a cigarette was a cocktail that brought inevitable health questions. With the two-hour drive each night becoming challenging and Hamlyn Rangers remaining in the lower leagues, it was another

MacLaren link that saw Frank return to coaching at Northcote City, where he hooked up with former Aston Villa coach Roy MacLaren (Dave's brother).

"The signs were there and Frank received a warning, although nobody had any idea that the devastating stroke which was to eventually take such a massive toll, was brewing. While at home with son Stuart, he suffered a mild heart attack and was rushed to Royal Melbourne Hospital. Although it proved minor, it meant Frank suddenly became mortal. It was followed by the sudden loss of his close mate, the former Hull midfielder Billy Wilkinson, whom Frank had been with a day earlier. Further personal pain followed when his wife Margaret returned to Scotland and made the decision to remain there, ending their long marriage and leaving a hole that Frank would find impossible to fill. Both Stuart and Grant had by this time moved out and were developing lives in Australia and Frank had moved on to coach at Keilor Austria. Ten years in Australia had been kind to him but, for the first time, there was a feeling it was no longer home. The call of Wolverhampton and the folks back home became stronger. Frank called it a day, leaving behind memories and experiences both on and off the field for many who had met him on his Australian venture."

Chapter Fifteen

After The Ball

Frank made a brief return to the UK in January, 1982, courtesy of The People. The newspaper was being sued by ex-Leeds skipper Billy Bremner over an article done with our former midfielder Danny Hegan harking back to 1972 and those famous allegations about our game with Don Revie's side that denied them the Double. Frank and former Leeds players Gary Sprake and Bill McAdams were among those who gave evidence on behalf of the newspaper. Lining up to give evidence in favour of Billy were Johnny Giles, Jack Charlton, Allan Clarke and Doug Fraser, as well as our own Derek Dougan, who was the chairman of the Professional Footballers' Association for much of the 1970s. Danny had alleged in the article that Billy had offered him a 'grand' to give away a penalty. It was a tough cross-examination in court for Frank, who also alleged he had been offered money if he conceded a penalty. He denied agreeing to give evidence against Bremner in order to get him and his family back from Australia on a visit. He admitted The People had paid air fares totalling £4,000 but said he had been thinking of coming over anyway. The High Court jury in London awarded Billy, by then manager of Doncaster, £100,000 in damages. Publishers Odhams and Danny were also ordered to pay costs of over £60,000. The libel award was at the time one of the highest ever.

The last time I played against Frank was for Blackburn against Wolves on Saturday, April 16, 1977. It was at Ewood Park and Wolves won 2-0 on their way to winning the Second Division title under Frank's captaincy. It was also our fifth defeat in a row and we were to finish in mid-table. Frank and I parted after the game not knowing when or where we would see each other again. That is the thing with footballers. For years, you live in each other's pockets, then you go your separate ways and you don't see each other for ages. But, often when you do meet again, it's as if it was only yesterday when you were last together. That is certainly how it was with Frank.

Many years later, I was steward at a sports club in Wolverhampton, the Old Wulfrunians in Castlecroft. I was locking up when somebody walked through the front door. He was about eight yards from me – and I did not recognise him at first. It was his hair. Last time I saw him, it was dark brown and now it was snow white. "I'm just locking up," I said. "Well, I'll just have a vodka and tonic before I go," he replied. It was then that the penny dropped. It was the white hair that had fooled me but there was no mistaking that Scottish drawl. I rang over to the bungalow and Barbara, my wife, joined us for a drink and then another, and then another. Instead of closing at 11.30, it was 2.30am when we emptied our glasses and put Frank in a taxi. After a gap of 11 years, it was like yesterday once more. Big Frank was back!

Some might wonder why he chose to settle back in Wolverhampton and not Dundee or Aberdeen. He had often said while playing for Wolves how much he missed Scotland. It must be something about the area or the people but it was amazing how many former players from many different parts of the country put down roots in or around the town, or city, as it became in 2000. Among them were Geoff Palmer, Phil Parkes, Gerry Taylor, John McAlle, Steve Daley, Derek Parkin, John Richards, Willie Carr, Derek Dougan and me. Then Frank decided to join us. He was back but without Margaret. She had for some time been displeased with the way he was conducting his life. Days off from his job were too often spent drinking with his pals and, consequently, Frank and Margaret hardly had a social life. Eventually, Margaret decided enough was enough and made up her mind to leave. She went back to Scotland to visit her mother, never to return to Australia while Frank was still there. She now makes a regular trip every Christmas to see her son Stuart, his wife and her grandchildren, who still live out there.

It was not long before Frank decided he was going to wave goodbye to Australia, too. With the proceeds of his house, £45,000, in his pocket, he came back to Wolverhampton. It sounds a lot of money but it's not so much when you have no job and no other income and you have to set about buying a property. At first, his return was one long booze-up, with Frank subsidising one or two people along the way, and his money dwindling fast. "I lent one friend £8,000 and have never had a penny back," he once told me. By this time, Frank had met Naomi Hackner, who was to be his partner and who would, hopefully, be a calming influence on him. Alas, Frank being Frank, he continued with the booze and fags. "I've made a mistake, Waggy," he told me. "I should never have left Australia." Frank's drinking and smoking were bound to have an effect on him and one day it all came home with a vengeance. He was at a friend's enjoying a game of cards when his life changed forever. "I was having a drink," he recalled, "but the drink was all running down my chin. My face had gone numb down one side. I knew I was having a stroke."

Although he was taken to hospital, Frank, I believe, did not realise the significance of what was happening. Let's face it, not all of us would. I am sure he thought he would be discharged in a week or so and would be as good as new. Alas, it was never going to be that way. Frank phoned me from West Park Hospital in Wolverhampton, and his voice was casual and relaxed. "When are you coming to see me?" he said. I was at that time working at Waggy's Bar in the North Bank Stand at Molineux but I arranged to go and see him the next morning. He was sitting up in bed when I got there, not looking pleased at all. "How are you feeling, Frank?" I asked. "Not too bad," he said, "but I'm bored. I have not even got a television." Fortunately, two days previously, I had taken delivery of two dozen sets for Waggy's Bar. I reckoned they would not miss one. Besides, Frank deserved one for all the time he had spent at Wolves. We were fortunate there was already an aerial socket in his room and soon he had sound and vision. He was really made up with the new fixture by his bed but, health-wise, I am sure he did not realise what lay ahead.

At first, he could just about walk with a stick – very slowly. However, he found it hard to adjust to this slower pace of life. He was a big lad and it was very difficult for him to move with only half his body able to respond. The money was by now virtually all gone. Once again, he said to me: "I wish I had never left Australia." It was The Doog who got him to phone Gordon Taylor, the head of the Professional Footballers' Association, to see if they could help him with the money for his fare to Australia in order that he could see his son Stuart and his family. His wish was granted and a ticket was dispatched to him. On the plane, he met one Martin Wilson, a well-known gambler who was on his way to adjudicate in a tournament for poker players. Martin was a very easy-going and accommodating guy who, after listening to Frank's plight as far as money was concerned, came up with a plan. He would buy Frank's cups, caps, medals and mementoes with the agreement that, should Frank become solvent again, he could buy them back. It was a very generous offer, which Frank readily agreed to. Alas, many years later, when Frank was in a position to buy them back, Martin had been burgled and among the things taken was Frank's memorabilia. It was a blow, not because Frank was particularly sentimental but because he was going to give all the keepsakes from his career to Stuart. The PFA were good enough to fund another trip to Australia but turned down a third request.

Financially, things did improve and Frank and Naomi acquired a flat in

Compton, not far from where he lived when he played for Wolves. His health was deteriorating and he had to be pushed in a wheelchair whenever we went out. He liked living there and felt comfortable in a place where he was able to enjoy visits from several of his old pals from football, including John Richards, The Doog, Steve Kindon, when he was near Wolverhampton, Phil Parkes and me. Football was always the main topic of conversation. Initially, Frank had been refused a testimonial match at Molineux, simply because he did not complete the necessary period of ten years with the club; this despite the fact he had been promised one. The more the years went by, the more Frank saw red about it and cursed the powers-that-be at Molineux. He never really lost his temper but he did feel very strongly about the testimonial issue. He also had a very good memory for all things football, although, as time went by, this began to fade.

There was, eventually, a testimonial match for him in October, 1994 – not at Molineux, but at Willenhall Town's tiny ground in Noose Lane, where a Wolves XI met an All Stars XI. The idea for the game was spearheaded by his old pal Kenny Drakeford, a well-known figure in non-League football, who had been with him in Australia. He recruited a few others to the cause to make sure it happened. The Wolves side included some familiar names from Frank's time – Parkes, Palmer, Parkin, McAlle, Hibbitt, Knowles, Carr, Richards, Eves and Daley. It says much for the affection in which he was held that Peter Knowles made a rare comeback. The All Stars included former Villa men Tony Morley and Des Bremner as well as ex-Blues and Nottingham Forest man Kenny Burns. About 1,500 turned up to watch and it was reported that the game would raise £1,600, a welcome sum for Frank as he recovered from his stroke. Wolves donated some shirts and footballs as raffle prizes.

It is in tough times that you find out who your friends are and one group who most definitely fell into that favourable category, as far as Frank was concerned, were the London Wolves' Supporters Club. Every so often, they invite the team of the late 1960s and early 1970s to the capital for a lovely weekend, comprising a dinner on the Saturday evening and a boat trip on the Thames on the Sunday morning. On one trip, we were all walking along the embankment in the sunshine when a jogger suddenly ran between Naomi and Frank's wheelchair, knocking over Naomi and causing her to bang her head on the pavement. Before anyone could do anything, the jogger had disappeared among the throng. Our main concern, however, was Naomi. An ambulance was called and she was taken to hospital. Obviously, Frank was very upset and worried and there was the added problem of needing to be accommodated for an extra night in London. This was all kindly taken care of by Stuart Earl and London Wolves. Small wonder that Frank always had a lot of time for them, as, indeed, did we all. Whenever they put something on, everybody had a good time and we were well looked after. The late '60s and early '70s era was great for Wolves and for those London Wolves members. They are still going strong and travel in big numbers to this day to watch Wolves games.

Another example of people rallying round for Frank came in February, 2004, when a dinner was staged at Goodyear's splendid Pavilion restaurant thanks to the efforts of old pals Steve Kindon and John Richards. 'Kindo' and Steve Daley, who have reached the very top as after-dinner speakers, donated their services free to entertain the large gathering, as did Tommy Docherty, Frank's old boss at Chelsea. Another character from those brief Stamford Bridge days, George Graham, could not attend but sent a letter, which was read out. There was also a message from Peter Osgood, which referred to the fact Frank now had to use a wheelchair: "Look on the bright side, mate, you're probably quicker now than when you were playing!" Frank laughed as loudly as anyone at that. As well as the two Steves and JR, the turn-out included Phil Parkes, Derek Parkin, Geoff Palmer, Mike Bailey, John McAlle, Willie Carr, Derek Dougan, Phil Nicholls and me. Also there were rock legends Robert Plant and Bev Bevan. It was a special night. The message from Osgood proved there were no grudges borne after their previous battles, particularly their spat in that game at Molineux in 1973. Frank said: "I didn't think I would be on Osgood's list of friends after that, so it was great of him to write."

Frank's disability did not stop him leading as normal a life as he could. He did not shut himself away as some would – quite the opposite. Socially, he was out there with everybody else. He and I would go to a pub in Wednesbury, where we sometimes did a question-and-answer session. He loved it. He was very naïve in some ways and very clever in others. I once took him in my car to a shopping mall and was looking for somewhere to park. "Here we are," said Frank, "right outside." "Those are invalid bays," I said. "I'm an invalid," said Frank, "anybody can see that." "Yes, but once you're out of the car and in the shops, the traffic warden won't know the difference," I replied. "You should have brought your stickers with you." "It won't matter for five minutes," said Frank. "We'll tell him we have only been five minutes." "Five minutes or five hours," I said, "once that notice goes on my car, I've had it, so you can pay the fine." With that, Frank finally kept quiet and we found a legitimate parking space before we went into WH Smith 20 yards away. Trying to get him to understand something like this could be hard work but ask him to work out the most intricate of betting slips and it would be done in a flash.

The sudden death of our old pal Derek Dougan really shocked Frank, as it did us all. "Out of that team," said Frank, "I thought I would be the first to go." The Doog had been a good friend to Frank. His frequent visits cheered him up no end and his knowledge of the workings of the PFA got Frank back to Australia to visit his family. I was very privileged to be asked to be a bearer at Derek's funeral but had reservations about saying yes because of the nervousness I would feel carrying the coffin. I was not sure I could go through with it but changed my mind immediately after I mentioned the matter to Frank. His answer was: "I would give anything to get out of this wheelchair and help carry that coffin." That summed it up for me and, from that moment on, I felt very proud at being asked to carry out the role. Frank did not miss out completely, though. He was given the task of handing out the order of service programmes from his wheelchair at the entrance to the packed St Peter's Collegiate Church in the centre of Wolverhampton on what was a very emotional day.

On another occasion Frank, Phil Parkes and I were asked to do a signing session in the Merry Hill shopping centre, Brierley Hill, so off we went in my car, this time not forgetting the disability cards to display on the dashboard. After finding the lift to get to the floor we needed, Frank suddenly decided he needed a smoke before we went into WH Smith's. So it was back down to the ground floor while he lit up. Then up we went again and Frank decided he needed the toilet. So off we went to find the toilets. It was just like Lou and Andy in the Little Britain TV show. Finally we arrived at the store again and proceeded with the signing for two hours or so. It was time to go but Frank decided he needed the toilet again. By the time we finally got back down to ground level and reached the door to the car park, there was torrential rain. I had an appointment that night, so I really had to get back as soon as I could. We needed to get Frank into the car but it was not easy. I gave Phil the keys to the car, not to drive it (he has never passed his test) but to open it, while Frank and I stood in the rain. By now, I had got him out of the wheelchair and was holding him upright. The rain was absolutely tipping down but, once we had started, we had to finish the job. Phil opened the passenger door and I was still holding 16st Frank up with great difficulty. "Waggy," shouted Frank, "I'm going to fall. Shove your hand down the back of my tracksuit bottoms, it's easier that way." By this time, the three of us were laughing uncontrollably and we were absolutely soaking wet, me with my hand down the back of Frank's tracksuit and Phil holding open the passenger door. Suddenly, Frank broke wind violently. I dared not let go, otherwise he would have fallen over and the three of us just burst into even bigger fits of laughter. A crowd had gathered in the doorway of the centre, waiting for the rain to ease off. Goodness knows what they must have thought of us three, laughing our heads off in the pouring rain. Anyway, our next priority was to get Frank back to his flat and into some dry gear. This we did with many more fits of laughter before we left him for the night.

That incident was typical of Frank's later life. I had many more days and nights of laughter with him because he was not put off in the slightest by his serious condition. Almost overnight, he moved from his flat in Compton to a bungalow in nearby Finchfield. It had a large back garden, where Frank could sit in the sun, and there was plenty of room inside for him to get about in his wheelchair. As the saying goes, everything in the garden seemed rosy. Alas it was not. From thereon, everything seemed to go downhill. Naomi was taken ill with a form of depression and could not possibly look after him. Having only just moved into a new place, Frank began to take a dislike to it. It was partly because Naomi was not there to look after him and partly because he did not feel comfortable in the surroundings. Meanwhile, John Richards, was trying to organise some carers. Looking after him was no easy task. Being so big, Frank was really hard to handle when he was out of his wheelchair. By now, he could manage only three steps under his own steam and it was imperative someone was by his side in case he overbalanced. Fortunately, I was quite used to it, having visited him many times, and we still had plenty of laughs, especially when I had to take him to the toilet. I used to say: "Who would have thought this 30 years ago, me having to bring you in here?"

Like it or not, I was in charge now and would wind Frank up by pretending to be in authority. "Have you had your tablets this morning?" I would ask with a straight face. "Course I have," he would reluctantly reply. "That's a good lad," I would answer. All I got from him was a grunt and I would walk into the kitchen to have a little snigger. "Will you pop down to the shops for me?" he would say. "I need some cigarettes." "Anything else, Frank?" I would reply, knowing full well what was coming. "Er, see if they have any of those French fancies while you're there....." They were his favourite but he would not admit it. "OK, Frank, is that it then?" "That will do for now," he would say. Night time is when there were problems, so I had to play it cagey. It was not so much getting him ready for bed that I was bothered about but the number of things that he had to have beside his bed within his reach. His cigarettes, his lighter, his tablets, his drink, his remote, his phone and, most important, his bed pan all needed to be within arm's length. I knew it was dangerous to leave him with his cigarettes and lighter but he insisted

I did. However, I compromised. I left him with five cigarettes only – and he moaned about that.

I turned up each morning at 8am, only for Frank to say: "Where have you been? I've been awake for ages." What he meant really was that he had smoked all his fags and was dying for another one, which he could not have until I got there. After breakfast, it was the same routine. "Will you get me 20 cigarettes from the shop? Oh, and see if they have any of those French fancies while you're there – and this time don't forget my paper." Back from the shops, I would take him to the bathroom and get him ready for the day. His television, which he enjoyed, was constantly turned on – to the sports channel, of course, and often the horse racing – and it was his main source of entertainment. John Richards did succeed in organising some carers for him, which released me from my duties; well, most of them, anyway. Even at this time of our lives, we were proud to think it was a good team effort.

Although the bungalow in Finchfield had everything to offer, Frank wanted to move back to the flat at Sandy Hollow, Compton. Then came a blow. Naomi, who by now was living with him, said she no longer felt she could cope with her illness, her job and looking after Frank. She had cared for him for many years and the strain was beginning to tell. Consequently, Frank would have to go into sheltered accommodation on the other side of the city. So began another chapter in the life of Francis Munro. Bridge Court in Wednesfield is a purpose-built residential home for those needing care. Each flat has all the up-to-date amenities and, above all, a very friendly staff are on duty throughout the day and night. I know Frank wanted to go back to the flat in Compton but here at least he had somebody to look after him should anything happen. He accepted it and quite liked it in the end. Naomi went to see him after work and John and I were among other frequent visitors.

Frank was no couch potato and we went out to various functions and parties. One lovely summer's evening, my son had a party in the back garden of the house he was renting. Frank enjoyed it because he could drink and smoke with it being outside. There was just one thing everybody had overlooked.....after an hour, Frank needed the toilet, which was upstairs. There was no chance of him getting there, so we had to compromise. Frank would have to use a corner of the garden for a wee and I had to hold him up – but not with my hand down his tracksuit bottoms! By the time I got him to the appropriate place among the shrubbery, he was really desperate and yanked his tracksuit down with his good hand and let it flow. Unfortunately, he forgot one thing – everybody could see his bare backside. This did not faze him one bit and he laughed along with the rest of us.

We had a couple of nights out at Billy Pilbeam's social club, once for a q & a session and another for Billy talking about the time he was Wolves' groundsman. Frank really enjoyed that as Billy was a down-to-earth character, the type Frank liked. Of course, there was a lot of reminiscing. Frank used to go to most home matches and sit in his wheelchair in the lounge which looked out from the Billy Wright Stand. He was also in the front seat when the Former Players Association went off in big numbers to Cardiff to see Wolves win the 2003 Championship play-off final. It really upset Frank when he was told he would have to watch from the front row of the Steve Bull Stand. It was draughty and, if it was raining with the wind blowing in a certain direction, he got drenched. He was a man not in the best of health and being soaked for an hour and a half was just not on.

Let's be fair, Frank was the only ex-player in a wheelchair, so he hoped he could continue to sit in the Billy Wright Stand lounge to watch in comfort. He loved football and could never quite understand why the rules dictated otherwise. Consequently, he stopped going regularly and mostly watched Wolves when they were on television. He really felt the club had a downer on him, what with the refusal to give him a testimonial and then this unreasonable – he reckoned – request. He did occasionally get invitations to watch from executive boxes, for which he was always grateful. Two supporters were very kind to him – Bachitter Singh and his son Ravinder (Rav), who took him to Molineux when he was invited and also ran him to many dinners and other events. Rav and his dad met Frank at the dinner to raise cash to help provide care for Peter Broadbent, who by then had Alzheimer's. The Singhs and Frank became friends. Many others offered valuable help, too, such as Dave Dungar, Bob Laslett and Ivan Laslett, who invited him to their boxes on match days. Rav reminded me: "I remember once we took Frank to a dinner at the Park Hall Hotel in Wolverhampton when Bobby Charlton was the guest. He really enjoyed that."

Frank was in trouble at Bridge Court for burning the carpet in his room – not once but twice – when he fell asleep with a cigarette in his hand. But the smoking had to stop when the oxygen bottles were installed in his room. From then on, when I visited, the first thing Frank would say was: "Take me in the garden for a cigarette." I did not mind at all but sometimes it was freezing. He relied more and more on the oxygen and, each time I visited, he seemed to have the tube attached. Once again, he said to me: "I wish I could go back to Australia and see Stuart and his family."

One thing Frank really hated was missing was the London Wolves dinner, which, in 2011, took place at the Travelodge Hotel in Greenwich. It was too much to ask of him to travel to London with his oxygen bottles and other equipment. However, it was still a shock to me to learn in August of that year that his health had taken a considerable turn for a worse. Val, my partner, and I had just returned from a break at our caravan near Morecambe, when I received a call from Phil Parkes. "Frank's in hospital," Lofty said. "It's probably just breathing problems," I replied. "It's a regular occurrence since he has been on oxygen." "No, this time it's serious," said Phil, "he's had another stroke." With this news, Val and I drove straight over to Fordhouses, picked Phil up and proceeded to New Cross Hospital. Naomi and her brother were there, so were Bachitter and Rav Singh.

Apparently, Frank had rung the Bridge Court night staff at 5am and they immediately phoned for an ambulance to whisk him to New Cross. The doctor who attended him did not know Frank's history. After discovering that this was his second stroke, he explained that, should Frank recover at all, he would be too far gone to have any quality of life. So it was decided that nature be allowed to take its course. We all sat around the bedside waiting for the inevitable but big Frank was not going to go quickly. Naomi and her brother, who had been there from the small hours of the morning, decided to drive home, have a quick change of clothes and a bite to eat, then come back. While they were away, Margaret, Frank's estranged wife, arrived from Scotland, having received a phone call informing her of the situation. Throughout all this, Frank remained unconscious and, unfortunately, Naomi did not make it back in time. Just before 9pm, the referee blew the final whistle and big Frank slipped away.

There was, fittingly, a large turnout for the funeral at St Anthony's Roman Catholic Church in Fordhouses, just off the Stafford Road out of Wolverhampton, with people travelling from as far away as Scotland and London to pay their last respects. There was nostalgia in the air, as there always is when the old players get together. Frank would have loved that. Danny Hegan and Peter Knowles, two talented inside-forwards who usually prefer to keep a low profile, were there, Danny accompanied by Bobby Thomson, the Scot who was on Wolves' books in the 1950s before carving our a career with Aston Villa. Our team of the 1970s were out in force, too with Kenny Hibbitt, Steve Kindon, John McAlle, Derek Parkin, Geoff Palmer, Steve Daley, Jim McCalliog and Gerry Taylor all in attendance. Mike Bailey, John Richards, Phil Parkes and I were among the pall bearers. From other Wolves eras came Fred Davies, Graham Hawkins, Terry Wharton, Roy Swinbourne, Gerry O'Hara, Les Cocker, Mel Eves, Colin Brazier, Alf Crook, one-time Molineux reserves Phil Nicholls, Doug Devlin and Kenny Drakeford and, from the present-day club, director John Gough, secretary Richard

Skirrow, programme editor John Hendley and fellow historian Graham Hughes.

The congregation, among whom several supporters wore Wolves shirts from our era, were reminded of the tough start Frank had had in life, what with losing both parents at a very early age. Mike Bailey recalled: "Frank came to Ronnie Allen's attention in America in 1967. The fact that he scored a hat-trick against us for Aberdeen in the final of that USA tournament might have had something to do with it. His greatest asset in my view was his ability to read the game so well. He had a quick football brain that put him one step ahead of his opponent and, like all great players, he found himself with more time on the ball. At Wembley against Manchester City in 1974, I thought he produced his finest Wolves performance. He and John McAlle were simply brilliant." Our skipper regretted the fact there would be no more phone chats with his trusty no 5 and added: "Our team is decidedly weaker today with the loss of one of our best mates."

The singing of football's most famous hymn, Abide With Me, was another part of a service that concluded, as it had started, with a moving lament from a bagpiper. Among the floral tributes was one from Alan Sunderland in Malta. He and Gary Pierce were the only surviving members of the 1974 League Cup starting side not present. The local press were eager to grab hold of the lads after the funeral and there were plenty of quotes which summed up what Frank meant to so many both during his playing days and for a long while afterwards. Derek Parkin said: "He was a terrific player. We joined Wolves within a few weeks of each other in 1967-68 and were put up in a hotel together for a while. He used to bully me with his banter at times but he was fairly quiet on the pitch. He just had a calmness and composure about him that helped keep things together at the back."

Mike Bailey, our inspirational skipper in the late 1960s and early 1970s, said: "He was as good as anyone around in his position and a fantastic player. He had such quick, brilliant feet and he could read a game so well." John Richards had no doubts about where Frank stood among his contemporary central defenders: "People talk about the great centre-halves of his day, such as Bobby Moore, Jack Charlton and Roy McFarland – well, Frank stood alongside them. He was a quality player and tough, too – but also the most skilful player in our dressing room." Phil Parkes, one of those who kept in close touch right to the end, said: "Frank was a lovely fellow and a quality player. We were talking recently and I said I'd just turned 64. He wanted to live until he was 65 because he said none of his family had lived to be as old as that. He would have been 64 on October 25."

So we said goodbye to our old pal.

Chapter Sixteen

What Others Said

To end our tale of a very special footballer, we have assembled some of the many tributes paid to Frank at the time, together with others written specially for us. They help paint the picture of a player who deserves to be listed with the very best who have ever worn the famous gold shirt of Wolverhampton Wanderers. Long-time Express & Star Wolves corrsepondent David Instone, who now runs, with John Richards, the www.wolvesheroes.com website which does so much to keep fans in touch with former players, visited Frank many times and wrote: "He was better off than most of us in terms of memories. He was full of them; revealing, controversial, funny and never dull or melancholy. That partly explains why he had a steady stream of regular visitors – Dave Wagstaffe, Phil Parkes and John Richards among them – to the Wednesfield care home at which he saw out his time.

"I was always a sucker for the tale he told about Derek Jefferson scrambling round looking for his contact lens in the penalty area while Wolves were taking a right pounding. His spats with Bill McGarry, whom he once had by the lapels as he reached over the manager's desk, were compulsive listening, too. Somehow, you always felt uplifted by a trip to his place. What could have been a maudlin experience, seeing him sat there with a shawl over his legs, a fag in his mouth and a cough on his chest, was always an hour guaranteed to fly by. It's why Waggy put up with running errands for him at unusual hours of the night, why Derek Dougan had a video of the 1967 USA final between Wolves and Aberdeen specially recorded for him and why he was top of the 'people to see' list when Brian Garvey and Gary Cutler came back to these shores from Australia. He was much more than a damned good player.

"Frank, after a bust-up with Sammy Chung, first went back up to Scotland, then Down Under to Oz. Wolves were barely recognisable by the time he came back after several years in Melbourne, where he combined football with a job as a traffic officer at a local airport. As he recuperated in hospital at the start of his chronic health problems, his numerous get-well cards included one from Billy

Wright. It was a welcome tonic on a long uphill road. Thank goodness Munro didn't do self-pity because he had a lot to bear. He enjoyed welcoming house callers and relished those regular trips to Wolves games but there was obviously such a lot he couldn't do. He had long since lost the letter from former chairman Harry Marshall promising him a testimonial and he didn't have much to show, financially or in terms of souvenirs, from the game he had graced for almost two decades. Although I was delighted in recent years to see a well-stocked photograph album on his coffee table, other keepsakes, like the Scottish caps, had melted away and that cherished tape from The Doog had been sent to Australia for the enjoyment of other members of the Munro clan."

South Melbourne Hellas president Leo Athanasakis said: "We were blessed to have had such a gifted player like Frank Munro represent our club considering he played for some great European clubs. We are so proud that a player who was so highly regarded by those clubs decided to come out to Australia and play for South Melbourne. On behalf of everyone at the club, we wish to express our sympathies to the Munro family for the passing of a wonderful man."

The late Jim Heath, a regular contributor to the much-lamented fanzine, A Load of Bull, also had warm memories and wrote on his website Junk Archive: "I was richly privileged to see most of Frank Munro's games for Wolverhampton Wanderers. He'd played only a handful of games following his transfer from Aberdeen when he wore the no 11 shirt on my first visit to Molineux, for a 0-0 draw against champions-elect Leeds in 1969. A season later, Munro was successfully converted to a centre-half by manager Bill McGarry and he simply oozed class as he starred in a great Wolves team. Frank Munro had that touch of arrogance that endeared him to the fans – comfortable on the ball and highly skilful, he was coolness personified. It was a sad day when I met him. A small group of fans were invited to the QPR match in 1997 by entrepreneur Des Desai to share his executive box in the Billy Wright Stand for the afternoon. We were all introduced to Frank and it was difficult to believe it was the same, fit, handsome man I had idolised from the North Bank as he sat forlornly in a wheelchair. But he was as bright as a button, regaling us with anecdotes as we were enlisted by Des to support an informal campaign to try to influence the club to award Frank a testimonial, something that was unjustly denied him at the time he left Wolves. Sadly, he never did get his reward but the memories cannot be erased."

Footballer writer and author Ivan Ponting also lauded Frank in The Book of Football Obituaries (Pitch Publishing). Ponting, whose tributes to footballers feature in The Independent newspaper, wrote: "Once described unforgettably by a Wolverhampton Wanderers fan with an inspired turn of phrase as 'an E-type Jaguar inside a Sherman tank,' Frank Munro was not only a redoubtable bulwark of the Black Countrymen's defence during the late 1960s and most of the 1970s, but also a stylish and occasionally audacious entertainer. Munro was an imperious cornerstone of the accomplished Wolves side which reached the UEFA Cup final in 1972, then won the League Cup two years later. After they were relegated in 1976, he captained them back to the First Division – the equivalent of today's Premier League – at the first attempt. The rock-like six-footer from Broughty Ferry was strong enough to slug it out with the most physical of centre-forwards when required, never yielding an inch. When not tackling ferociously or soaring combatively into aerial duels, Munro could control the ball assuredly, pass it perceptively and even embark on a deft dribble which was clearly a legacy of his earlier days as an inside forward."

Ponting, also the obituary writer for the Backpass nostalgia magazine, added: "Invariably, too, he radiated confidence and composure, precious qualities at the heart of any rearguard, and beyond that, for all the raw physical endeavour demanded of any top-flight defender, somehow his play was infused with his own personality, which was sunny. He loved playing football for his living, the Molineux fans picked up on that happy circumstance, and they adored him for it. The Munro career, which yielded caps at youth and under-23 level, and then a further nine for the senior team, got off to a false start when he headed south to join Chelsea as a promising teenage forward in 1961. He failed to make the grade and never turned professional at Stamford Bridge, instead heading back to his home city to sign for Dundee United in July, 1963.

"Now his star began to rise rapidly, so that soon he was spoken of as 'the Scottish version of Duncan Edwards,' a memorably daft and unrealistic tag of which he made light to become established at Tannadice as an attacking midfielder in 1964-65. Somewhat surprisingly, Munro was sold to top-tier rivals Aberdeen and made a rapid impact, appearing in that season's Scottish Cup final defeat by Celtic. That qualified the Dons for the European Cup Winners' Cup and Munro made the most of the opportunity, netting a hat-trick, including the club's first goal in continental football, as they kicked off the campaign with a 10-0 annihilation of Icelandic side Reykjavik. By then, the young Taysider's destiny had been decided by an eye-catching display, and another hat-trick, during a tournament that summer in the United States. While playing for Aberdeen, he shone against Wolves in the final, in the process riveting the attention of their manager Ronnie Allen and the upshot was a £55,000 transfer to Wolverhampton in January, 1968.

"Mirroring his previous under-achievement in England, at first he struggled to make a mark and it was not until he was converted from midfielder to centre-half by Allen's successor as boss, Bill McGarry, that he began to excel. First partnering John Holsgrove and then, for three-quarters of a decade, John McAlle, Munro became a key figure in an exhilarating side. There were those who believed he deserved to be an international regular throughout his prime but, given that his competitors for a central-defensive berth included Billy McNeill (at first), Martin Buchan, Gordon McQueen, Jim Holton, Bobby Moncur and Colin Jackson, that was never likely."

David Innes paid a fond tribute to Frank on the website Aberdeen Voice. He wrote: "The statistics show that Francis Michael Munro played (started) 59 games for the Dons and scored 14 goals. In today's multi-media analytical world, his number of assists, the yards he covered during 90 minutes, his percentage successful passing rate would all be monitored and published. Had such analysis been available in Franny's time at Pittodrie, his value would have been far more obvious now. But it still wouldn't have told the full story. When I interviewed Eddie Turnbull in 1997 about the Dons' 1967 USA adventure as the Washington Whips, I asked about Franny in particular. Why? Because on Christmas Eve, 1966, I witnessed this teenager rule the midfield in a top-of-the-table head-to-head with Celtic, a mere five months before Jock Stein's team lifted the European Cup. Stein's midfield of the time included luminaries such as Bertie Auld and Bobby Murdoch, yet it was Munro who bossed the game and, had it not been for Ronnie's Simpson's breathtaking save just before the end, Munro's pile-driving late goal attempt would have secured a rare victory over Celtic.

"He wasn't about blood and thunder, though. He was as graceful an athlete, despite an on-going weight problem, as any of the more high-profile figures of the time. During the 1997 interview, Turnbull told me: 'In the early days, before I came to Aberdeen, I was in charge of Scotland under-18s and remember Francis as a 15 or 16-year-old. I thought 'This is some player'. Of course he was a Dundee boy and went to Dundee United but Jerry Kerr couldn't handle him and he started getting into the wrong company. He was one of the finest long passers of a ball that I ever saw, that I ever had under me, that I ever played against. He would say, 'I can't do that', and I would say, 'You're the most skilful of the lot.' That was when he first came in, he was an introvert, a lovely lad. For a big man, he was so light on his feet. He'd great vision, could see everything on the park.' In his pen picture of Franny in a Washington Whips programme in 1967, the boss described his protégé as being as 'nimble as a ballerina'. That he shares his date of death with Elvis is a coincidence that I will regard as wholly indicative of the level of Franny Munro's talent."

David Slape, of London Wolves, used to stand on the North Bank in the 1970s and can remember the tussle between Frank and Chelsea's Peter Osgood. "Osgood was chasing a through ball towards the North Bank goal. Frank waited until Osgood had almost reached the ball, before calmly pulling the ball right, leaving the forlorn forward on his backside. The crowd laughed but Osgood got his revenge at a Chelsea corner by kneeing Frank in the thigh."

Charles Ross, editor of A Load of Bull, the Wolves fanzine that is sadly no longer published, gave us his splendid reflections on Frank: "I never did see Frank Munro play. Not strictly true, perhaps but it feels that way and it feels that way to this day. I could look up the stats in a book but memories of greatness glimpsed all too briefly through a boy's eyes are made of more than cold, hard numbers. Most Wolves fans inherit their burden through an accident of birth, not promiscuous choice. My time and place meant that I was a nervous but excited ten-year-old Shropshire lad when I first went to Molineux on Boxing Day, 1970, to see Wolves play Everton, then League champions. I knew all the names, as any football-mad ten-year-old would, but they were just that – names. Thick snow blanketed the pitch, I was freezing but agog, eyes wide at the vast heaving terraces of the South Bank. Wolves won 2-0 with The Doog getting both. I can't claim to remember anything about what Frank Munro did that day but, by 4.40pm (when games used to end), I was hooked on Wolves. To keep Everton scoreless, Munro had played a blinder. You didn't have to be there, or to be there as a kid not really understanding the game, to just know that. It must have been true.

"Frank Munro was already a hero come the next big game and this one I really wasn't at. I was still at the stage of only being taken as a Christmas treat, or to the very occasional game. So a Monday night match in May 1972 was never going to happen for me. However, I knew all about it. All the glory hunters (yes, they existed even back then) at school were Leeds 'supporters.' They had, of course, never been to a game. Not like me. And Leeds would inevitably beat us to do the Double. Or so they thought. But I, with my precious little radio and its aerial dangling out of a window to pick up the crackle of a commentary – I knew better. We had the likes of Frankie Munro playing for us, so we were going to win . . . AND we did, AND he scored – so there. Take that!

"Four years later, it's still a school night. I still can't go. Still school is full of glory hunters but this time it's Liverpool they are 'supporting' for the final game of the season and I know the permutations. It's death by a thousand radio crackles.

Four years is a long time as a kid. I have read all that too-good-to-go-down stuff and know there ain't no such thing. It's going to be my first time. I am not seduced by Steve Kindon's opener or by the half-time scores. I know we haven't got John McAlle and Frank Munro at the back and that means something is not right and it will end in tears. It does and I don't suppose mine were the only ones. Equally, I know that in the next season, 1976-77, we will go straight back up. And this is my season. I am 16 now and am going to go on my own, on the train, every home game. How can we fail? Pierce, the hero of Wembley '74, is in goal. Not that we'll need him – not with Palmer, Parkin, Munro and McAlle in front of him. Not with Kenny Hibbitt in midfield and John Richards up front. Doubt does, however, creep in, when we contrive to lose 6-2 at home to Southampton. Rationalising it does not take me long. Frank Munro hasn't been playing so far. That's the reason. But he will be soon and it will be OK. And he was. And it was.

"At some point early in the season, I must have asked for more pocket money, because I was told to keep a check of how, where and when I spent it; football, a football magazine, sweets or whatever – life in Shropshire aged 16 was pretty racy in the mid-1970s. A month later and I knew that 83 per cent of it (I think that was the number) was spent on football. And no, I still don't know where I wasted the other 17 per cent. It wasn't that I was extravagant – I didn't always pay to sneak on that train, or how else could I afford to go to games? I was entering a different world now on Saturday afternoons. I can still remember the bouncing of the North Bank during matches as we won game after game. Those primal chants of "Munro, Munro – Frankie Munro, Frankie Munro!" still reverberate decades later. As indeed they did one autumn day that season at Bloomfield Road.

"I'd cut out some of the 17 per cent I was wasting on fripperies like sweets so I could pay my Don Everall's coach fare for my first away day, at Blackpool. It was around Bonfire Night, the clue to that being in the exchange of rocket fire and other projectiles between the two sets of fans on that giant old terrace. The bloke behind me yelped at one stage and I turned round to see blood pouring from a nasty cut below the eye. I could see what had done it. There on the floor was a shiny new 10p piece, looking oddly twisted now. Pocket money issues or not, I didn't stoop (literally or metaphorically) to pick it up. I reckoned it belonged to him if anyone. Anyway, there was a game to try to watch. And we drew. And Frankie Munro scored. And I saw it.

"I'd like to say I was finally watching him play. The truth was a little different. I was there but I was too young to appreciate his talents and we were in the wrong division to see him at his best – against the best. Yes, I could chant his name, could look lovingly at that name on the programme, could see this tall, graceful player in that gold shirt elegantly take no prisoners. However, I could not see, really see, what it was he did. Incredibly, I missed the final home game, 1-1 against Chelsea. I was playing cricket, the other love of my boyhood life. And that was why going up to Bolton for the final game was not an option; the game where Kenny Hibbitt scored to stop them going up and let Forest sneak through instead. I didn't really mind missing those celebration games. We were champions, we were up. I'd seen them lose 6-2 at home, seen them grab a point away from home. I had been there from the off. I had come of age. And I would get to see them all again soon, back in Division One where we belonged, in August, 1977.

"What I did not know was that, at home against Chelsea and away to Bolton, I had just missed Frank Munro's last two games in a Wolves shirt. They say you should never meet your heroes. Not necessarily so. Years later, when I was editing A Load Of Bull, I got the opportunity to interview Frank for the mag. Don't ask me how the opportunity arose, or even when it was. I haven't a clue. It doesn't matter. All that matters is that I was finally going to come face to face with a boyhood icon. Frank was by then living in a flat in Compton. I knew he was in poor health and was apprehensive, in a way that I never was meeting well-known senior people in the day job. This wasn't the adult ringing his doorbell one morning – it was that young boy. It was not an easy interview to do. Sat opposite me was this giant of a man. Some might say diminished by the passage of time. His lack of mobility was hard to witness and his thick Scottish brogue a wee bit hard to fathom clearly at times. This sort of fate should not, I felt, befall an athlete like Frank Munro who so adorned his playing stage. It should be reserved for us ordinary folk.

"However, that only paints a superficial story. His handshake was not just firm (ouch!) but warm, his welcome in his own home so genuine. This, to someone he had never met and had no need to see. His eyes still burned bright, fiercely at times. I raised the subject of that Leeds game. Frank remained professional and I respected him immensely for it. However, the look in his eyes as I dared broach that or other subjects told me that for an opposition player, here was a centre-half with whom the taking of liberties would have been unwise. I caught but a glimpse of the steel that lay beneath the elegant surface of his playing days, days I regretted missing so many of. When today's multi-millionaire stars retire behind the remotely controlled gates of their private mansions, will they ever realise what they are missing out on? Today's kids won't be seeking them out in decades to come, nervously ringing their bell, pen and paper in hand as if they were still schoolboys. Keen to see them not because of their circumstances but despite them. To this day, I still don't really feel like I ever truly saw Frank Munro play. But I met him. And that burnishes the legend rather than tarnishes it. A mark of the man, not just of the footballer. Munro, Munro – Frankie Munro, Frankie Munro."

Clive Corbett, author of two fine Wolves books, Those Were The Days and Out of Darkness, watched Frank in action many times and looks back on him with admiration and affection. He wrote: "Quite simply, to a teenage Wolves fan in the late 1960s and early 1970s, Frank Munro was a giant in a team of giants. I had the privilege of spending a few hours with him at his Sandy Hollow home in Compton in early December, 2006. The only sadness was to see at first hand his physical deterioration but his mind was as sharp as ever and the mischievous humour and twinkle in the eye were very much intact. He remembered how things suddenly went sour in Scotland: 'I was very surprised. I had only been married a couple of months and I really liked Aberdeen. On New Year's Eve, 1967, I said to my wife, 'We'll not go out because one of four fellows will turn up'. Stuart Fraser did and we each had a glass of Harvey's Bristol Cream. The next day on the coach to Dundee, we stopped at Montrose and manager Eddie Turnbull said: 'I'm going to leave you out today. I think you've been drinking all night.' I was staggered and it was only three or four years ago that he finally accepted I hadn't been.'

"Interest from the Wolves was revealed so quickly that Munro himself was taken aback: 'January 5 will always be a special date in my life. I'm always glad to get to January 6 now because, on January 5, 1968, I signed for Wolves and then, on the same date many years later (1994), I had a stroke.' It was clearly not love at first sight for the big Scotsman at Molineux; 'In my first match I was virtually at outside-right and thought 'What am I bloody doing here?' At that time, Frank was particularly frustrated at being played out of position. 'The midfield when I came here was Bailey, Knowles and me,' he said. 'Although I was bought as a midfield player, I thought I should play central defence. Even before my first game, I said that to Ronnie Allen but he said: 'You've got too much ability to play centre-half.' I disagreed – I think that was an advantage.'

"Although I have always admired Dr Percy Young's seminal work on the first 100 years of Wolverhampton Wanderers, I cannot agree with his somewhat uncharitable assessment of Frank and Derek Parkin, who arrived at Wolves a few weeks later. 'Both these players were adventurous, inclined at times to prefer imagination to industry' was Young's verdict. However, in my opinion those two just oozed class and composure. The 1968-69 season was a particularly frustrating time for Frank. But it was then that Ken Hibbitt made his bow in the Central

League side alongside him and Kenny told me: 'My first game was at Manchester United in the reserves with Frank Munro. I was five grand from Bradford and played alongside a sixty grand signing from Aberdeen. It was a wonderful occasion, running on to Old Trafford and playing in midfield with Frank and it all started from there. I'd had 16 games at Bradford and it was my first bonus, the first time I'd been in a winning or drawing side – 2-2 and I got a fiver, quite a good bonus in 1968. It all really took off from there.'

Clive continued: "In July, 1969, Wolves returned to the USA and one tangible benefit of the tour was new boss Bill McGarry's discovery of Frank Munro's defensive skills. Speaking to Neville Foulger of the Birmingham Evening Mail, the manager said: 'Munro's performances out in America were a revelation. He has often said he fancied playing in a strictly defensive role. I never pictured him in this sort of position but decided to give him a try.' This was of course a discovery that was to serve Wolves well for the best part of a decade. An abiding memory of my time with Frank was not only the respect that he engendered in his fellow players but also that which he had for them. He felt that Knowles was a huge loss: 'If Peter had continued playing, we would have won more things. I'm convinced. When I was in hospital after the stroke, he was one of the first to come and see me.'

"John McAlle remembered with affection just how well he and Frank worked together, with Munro the skilful reader of the game and distributor, and him the ball winner: 'Wherever he went, I covered him. Frank Munro and myself played very well together.' Frank agreed: 'John was one of the best tacklers I've ever seen, so brave.' John Richards adds: 'Frank must have been dreadful for someone like John to play alongside. John was a straightforward player; defend, win the ball, lay it off. Frank had so much time, he was always looking to take players on and beat them.' The consistency of team selection in the early 1970s was well remembered by Munro: 'We were together for eight to nine years. For a season or two, our team virtually never changed, you knew exactly what it was going to be. It's not that I would hate to play now and I love to watch it on Sky, but I couldn't go with this rotation. I'd hate to be in one week and out the next.'

"Derek Parkin, who played alongside Munro and McAlle on countless occasions, offered these thoughts: 'John was great to play with because he was so consistent. He was probably the most left-footed player I ever played with; he couldn't kick the ball with his right foot to save his life. But he had a heart like a lion and worked hard. Frank was easy to play with, a class player. He was never the quickest but read the game well and had a tremendous touch for a big man, better than John Richards! He was so skilful that he made the game look easy. He and John (McAlle) complemented each other. That's what it's all about.' Willie Carr greatly admired Frank's skills: 'He was a footballing inside-forward playing at centre-half and used to scare the shit out of Lofty when he went to head the ball, then duck and leave it.' Steve Daley remembered the same party piece and a fabulous defensive pairing: 'I used to love the tricks Frank would do in training. In a match, their goalie would ping a free-kick to the striker and Frank would shout 'My ball!' and then duck. He would do that three or four times a game. He wasn't the most mobile of players but, like Bobby Moore, his reading of the game got him there early.'

"My favourite Wolves season was the great European adventure of 1971-72 and Frank Munro made stand-out contributions on so many occasions. November, 1971, saw two memorable home games, against Derby and Arsenal, on successive Saturdays and covered on TV by Star Soccer and Match of the Day respectively. Fighting back to gain parity just before half time against Derby, Wolves laid siege to the South Bank end in an exciting second half. It was the colossus Frank Munro who strode imperiously out of defence to set up Ken Hibbitt. His fierce drive was parried by Colin Boulton to set up a terrific scramble on the floor involving Dougan and Colin Todd. As the ball squirted clear, John Richards prodded the ball over the line to spark ecstatic celebrations. The following Saturday, Wolves demolished Double winners Arsenal 5-1 in a second-half snowstorm and, although Kennedy had given the visitors the lead, Frank considered it a great achievement to keep the Arsenal strikers mainly quiet: 'Talking with John McAlle recently, we think the only pair to really got the better of us were Radford and Kennedy. I think Chivers and Osgood had more ability and were probably better players but, for some reason, I found it difficult with Radford in the air, on the ground, everywhere. To make it doubly difficult, John found it difficult against Kennedy.'

"Into January, 1972, and I experienced the joy of a rare win on my first visit to Old Trafford. The Doog put Wolves ahead on 20 minutes and, just nine minutes later, Frank Munro took a free-kick well inside his own half and, with pinpoint accuracy, found Dougan 20 yards out. John Richards seized upon his flick-on, shielding the ball from his marker before clipping a marvellous rising half volley into the United net. The first leg of the UEFA Cup quarter-final In Turin was another cherished memory, if only 'witnessed' from afar. Frank considered the match against Juventus 'the best game we ever played.' He added: 'We all did well and drew 1-1 but we should have won easily.' Bitter disappointment, of course, followed in the all-British final but the extraordinary finale to the League season, against Leeds, saw another significant Munro contribution. He scored the opening goal in that 2-1 win which denied Leeds the Double. However, he had sympathy for the fact their opponents had to play just two days after the FA Cup final: 'They were the best team. I don't think it should have been played on the Monday night after the final. It was a good game, played at 100 miles an hour.'

"Leeds featured heavily in the 1972-73 season too, knocking Wolves out in a very closely-fought FA Cup semi-final at Maine Road. The only goal was scored by Billy Bremner, a memory that haunted Frank when I met him: 'I still have nightmares about that goal. I'm screaming to Ken Hibbitt to leave it, I know I can head it clear or catch it on my chest and walk out of the area with it. I can see it all now, I was screaming but Kenny couldn't hear me with the crowd noise. He tries a bloody bicycle kick, it goes straight up in the air and where does it fall? Bremner smashes it home and that was it.' Ken Hibbitt adds: 'We went to Maine Road and got beat 1-0. Every time I saw Frank Munro, he said: 'Your fault!' The cup disappointments were eventually put to rest by the League Cup final victory in 1974. Frank told me he was pretty confident at the time: 'I didn't think Man City were favourites. I know people said about their forward line but I think they were all getting a little past it, even Denis Law, who I thought was fantastic. I always thought Franny Lee was a really great player, though, so was Colin Bell – and you had to watch Rod Marsh, who could get a penalty by tripping himself up. We were 11/8 against, they were 7/4 on but I really fancied us.'

"Munro described the amazing scenes as the team coach crawled up Wembley Way: 'Waggy and I were always card partners and there were so many Wolves fans that it was unbelievable. They were banging on the coach windows. It was at this point that Dave said: 'It's OK for them, I wish the game was at Castlecroft!' It was entirely appropriate to me that the match ended with Munro outjumping Denis Law in the Wolves area to head clear. Mike Bailey fully appreciates the key role played by Frank and John: 'Gary Pierce's part in our win is deservedly remembered but Frank Munro and John McAlle in front of him were magnificent.' Geoff Palmer is fulsome in his praise of those around him: 'The way Mick Bailey, Derek Parkin, Frank Munro and John McAlle played that day, and obviously Gary, was amazing.'

"The 1975-76 season of course ended in relegation, with a last-day home defeat to Liverpool hammering home the final nail in the coffin. Crucially, Wolves were shorn of the Munro-McAlle partnership, as Ken Hibbitt reflects: 'They were the backbone of our defence. They had played together for so long that they knew each other's game and how to play off each other. You'd got Scouse, who was tough and aggressive, and Frank, who was a real football player with a real brain. We didn't have them and it didn't help against Keegan and Toshack, who were part of an amazing side. We did our best but shouldn't have been in that position anyway.' The makeshift defence had Alan Sunderland at right-back but why McGarry played him there even in this crisis was beyond Frank Munro: 'No-one was more skilful than Alan Sunderland. McGarry wasted a year of his life playing him at right back. It was a crying shame. He was such a talent. He should have been playing midfield or up front.'

"Frank recalled the circumstances of his move to Celtic with some anger over the testimonial issue. 'Wolves promised me a testimonial match. I had a letter from the then chairman Harry Marshall but, over the years, lost it. Billy McNeill, then manager of Aberdeen, phoned me and I was tempted (to re-join them). The only reason I didn't go there was because I had given Jock Stein my word.' I remember that Frank expressed just one regret during the interview and asked for his team-mates to make a promise to each other: 'The only time we will meet is when somebody dies, sad to say. But if we don't keep in touch, this is what will happen.' All that Frank wanted was a promise – to see each other more often. It is sadly too late for him but not for them."

A Wolves fan of many years, David Dungar proved a good friend to Frank in his later life and recalls: "As a young fan watching my favourite Wolves players from the stand, it was beyond my wildest dreams that I would ever get more than a fleeting off-field opportunity to see them close up, let alone actually speak to them at some length. Although my father had passed the Wolves supporting baton to me at the age of three, I had been far too young to form favourites among the great 1950s players, other than I know I took to Eddie Clamp because of his combative style and the fact he obliged me with an autograph as I sat on the small wall at the front near the touchline. It was more the Wolves players from the middle of the 1960s to the mid-1970s that I grew up on. It was only later I realised how good those players were. Over that decade, they had terrific loyalty to the team as well great ability. I managed to get tickets for all the big games in that time, including both legs of the UEFA Cup final and the 1974 League Cup final. Imagine my delight when, in 2006, my then employers, Chaucer, said I could represent us at London Wolves' 40th anniversary party in London, knowing my heroes would be there. I had met The Doog some years earlier through a mutual friend and, in doing so, I met Waggy and Frank: the three were great pals. Frank was a terrific player for Wolves – one of those who, if I had been the manager, would have been an instant pick. He had the lot. He read the game so well, was strong and you just felt as a fan if he was in the team, we always stood a chance of winning.

"Frank was calmness personified and hoofing the ball was the last thing on his mind. He was always looking to set up an attack immediately after breaking up one by the opposition. He was Wolves' Franz Beckenbauer. Perhaps I should have called him Franz. By the time I met him, he was confined to a wheelchair, which seemed so unfair on someone who had been so majestic on his feet on the pitch. I immediately hit it off with him and, along with our partners and other friends, had a number of meals out with him. The thing about Frank was that he would talk about Wolves as much or as little as you wanted. So we talked about Wolves a lot! When I first met him, I mentioned we had the same birthday, October 25, and we also shared it with Stan Cullis. Frank said he was very proud to share the same birthday as Cullis, such a legendary Wolves defender as well as manager.

"I was honoured to be invited to Frank's 60th birthday party alongside all his old playing colleagues. Sadly, I was also there with him the day he died and was at Molineux to see his ashes interred. Apart from the birthday do, I had the pleasure of other meals out with Frank. He never bigged up his playing days. He didn't need to as we all knew he was a legend. Imagine how humbled I was by Frank buying me a birthday present, too! His legendary status was illustrated on one of our meals out to a curry house in Wednesfield. He always wanted to pay his corner and was disappointed when the bill arrived with no After Eight mints. Jokingly, I told the restaurant manager it wasn't good enough. Quite rightly, the manager viewed Frank as an A list guest and immediately sent out for a box of After Eight. Such was Frank's status!

"I always drink a toast to Frank on our birthday and insist we have After Eight mints on the table. Surprisingly, for a proud Scotsman, Frank preferred vodka to scotch. At his ashes interment, I was honoured to meet his lovely family. His son Grant's body art says it all – he has a picture of Frank in a Wolves shirt tattooed on his tummy with the words 'Six foot two and eyes of blue' – part of the song fans would chant at Molineux."

Long-standing Wolves fan John Lalley, a regular and incisive contributor to the Express & Star sports pages, recalls visiting Frank for the final time at the care home in Wednesfield where he spent the last few years of his life battling against illness without a word of self-pity. He said: "It was a bitter-sweet experience sharing his always ebullient company; a delight to chat with a Wolves hero but at the same time, heartbreaking to see this colossus of a player prematurely deprived of his considerable physical stature. He appeared noticeably frailer than the last time I had enjoyed his company but, as ever, he had a welter of football tales and reminiscences to impart, his enthusiasm for the game undiminished to the end. He loved Wolves, spoke with admiration and affection about his playing colleagues and rued the day he left for Celtic, an experience that, remarkably, he said he hated. One thing did rankle; he remained exasperated that he was never awarded a testimonial by the club. 'All the others got one, I didn't.' He had left Molineux just before completing the statutory ten years of service but, given his exceptional circumstances, he felt protocol should have been set aside.

"Just the same, he barely missed a match at Molineux in recent years and listening to his perceptive and fair-minded views about the current Wolves team was an education. He wasn't the type to insist everything was better in his day; he didn't much care for them playing only one up front but he recognised skill when he saw it. It was a regular feature at half-time to see Frank with a small Wolves flag fluttering from the back of his wheelchair making the journey around the perimeter of the pitch. Pockets of spontaneous applause broke out from older fans who recognised him. He waved his acknowledgement and smiled in recognition. It brought a lump to the throat and a recollection of so many marvellous days when he graced the pitch in front of him. He loved his visitors to pore over a meticulously preserved scrapbook of press cuttings beginning with his exploits as a junior player right through to his success with Aberdeen. It always amused me that many of the Scottish papers back then referred to Frank as 'Francie.'

"Moving into the pivotal role in the back four transformed his career. For a couple of seasons around 1973 and 1974, he was absolutely peerless; as good as any centre-half in the country. He was magnificent on the ball, classy and assured almost to the point of arrogance, such was his mastery. His elegance and his storming attacking runs from the depths of defence thrilled the Molineux masses and he became an absolute hero. He was a hard nut, too, and, if any forward wanted to 'mix it,' Frank was more than happy to oblige. He was belligerent and had a short fuse when he was riled. Such was his confidence that he always insisted he was baffled as to why Manchester City were considered favourites prior to the League Cup Final in 1974. 'We had the better players; I couldn't fathom why we weren't favourites to win,' he said. "A Wembley cup final was an ideal setting for Munro – then operating at the absolute pinnacle of his powers. On the day, he was brilliant. He marshalled a magnificent defensive show to snuff out the galaxy City forward line.

"Soon afterwards, knee trouble severely restricted his ability to train regularly and an already strained relationship with Bill McGarry deteriorated further. After

Sammy Chung replaced McGarry, Frank admitted that, much as he admired Sammy as an absolute gentleman, he took liberties and against his better judgement, made the ill-fated move to Celtic. There are so many happy memories of sitting with him in his flat before he moved into care and watching the video of the fabulous Wolves v Aberdeen American final in Los Angeles, where he scored a hat-trick against Wolves. It was absolutely priceless hearing him repeat the same story a thousand times about Billy Bremner in the infamous match against Leeds in 1972. After 30 years plus in the Midlands, Frank never lost the thick Scottish lilt. Many a time, I had to ask him to repeat himself as I still struggled to catch his drift!

"He really did carry his burden with immense courage and dignity and deeply appreciated the company of friends and former team-mates who visited him. At that final meeting, he told me how much he was looking forward to travelling with his old colleagues to Charlton's ground as a guest of the London Wolves supporters who always made such a tremendous fuss of him. Alas, he was simply not well enough to undertake a trip to London, which saddened him deeply. My last words to him concerned the '74 Wembley final. 'It was a fabulous day, wasn't it, Frank?' I said. 'It was wonderful,' he replied. So it was and that's how I and thousands of other Wolves fans will remember him now the final whistle has blown. No more suffering. Frank, you were an absolute champion; a fabulous player and a Wolves man to the end."

A more than useful utility player, Les Wilson soon became friends with Frank on the Scot's arrival at Molineux and recalled: "My first meeting with him had been on the playing field at Washington DC's massive District of Columbia Stadium in June, 1967 – and what a confrontation it proved to be! That meeting was a hard-fought, no-prisoners game, which included a number of young and promising Wolves and Aberdeen players, like teenagers Graham Hawkins, Pat Buckley, Alun Evans, Gerry Taylor and myself, along with Martin Buchan and young Frank for Aberdeen. Frank impressed so many of the Wolves players during this highly competitive game, as well as our manager Ronnie Allen. His hard tackling, solid defending, attacking prowess, quality pinpoint passing and football intelligence were evident throughout. Who would have thought that the best was yet to come from this Scottish teenager? One who did was Ronnie Allen, who was incredibly smart in spotting raw talent, as well as quality experienced players. His track record was outstanding.

"Our Wolves team were delighted with the 1-1 draw but it was wiped from the records because we had used three substitutes when only two were allowed, so we had to meet again. The Wolves players had given their all in Dallas 24 hours before the sides replayed and it was no surprise a tired team lost 3-0 to Aberdeen. Once again, young Munro stood out with his style, confidence and intelligent running off the ball. I was one of the Wolves substitutes and was impressed greatly by the outstanding play by him, Jimmy Smith and young Martin Buchan. There was no doubt that these three had what it took to play at the very top of British and world football. Their performances were excellent and their will-to-win was there for all to see. I was sitting next to Ronnie Allen and hung on to every word and technical comment that he and his assistant Jack Dowen uttered. Both were impressed with Frank.

"When Wolves and Aberdeen met again in the final, it produced a classic and the two individual stars of this pulsating and memorable game were Frank, whose play was simply brilliant, and our own David Burnside. I was a sub and again sitting next to Ronnie, who said: 'Get warmed up, Leslie. You will be going on to keep that Munro in check.' He told me to limber up on at least three occasions but I never did get on and I'm not sure I would have curbed Frank if I had. It was no surprise when Ronnie made Frank the first addition to our 1967-68 squad. It was rumoured he also made a very attractive offer for Martin Buchan which was turned down by the Aberdeen directors. What a great pity! Frank, Evan Williams, our Scottish goalkeeper from Third Lanark, and I became good friends and team-mates and we all did extra training sessions together in the afternoons at Molineux or at the Castlecroft training ground. The three of us were determined to make the grade in the big time of British football.

"The other two reckoned that Jock Stein was having them watched and wanted to take them to Celtic. Evan, especially, had some inside information on their interest in him, possibly through his family relationship with former Sunderland and Derby striker John O'Hare. In 1969, Frank and I were regulars in the Wolves first team, so I could observe him at first hand. He had a great memory of incidents on and off the field, plus outstanding tactical and technical knowledge of the game. When it came to some football matters, he was encyclopaedic and had a brilliant memory. Evan Williams went on loan to Aston Villa for a short period and, once again, both Evan and Frank were constantly telling me Jock Stein was watching them. So it was no surprise when Evan did go to Celtic, where he won five medals – three League titles and two via the Scottish Cup. Frank and I played in some 85-plus Wolves first team games together, including pre-season tours.

"There is no question that Francis Munro was a very loyal, outstanding and dedicated player with Wolverhampton Wanderers, possibly one of their best ever defenders. He was always finding ways to make things work on the field and was never afraid to take a chance. He always expected to win and it has been said many times that professional football is a self-fulfilling prophecy. On and off the field, Frank always told it as it was. He was no flim-flam merchant. He had bags of courage and determination. He was, without question, his own man. He was brave and true and always spoke his mind in the dressing room. It always seemed that nothing was too difficult for him on the field. Football was the love of his life.

"When we heard Frank had suffered a stroke, David Burnside and I visited him in his flat in Wolverhampton and we spent a good five hours together. You can imagine Frank and David talking about their hat-tricks in the Aberdeen v Wolves game in 1967. Needless to say, I loved listening to their recollections. I found Frank always to be straightforward, honest and to the point. Meeting him on so many occasions after our retirement gave me the opportunity to tell him what a wonderful and outstanding player he really was. His greatest asset was his reading of the game and his anticipation. He was simply one of the very, very best of his generation in British football."

Appendices

Frank's international appearances:
HC = Home International Championship, EC = European Championship

1970-71
May 18, Hampden Park: Scotland 0 Northern Ireland 1. Attendance: 31,643. HC
Scotland: Clark (Aberdeen), Hay (Celtic), Brogan (Celtic), Greig (Rangers), McLintock (Arsenal) sub MUNRO (Wolves) 71, Moncur (Newcastle), Lorimer (Leeds), Green (Blackpool), O'Hare (Derby) sub Jarvie (Airdrieonians) HT, Curran (Wolves), Eddie Gray (Leeds).
Northern Ireland: Jennings (Tottenham); Rice (Arsenal), Nelson (Arsenal), O'Kane (Nottingham Forest), Hunter (Blackburn), Nicholson (Huddersfield), Hamilton (Linfield), McMordie (Middlesbrough) sub Craig (Newcastle) 67, Dougan (Wolves), Clements (Coventry), Best (Manchester United).
Goal: Greig own goal 14.

May 22, Wembley: England 3 Scotland 1. Attendance: 91,469. HC
England: Banks (Stoke); Lawler (Liverpool), Cooper (Leeds), Storey (Arsenal), McFarland (Derby), Moore (West Ham), Lee (Manchester City) sub Clarke (Leeds) 73, Ball (Everton), Hurst (West Ham), Chivers (Tottenham), Peters (Tottenham).
Goals: Peters 9, Chivers 30, 40.
Scotland: Clark (Aberdeen), Greig (Rangers), Brogan (Celtic), Bremner (Leeds), McLintock (Arsenal), Moncur (Newcastle), Johnstone (Celtic), Robb (Aberdeen), Curran (Wolves) sub MUNRO (Wolves) HT, Green (Blackpool) sub Jarvie (Airdrieonians) 82, Cormack (Nottingham Forest).
Goal: Curran 11.

June 9, Copenhagen: Denmark 1 Scotland 0. Attendance: 37,682. EC
Denmark: Sorensen, Torben Nielsen, Berg, Arentoft, Rasmussen, Bierre, Laudrup (sub Outzen 75), Bjornmose, Le Fevre, Benny Nielsen (sub Pedersen 75), Kristensen.
Goal: Laudrup 43.

Scotland: Clark (Aberdeen); MUNRO (Wolves), Dickson (Kilmarnock), Stanton (Hibernian), McKinnon (Rangers), Moncur (Newcastle), McLean (Rangers), Forsyth (Motherwell) sub Robb (Aberdeen) HT, Stein (Rangers), Curran (Wolves), Forrest (Aberdeen) sub Scott (Dundee) 75.

June 14, Moscow: USSR 1 Scotland 0. Attendance: 20,000. Friendly
USSR: Rudakov, Istomin, Shesternev, Matvienko, Kaplichny, Kolotov, Konkov, Nodija (sub Dolgov 70), Fedotov, Shevchenko, Evriuzhikan (sub Khmelnitsky HT).
Goal: Evriuzhikan 25.
Scotland: Clark (Aberdeen), Brownlie (Hibernian), Dickson (Kilmarnock), MUNRO (Wolves), McKinnon (Rangers), Stanton (Hibernian), Forrest (Aberdeen), Watson (Motherwell), Stein (Rangers) sub, Curran (Wolves) 71, Robb (Aberdeen), Scott (Dundee).

1974-75
April 16, Gothenburg: Sweden 1 Scotland 1. Attendance: 15,574. Friendly
Sweden: Hagberg, Bjorn Andersson, Karlsson, Nordqvist (sub Linderoth HT), Augustsssen, Thorstenssen, Fredriksson, Edstrom (Roy Andersson HT), Ahlstrom (Nordahl 65), Sjoberg, Matsson.
Goal: Sjoberg 44.
Scotland: Kennedy (Rangers), Jardine (Rangers), McGrain (Celtic), MUNRO (Wolves), Jackson (Rangers), Robinson (Dundee), Dalglish (Celtic), Souness (Middlesbrough) sub Johnstone (Rangers) 54, Parlane (Rangers), MacDougall (Norwich), Macari (Manchester United) sub Hughes (Sunderland) 54.
Goal: MacDougall 86.

May 17, Cardiff: Wales 2 Scotland 2. Attendance: 23,509. HC
Wales: Davies (Everton), Thomas (Derby), Page (Birmingham), Mahoney (Stoke), Roberts (Birmingham), Phillips (Aston Villa), Yorath (Leeds), Flynn (Burnley), Toshack (Liverpool), Reece (Cardiff), James (Burnley).
Goals: Toshack 28, Flynn 36.
Scotland: Kennedy (Rangers), Jardine (Rangers), McGrain (Celtic), Jackson (Rangers) sub MUNRO (Wolves) 77, McQueen (Leeds), Rioch (Derby), Dalglish (Celtic), Macari (Manchester United), Parlane (Rangers), MacDougall (Norwich), Duncan (Hibernian).
Goals: Jackson 52, Rioch 61.

May 20, Hampden Park: Scotland 3 Northern Ireland 0. Attendance: 66,496. HC
Scotland: Kennedy (Rangers), Jardine (Rangers) sub Forsyth (Manchester United) 89, McGrain (Celtic), MUNRO (Wolves), McQueen (Leeds), Rioch (Derby), Dalglish (Celtic), Robinson (Dundee) sub Conn (Tottenham) 76, Parlane (Rangers), MacDougall (Norwich), Duncan (Hibernian).
Goals: MacDougall 15, Dalglish 21, Parlane 80.
Northern Ireland: Jennings (Tottenham), Rice (Arsenal), Nicholl (Aston Villa), Hunter (Ipswich) sub Blair (Oldham) 83, O'Kane, (Nottingham Forest), Clements (Everton), Finney (Sunderland), O'Neill (Nottingham Forest) sub Anderson (Swindon) 87, Spence (Bury), McIlroy (Manchester United), Jackson (Nottingham Forest).

May 24, Wembley: England 5 Scotland 1. Attendance: 98,241. HC
England: Clemence (Liverpool), Whitworth (Leicester), Beattie (Ipswich), Bell (Manchester City), Watson (Sunderland), Todd (Derby), Ball (Arsenal), Channon (Southampton), Johnson (Ipswich), Gerry Francis (QPR), Keegan (Liverpool) sub Thomas (QPR) 85.
Goals: Francis 6, 64, Beattie 7, Bell 40, Johnson 73.
Scotland: Kennedy (Rangers), Jardine (Rangers), McGrain (Celtic), MUNRO (Wolves), McQueen (Leeds), Rioch (Derby), Dalglish (Celtic), Conn (Tottenham), Parlane (Rangers), MacDougall (Norwich) sub Macari (Manchester United) 71, Duncan (Hibernian) sub Hutchison (Coventry) 61.
Goal: Rioch (pen) 42.

June 1, Bucharest: Romania 1 Scotland 1. Attendance: 52,203. EC
Romania: Necula, Cheran, Sandu, Anghelini, Satmareanu, Dinu, Crisan, Georgescu (Balaci 38), Dobrin (Kun 82), Dumitru, Lucescu.
Goal: Georgescu 22.
Scotland: Brown (Sheffield United), McGrain (Celtic), Forsyth (Manchester United), MUNRO (Wolves), McQueen (Leeds), Rioch (Derby) sub Hutchison (Coventry) 66, Dalglish (Celtic), Miller (Aberdeen), Parlane (Rangers), Macari (Manchester United) sub Robinson (Dundee) 66, Duncan (Hibernian).
Goal: McQueen 89.

Frank's Under-23 international appearances

1969-70

December 3, Hampden Park: Scotland 4 France 0, Attendance: 5,004.
Scotland: Hughes (Chelsea), Malone (Ayr), Hay (Celtic), Blackley (Hibernian), Thomson (Heart of Midlothian), MUNRO (Wolves), Lorimer (Leeds), Carr (Coventry), O'Hare (Derby), Robb (Aberdeen) sub Marinello (Hibernian), Johnston (Rangers).
Goals: O'Hare 26, 74, Lorimer 43 (pen), 55.
France: Baratelli, Camerini, Varucci, Rostagni, Osman, Eo (Mezy), Hardouin, Huck, Vergnes, Lafrique, Dellamore.

January 14, Aberdeen: Scotland 1 Wales 1. Attendance: 14,500.
Scotland: Stewart (Ayr), Clunie (Hearts), Wilson (West Brom), Blackley (Hibernian), Thomson (Hearts), Campbell (Charlton) sub MUNRO (Wolves) 67, Lorimer (Leeds), Carr (Coventry), O'Hare (Derby), Robb (Aberdeen), Hartford (West Brom) sub Harper (Aberdeen) 67.
Goal: O'Hare 86.
Wales: Lloyd (Southend), Pearson (Southport), Thomas (Swindon), Davis (Wrexham), Morgan (Cardiff), Yorath (Leeds), Krzywicki (West Brom), Page (Birmingham), Price (Peterborough), Jones (Bristol Rovers), Hawkins (Shrewsbury).
Goal: Hawkins 11.

March 4, Sunderland: England 3 Scotland 1 (Abandoned after 68 minutes). Attendance: 12,885.
England: Shilton (Leicester), Smith (Sheffield Wednesday), Parkin (Wolves), Todd (Sunderland), McFarland (Derby), Nish (Leicester), Husband (Everton), Hudson (Chelsea), Osgood (Chelsea) sub Royle (Everton) 56, Kidd (Manchester United), Thomas (Burnley).
Goals: Osgood 25, 55, Kidd 59.
Scotland: Hughes (Chelsea), Clunie (Hearts), Dickson (Kilmarnock), Blackley (Hibernian), Thomson (Hearts), MUNRO (Wolves), McLean (Kilmarnock), Connelly (Celtic) sub Marinello (Arsenal) 56, O'Hare (Derby), Gemmill (Preston), Johnston (Rangers).
Goal: Own goal (Todd) 60.

1970-71

January 13, Swansea: Wales 1 Scotland 0. Attendance: 9,000.

Wales: Dai Davies (Everton), Roberts (Bristol Rovers), Derrett (Cardiff), Prince (Bristol Rovers), Davis (Wrexham), Thomas (Swansea), Hughes (Blackpool), Price (Peterborough), Phillips (Cardiff), Jones (Bristol Rovers), Cyril Davies (Charlton).

Goal: Price 67.

Scotland: MacRae (Motherwell), Hay (Celtic) sub Jardine (Rangers) 53, Hermiston (Aberdeen) sub Oliver (Hearts) HT, Kelly (Arsenal), MUNRO (Wolves), Buchan (Aberdeen), Hartford (West Brom), Carr (Coventry), Harper (Aberdeen), Connolly (St Johnstone), Hutchison (Blackpool).

Frank with Aberdeen in United Soccer Association tournament in 1967

Stoke 1-2, Washington, May 27 (Storrie); Hibernian 2-1, Toronto, May 31 (Storrie, Jimmy Smith); Cagliari 1-1, Washington, June 3 (Storrie); Cerro 3-0, Washington, June 7 (Jimmy Smith, Jimmy Wilson, OG); Glentoran 2-2, Detroit, June 11 (Jimmy Wilson, Pat Wilson); Stoke 2-2, Cleveland, June 14 (Shewan, Pat Wilson); Wolves 1-1, Washington, June 20 (Jimmy Wilson); ADO 0-0, San Francisco, June 25; Sunderland 1-1, Washington, June 28 (Munro); Dundee United 2-0, Dallas, July 1 (Jimmy Smith, Whyte); Bangu 1-0, Houston, July 4 (Jimmy Smith); Shamrock 1-2, Washington, July 8 (Munro); Wolves 3-0, replayed game as first game was declared void, Washington, July 10 (Storrie 2, Buchan); Wolves 5–6, Los Angeles, July 14 (Munro 3 (2 pens), Storrie, Jimmy Smith).

Goals: 6 Storrie; 5 Munro, Jimmy Smith; 3 Jimmy Wilson; 2 Pat Wilson; 1 Shewan, Own goal, Buchan, Whyte.

Frank with Wolves in North American League in 1969

West Ham 2-3, Baltimore, May 2 (Knowles, Bailey); Dundee United 4-2, Kansas, May 4 (Knowles 2, Wilson, Bailey); West Ham 4-2, Kansas, May 8 (McAlle 2, Bailey, Curran); Kilmarnock 3-2, Kansas, May 11 (Curran 2, Farrington); Aston Villa 2-1, Atlanta, May 14 (Knowles pen, Dougan); Kilmarnock 3-0, St Louis, May 16 (Dougan, Wagstaffe, Curran); Aston Villa 5-0, Kansas, May 22 (Curran 2, Dougan, Knowles, Woodfield); Dundee United 2-3, Dallas, May 31 (Dougan 2).

Goals: 6 Curran; 5 Dougan, Knowles; 3 Bailey; 2 McAlle; 1 Farrington, Wagstaffe, Wilson, Woodfield.

Frank with Wolves on North America, New Zealand and Australia tour in 1972

Aberdeen 1-3, San Francisco, May 21 (McCalliog); Aberdeen 0-3, Seattle, May 24; Aberdeen 3-0, Vancouver, May 26 (Richards, Hibbitt, Curran); Aberdeen 4-0, Los Angeles, May 28 (Richards 3, Munro); Auckland 3-2, June 3 (Dougan 2, Curran); Wellington 6-0, June 5 (McCalliog 2, Eastoe 2, Dougan 2); South Island 2-0, Christchurch, June 7 (Eastoe, Munro); Australia 0-1, Melbourne, June 11; Australia 2-2, Sydney, June 12 (Munro, Curran); Queensland 6-2, Brisbane, June 14 (Eastoe 3, Dougan, Hibbitt, McCalliog); South Australia 3-2, Adelaide, June 17 (Hegan, Hibbitt, Sunderland); Western Australia 3-0, Perth, June 18 (McCalliog, Eastoe, Wagstaffe).

Goals: 7 Eastoe; 5 Dougan, McCalliog; 4 Richards; 3 Curran, Hibbitt, Munro; 1 Hegan, Sunderland, Wagstaffe.

Frank's domestic League and cup appearances (figures in brackets denote substitute outings; A = appearances, G = goals)

Dundee	League		Cup		Lge Cup		Others*		Total	
	A	G	A	G	A	G	A	G	A	G
United										
1964-65	20	1	2	-	8	5	10	1	40	7
1965-66	28	13	1	-	6	3	-	-	35	16
1966-67	2	-	-	-	3	-	-	-	5	-
Total									**80**	**23**
Aberdeen										
1966-67	29	6	6	-	-	-	-	-	35	6
1967-68	13 (1)	2	1	-	6	1	4	5	24 (1)	8
Total									**59 (1)**	**14**
Wolves										
1967-68	7 (1)	-	-	-	-	-	-	-	7 (1)	-
1968-69	12 (4)	2	-	-	1	1	-	-	13 (4)	3
1969-70	32 (1)	1	-	-	3	-	4	-	39 (1)	1
1970-71	36	-	2	-	-	-	8	-	46	-
1971-72	37	3	2	-	1	-	10	2	50	5

FRANK'S FOR THE MEMORY

	League		Cup		Lge Cup		Others*		Total	
Wolves cont.	A	G	A	G	A	G	A	G	A	G
1972-73	32	2	5	-	6	1	4	-	47	3
1973-74	36	2	1	-	8	-	4	1	49	3
1974-75	35	3	1	-	1	-	2	-	39	3
1975-76	30	-	5	-	3	-	-	-	38	-
1976-77	33	1	4	-	-	-	-	-	37	1
Total									**365(6)**	**19**
Celtic										
1977-78	13 (1)	-	2	-	5	-	-	-	20 (1)	-
Totals	**395 (8)**	**36**	**32**	**0**	**51**	**11**	**46**	**9**	**524(8)**	**56**

* **Others**: Dundee United 1964-65 Summer Cup; Aberdeen 1967-68 European Cup-winners' Cup; Wolves 1969-70 Anglo-Italian Cup, 1970-71 Texaco Cup, 1971-2 UEFA Cup, 1972-73 Texaco Cup and Watney Cup, 1973-74 UEFA Cup, 1974-75 UEFA Cup.

Author's references
Aberdeen A Complete Record 1903-1987 – Jim Rickaby (Breedon Books)
Dundee United The Official Centenary History – Peter Rundo and Mark Watson (Birlinn)
Having A Ball – Eddie Turnbull with Martin Hannan (Mainstream Publishing)
Rothmans Football Yearbook – edited by Jack Rollin (Queen Anne Press)
Talking With Wolves – Steve Gordos (Breedon Books)
Those Were The Days – Clive Corbett (Geoffrey Publications)
www.wolvesheroes.com website

Photo acknowledgements
We are very grateful to the Press Association/PA Photos Limited (©PA Images) for providing the front-page photograph and material used inside; also, we thank the Derby Telegraph, Huddersfield Examiner, Southern Daily Echo, Bolton News, www.wolvesheroes.com and the families and friends of Frank Munro and Dave Wagstaffe. If you think we have inadvertently breached copyright, please contact us so we may take the appropriate steps.

In Tribute To Frank

(A roll call of the loyal customers to whom we are greatly indebted
for purchasing this title in advance as subscribers)

Arthur and Peter Adams
Gerald Allen
Simon Archer
Roy Ashton
Mark Astbury
Douglas Aulton

Jonathan Babb
Peter Bagley
Mike Bailey
Eddie Baker
Matt Bakewell
Charles Bamforth
Thomas Barlow
Neil and Sheila Barnes
Horace Barnfield
Christopher Bayley
Albert Belcher
Christopher Bennett
Dave Benton
George Berry
Steve Bills
John Black
Malcolm Black
Rob Blackhall
Gavin Blackwell
Vic Boffey
Tony Bond
Sandra Bottle
Chris Bowyer
Ulf Brenmo
Bryan Bridges

Alfred Camilleri
Willie Carr
Rob Cartwright
David Chester

John Clarke
David Cleveland
Vincent Coates
Les Cockrill
Gerry Collins
Paul Collins
Mick Conway
David Cooke
Clive and Tom Corbett
Mike Cox and family
Steven Cox
Bob Crockett
John A Cross
Gary Cutler

Steve Daley
Chris Dangerfield
Brian Daniels
Harry Davenhill
Rob Davies
Steve Davies
Glyn Stanley Davis
Kevin Defty
Dave Degg
Brian Dennis
Philip Dodd
Nick Downes
D Dungar (25th October Club)

Ian Eccles
Dean Edwards
Steve English
Everiss Family
Les Evans
Mel Eves

Paul Fairley

David Farmer
Jim and David Fielding
Andrew Flack
Anthony Flavell

Brian Garvey
Maurice Gelipter
Brian Gibson
Chris Gittins
Robert Goddard
Val Gordon
Bobby Gould
Robert Granbom
Les Green
Richard Green
Robert Green
Paul Greenfield
Ken Gregory
Andy Griffin
Shay Griffiths
Robert Gubbins
Stuart and Eileen Guest
Jason Guy
John Gwilliam

Antony Hackner
Jake Hackner
Keith Hall
Alex Hamil MBE
Nick Hamil
Tony Hammond
Graham Harridence
David Harriman
Steve Harris
Vernon Harris
David A Harrison
Darren Hartle
Gil Hartle
Graham Hawkins
Michael Hayden
Jim Heath (in memory of)
Odin Henrikssen
Irene and Ken Henson

Lisa and Michael Henson
Kenny Hibbitt
Alwyn Hill
John Holsgrove
Nick Hone
Anthony Hughes
Quentin Hughes
Graham Hughes
Rob Hunt
Mike Huntbatch

Marie Inkster

Pat Jackson
John James
Martin James
Rowland James
PA and JM Jennings
Derek Jervis
Tony Johnson
Chris Jones
Elvis Jones
Graham Jones
Jack Jones
Kenneth Jones
Mike Jones
Trevor Jones
Stan Journeaux
Robin Jukes

David Keeling
Steve Kindon

Mark Lagram
Graham Large
Kelvin Large
Mick Lavelle
Robert Leek
Ray Lees
Mick Lewis
Bror Loelv (in memory of)
London Wolves
Simon Lucas

FRANK'S FOR THE MEMORY

Lee and Bertie Lutton

Gwilym Machin
Manmohan Singh Maheru
Truls Mansson
John McAlle
Mel McBride
Jim McCalliog
Jeremy McCormick
Dave Meads
Tim Meese
Per Magnar Meyer
Jean Pierre Micallef
Louis Micallef
Eric Millington
Phil Murphy
Paul, Lisa and Issy Murray

John and Steve Oates
Gerry O'Hara
Dennis Oliver
Irene and George O'Neil
Keith Alexander Owen

Geoff Palmer
Terry Palmer
Phil Parkes
Derek Parkin
Ron Peacock
Douglas Pearl
Per Perers
Bjorn Persson
David Phillips
Roger Pitt
Mitchel Poole
Ian Potts
Robert Poulton
Barry Powell
Gordy Powell
Edward and Maurice Pritchard
Martyn Pritchard

Patrick Quirke

Toni Ragno
Keith Randle
Martyn Randle
David Rawlings
Mike Redfern
Brian Restall
John Rhoden
Bob Richards
John Richards
Mark Rigby
Ken & Phil Roberts
Mark Roberts
Mike Roberts
John Rogers
Kevin Rogers
Charles Ross
Riccardo Rossi
John Rowding
Arthur and Jane Rudge
Jenni Rullan

Chris Salmon
Peter Schofield
Jim Sharma
Nigel Shave
Tom Sheehan
Ben Sheriff
Dave Slape
Helena Smith (in memory of)
I W Smith
Richard Stafford
Roger Stafford
Ron Stevens
Barry Steward
Steve Swann

Carol Taylor
David Taylor
Gerry Taylor
John Taylor
Gloria Thomas
Ian Thomson
John Tilley

IN TRIBUTE TO FRANK

Mo Tinsley
Tony Turpin

Paul Utnik

Stig Arve Vangsnes

Clare and Mark Wadsworth
Bill Wager
Chloe Louise Wagstaffe
Joshua Scott Wagstaffe
John T Walker MBE
Paul Walker
Dave Wallington
Kevin Wallsgrove
Pete West
Mike Westwood
Sue and Terry Wharton
Paul Ronald Whitcombe
Ronald Whitcombe
Tony White
Adrian Whitehurst

Tony Wild
Claire Williams
Evan Williams
Ian Williams
James Williams
Judith A Williams
Nick Williams
Peter Williams
Les Wilson
Peter Wollam
Andy Wood
Peter Woodifield
Bernard Wright
Jan Wright
Martin G Wright and
Sean M Wright
Michael Wright
Steve Wright
Tony Wright

Penny Malik and Craig Yeoman

Our other Molineux-based literature

Thomas Publications have become by far the biggest producers of Wolverhampton Wanderers books and have also been responsible for the following titles, most of them by David Instone:

The Bully Years
Wolves: Exclusive!
Sir Jack
Forever Wolves
Running With Wolves – Peter Lansley
Wolves: The Glory Years
Wolves In Pictures
Billy & Bully
Wolves In 20/20 Vision – Jim Heath
When Football Was Football: Wolves

We also supported the 2009 production of the updated **Wolverhampton Wanderers Complete Record** and two Express & Star books (**Molineux Memories** and **Talking With Wolves**). In addition, the company were major sponsors in the production of the **Official DVD of Wolves** and are proud to have supported the **Promise Dreams** charity with a major donation from past projects.